Street by Stre…

MAIDSTONE,
CHATHAM
GILLINGHAM, SITTINGBOURNE, STROOD

Aylesford, Bearsted, Cliffe Woods, Coxheath, Ditton, Harrietsham, Higham, Hoo St Werburgh, Kings Hill, Newington, Rainham, Snodland, Sutton Valence, Walderslade, Wateringbury, West Malling

2nd edition May 2005
© Automobile Association Developments Limited 2005

Original edition printed September 2002

Ordnance Survey® This product includes map data licensed from Ordnance Survey® with the permission of the Controller of Her Majesty's Stationery Office. © Crown copyright 2005. All rights reserved. Licence number 399221.

Published by AA Publishing (a trading name of Automobile Association Developments Limited, whose registered office is Southwood East, Apollo Rise, Farnborough, Hampshire, GU14 0JW. Registered number 1878835).

Mapping produced by the Cartography Department of The Automobile Association. (A02246)

A CIP Catalogue record for this book is available from the British Library.

Printed by GRAFIASA S.A., Porto, Portugal

Ref: ML178z

Key to map pages	ii-iii
Key to map symbols	iv-1
Enlarged map pages	2-7
Main map pages	8-69
Index – towns & villages	70
Index – streets	71-80
Index – featured places	80-81
Acknowledgements	81

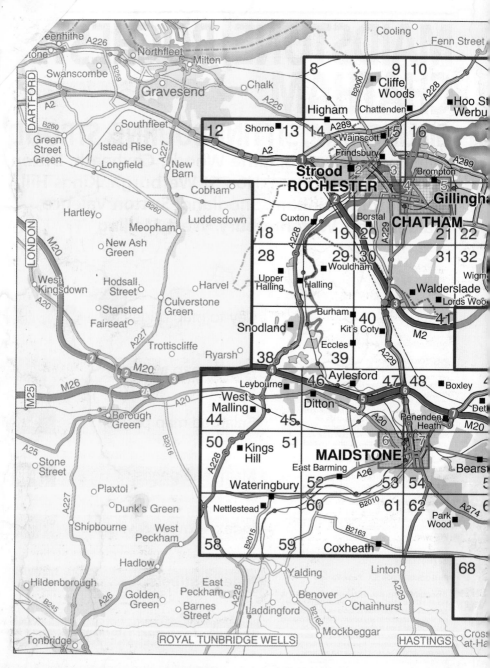

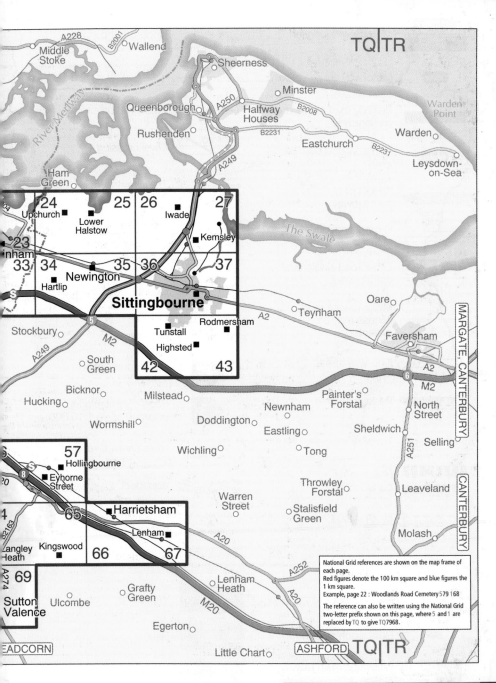

TQ|TR

A228
Middle Stoke
B2001
Wallend
Sheerness
River Medway
Queenborough
A250
Halfway Houses
B2008
Minster
Warden Point
Rushenden
B2231
Eastchurch
B2231
Warden
A249
Leysdown-on-Sea
Ham Green

24 25 26 27
Upchurch Lower Halstow Iwade
Kemsley
23
inham
33 34 35 36 37
Newington
Hartlip
Sittingbourne
Oare
Faversham
Stockbury
M2
Tunstall Rodmersham
Highsted
42 43
A2
Teynham

MARGATE, CANTERBURY

South Green
Bicknor
Hucking
Milstead
Newnham
Painter's Forstal
North Street
A251
Selling
Wormshill
Doddington
Eastling
Sheldwich
Wichling
Tong

57
Hollingbourne
Eyhorne Street
Throwley Forstal
Leaveland
Molash

CANTERBURY

65
Harrietsham
Warren Street
Stalisfield Green
Lenham
66 67
Kingswood
Langley Heath
A20
69
Sutton Valence
Ulcombe
Grafty Green
Lenham Heath
A252
M20
A20
Egerton

EADCORN
Little Chart
ASHFORD
TQ|TR

> National Grid references are shown on the map frame of each page.
> Red figures denote the 100 km square and blue figures the 1 km square.
> Example, page 22 : Woodlands Road Cemetery 579 168
>
> The reference can also be written using the National Grid two-letter prefix shown on this page, where 5 and 1 are replaced by TQ to give TQ7968.

3.6 inches to 1 mile   **Scale of main map pages**   **1:17,500**

0   1/2   miles   1
0   1/2   1   kilometres   1 1/2

Junction 9	Motorway & junction
Services	Motorway service area
	Primary road single/dual carriageway
Services	Primary road service area
	A road single/dual carriageway
	B road single/dual carriageway
	Other road single/dual carriageway
	Minor/private road, access may be restricted
← ←	One-way street
	Pedestrian area
============	Track or footpath
	Road under construction
[= = = ={	Road tunnel
P	Parking
P+	Park & Ride
	Bus/coach station
	Railway & main railway station
	Railway & minor railway station
⊖	Underground station
⊖	Light railway & station
+++++++++	Preserved private railway
LC	Level crossing
•—•—•—•	Tramway
-----------	Ferry route
....	Airport runway
— · — · — · —	County, administrative boundary
ᵛᵛᵛᵛᵛᵛᵛᵛ	Mounds
17	Page continuation 1:17,500
3	Page continuation to enlarged scale 1:10,000
	River/canal, lake, pier
	Aqueduct, lock, weir
465 ▲ Winter Hill	Peak (with height in metres)
	Beach
	Woodland
	Park
	Cemetery
	Built-up area

	Featured building			Abbey, cathedral or priory
	City wall			Castle
A&E	Hospital with 24-hour A&E department			Historic house or building
PO	Post Office		Wakehurst Place NT	National Trust property
	Public library			Museum or art gallery
i	Tourist Information Centre			Roman antiquity
	Petrol station Major suppliers only			Ancient site, battlefield or monument
†	Church/chapel			Industrial interest
	Public toilets			Garden
	Toilet with disabled facilities			Arboretum
PH	Public house AA recommended			Farm or animal centre
	Restaurant AA inspected			Zoological or wildlife collection
	Theatre or performing arts centre			Bird collection
	Cinema			Nature reserve
	Golf course		V	Visitor or heritage centre
▲	Camping AA inspected			Country park
	Caravan Site AA inspected			Cave
	Camping & caravan site AA inspected			Windmill
	Theme park			Distillery, brewery or vineyard

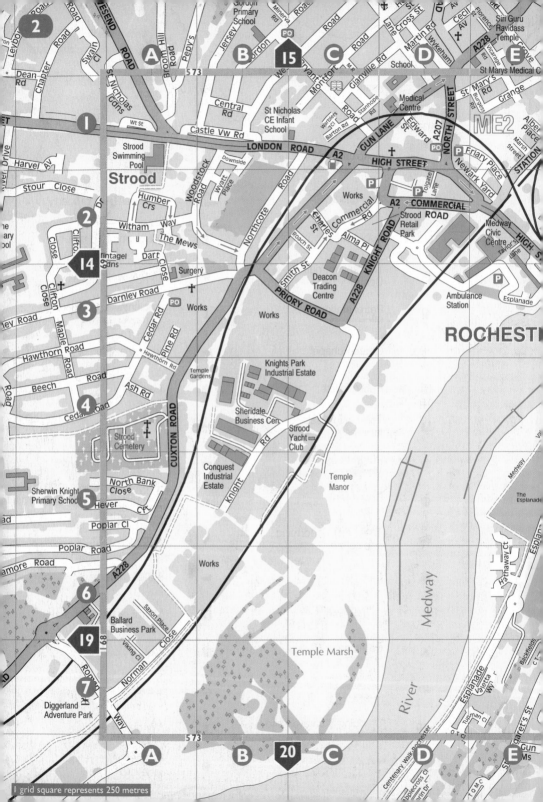

I grid square represents 250 metres

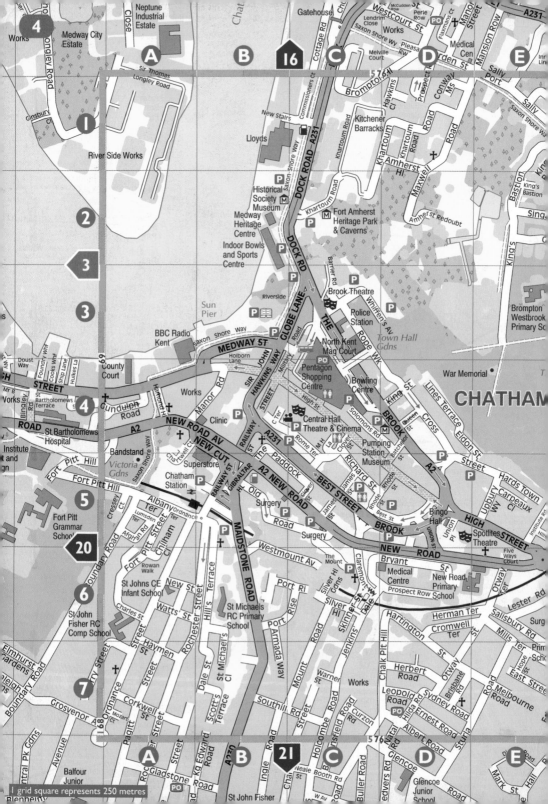

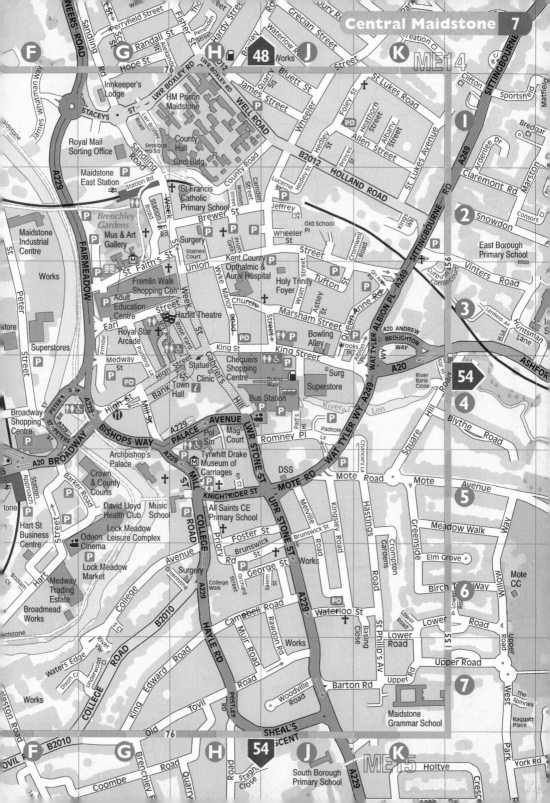

F G H J K

74 75

I

Cooling
Street

Spendiff
Farm

Cascade Close

2

Lodge Hill

South
Bank

Buck...
Road

ROAD

B2000

Perry Hill
Farm

Cooling Street

Perry Hill

Merry Boys Road

Cooling Common

Wentworth Drive

Milton Avenue

Mortimers
Avenue

Surgery

Cliffe
Woods County
Primary School

Cliffe
Woods

Great
Chattenden
Wood

Road

3

Ladyclose
Avenue

PO

Parkside

Shaw
Cl

Cardens Rd

View Rd

Reed Ham Crs

View Road

Tennyson Avenue

Brewer Road

Goodwin
Road

Sedley
Close

Ashwood Close

Lochat

10

Brookmead Road

Archery
Close

Hale
Road

4

View Road

Englefield
Crs

Hilton
Rd

Thames
View

Graveney
Close

Central

Ham River Hill

Common

Road

Lochat Road

Chattender

Kirby

TOWN ROAD

Lee
Green

5

Wack Road

Mockbeggar

Bunters Hill Road

Common Road

Haven Street

The
Mount

Woodfield Way

Upchat Road

172

6

LWR. ROCHESTER RD

Lane

Bunters Hill Road

Noke
Street

A Lee
Green
Rd

Higham Farm Road

ELMS HILL

Upchat Road

A228

B2000

Ditch Fields Wood

HASTED ROAD

Chaplin
Cl

Grant
Cl

Grant Rd

Higham Road

Stone House
Farm

F G H 15 J K

74 A289 75

F **G** **H** **J** **K**

79 80

I

Solomons Farm

Sharnal Street

Sharnal Street

74

2

RATCLIFFE HIGHWAY

Roper's Green Lane

Beluncle Farm

Roper's

Tile Barn Farm

3

Alpha Close

Stoke Road

73

Lane

Stoke Road

Jacob's

Stoke Road

Eshcol Road

4

Lane

Jacob's La

Saxon Shore Way

Grandsire Gardens

St Werburgh Medical Centre

Belly's Lane

Peal Cl

Coombe Road

Stoke Road

Jacob's

Lane

5

172

Flack Gdns

Peal Cl

Abbot's Court

6

Brookside

PO

Church St

Vicarage

Court Road

Abbots

Saxon Shore Way

Armytage Close

Everest Dr

Church Farm

Vicarage Lane

Works

Vicarage La

Berry Rd

Poplar

Saxon Shore Way

79 80

F **G** **H** **I7** **J** **K**

Marine Dr

Hoo Flats

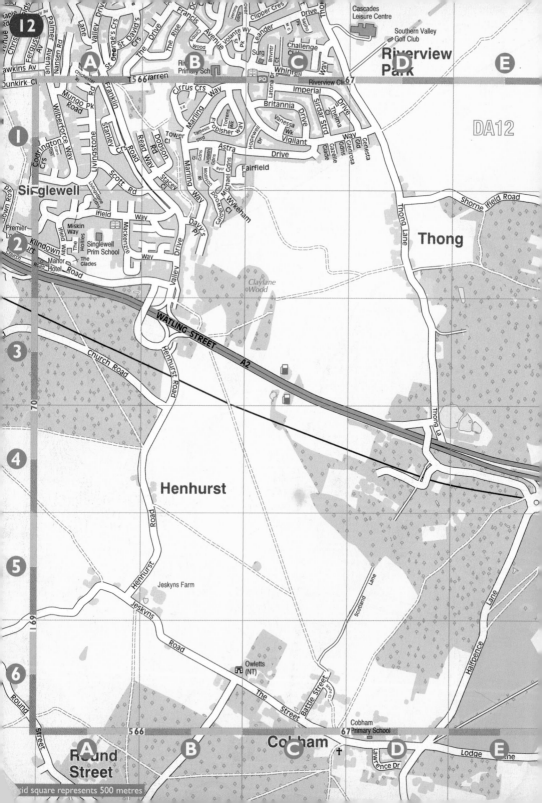

CRAVESEND ROAD
Coutts
Avenue
A226

F G H J K

Crown Lane

8 69 70 Walmers Aver

A226

Evergreen
Close

Mermoue La
Crwn Cn

Forge

1

Cob Drive

Shorne CE
Primary
School

Court
Wood

Mill Hill Lane
PO
The Street
Hollands
Cl
Surgery

Manor
Fld

Shorne

Upper
Ifield

Swiller's
La

Lodge Gd

Warren
View

Peartree Lane

2

Tanyard Hill

Randall
Wood

**Shorne
Ridgeway**

Lane

Racefield
Cl

Great
Crabbles
Wood

3

Woodlands

The Ridgeway

Pondfield Lane

Bowesden Lane

I4

Shorne Wood
Country Park P

Brewers Road

Bowesden Lane

Pale Park

4

WATLINC ST A2

ewers Road

Junction 1

5

Golf Course

Knights
Place

I 69

Cobham Hall

Rochester & Cobham Park
Golf Club

6

Kent

Cobham
Park

Lodge Point

F G H **I8** J K

8 69 70

F G H H J K

Church Farm
Church La
Lane
Vicarage La
Saxon Shore Way
Elder Cl
The Poplar
Oak Cl
Berry Rd
Poplar Cl
Marine Dr
Birch Rd
Vicarage
Works
Marine Dr

Hoo Flats

79   80

Lower Bush

Hoo
Ness

Pinup
Reach

The Strand

Gillingham Reach

St Albans
PO
A289
Baron
Christmas
Waterside La
Saxon Shore Way
Works
Strand Ap Rd
Holly Close
Cemetery
Margate Cl
Church St
Leeds Cl
Layfield Road
Court Ldg Rd
Eastern Rd
Edward St
Gillingham Green
Church Pth
Saxon
Grange
Dial Cl
PO
Hewitt Cl
Lwr Woodlands
Cypress Close
Pier Road
Danes Hill Rd
Grove Road
Lwr Rainham Rd
Saxon Shore Way

Grange

Saxon Shore Way

Springfield Road
Portland Ave
M Cavendish Av
Granville Rd
Ingram Rd
Elm Rd
Oak Av
Maple Avenue
Poppy Cl
The Vineries
Castlemaine Avenue
Carrington Close
Bluebell
Freesia Close
Griffin Cl
Morris Cl
Stanley Cl
Conliston Close
Plantation Road
Grange Road

Grmbrdg Dr
Grange Road

Lower Rainham Road
B2004

East Court Farm

79   80

F   G   H   22   J   K

LOWER RAINH

Lower
Twydall

Ferndale Rd
Linden Rd
Priestfield Road
Sunnymead
Cobham Rise
Redfern
Woodlands
Tangmere Cl
Hazlemere Drive
Buttermere Cl
Thinmere Cl
Sharps Green
stcourt Lane
LOWER RAINHE

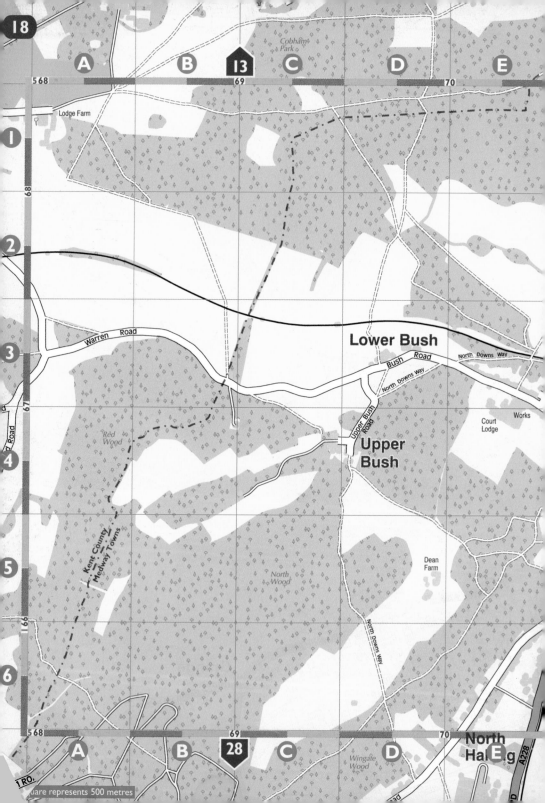

18

A   B   **13**   C   D   E

5 68   69   70

Lodge Farm

1

68

2

Warren   Road

Lower Bush

Bush   Road   North   Downs   Way

3

67

North Downs Way

Red Wood

Works

Court Lodge

4

Upper Bush Road

Upper Bush

Kent County Medway Towns

North Wood

Dean Farm

5

66

North Downs Way

6

5 68   69   70

A   B   **28**   C   D   North Hal E.g

Wingate Wood

Cobham Park

I RO.

A228

quare represents 500 metres

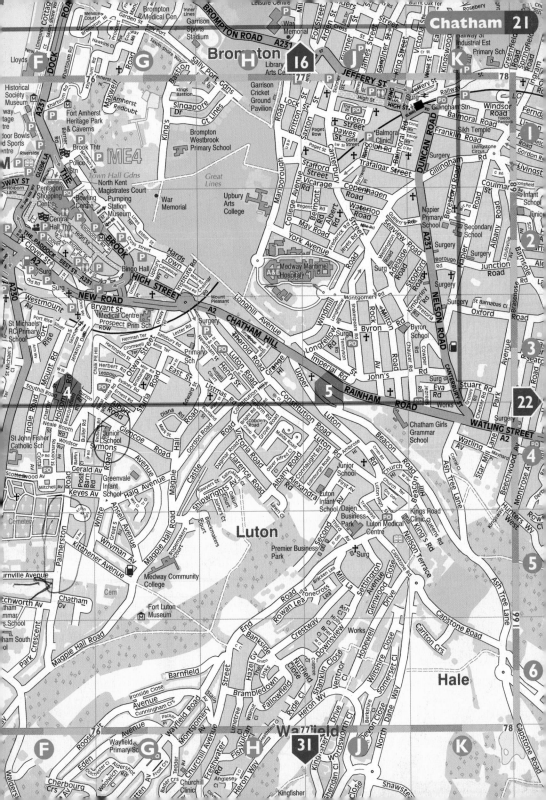

F G H J K

86 87 88

Barks Marshes

Funton Creek

1

68

Funton Brickworks

Saxon Shore Way

2

Barksore

Saxon Shore Way

Lapwing Drive

Curlew Avenue

Hero Cl

The

Street

PO

Vicarage Lane

Burntwick Drive

Westmo

Cumberland Drive

School Lane

Landrail Road

Lower Halstow

Callum Park

3

26

4

Elm Farm

Lower Halstow School

Wardwell Lane

Great Norwood

Belnor

Little Norwood

5

I 66

Parsona

Hawes Wood

High Oak Hill

Avenue

6

Bog Farm

Wardwell Lane

Cemetery

Oak Hill

Harbour Lane

F G H 35 J K

86 87 88

Newington CE Primary School

School Lane

We

Bedlams Bottom

A   **B**   **C**   **D**   **E**

Raspberry   Hill   Lane   Old Fe

5 88   89   90

Sheppey Way

I

68

Saxon Shore Way

Sanderling Way

Iwade Primary School

Iwade

Fans   Evergreen   Cl

Mds

La   Cl

2

Linkway

PO

Woodpecker Dr

Syn   Wa

Meadow   Rise

Springvale

Ferry

Helen Thompson Close

Funton

Sheerstone

Road

Kingfisher Close

School   Lane

Colson Dr

Grovehurst

Road

3

Coleshall

Sheppey   Way

Teal   Way

Pln

Orchard Farm

25

Featherbed La

Culnells

A249

B2005

4

Sheppey Way

Pheasant Farm

Stickfast   Lane

Cambray Farm

Bramblefield Lane

5

Cambray Works

Lane

John Goodhev Medical Centre

Howt Green

Kemsley Station

Parsonage

166

The Garden of England Crematorium

Nether Toes

Flint

Eclipse Drive

6

Parsonage

Sheppey Way

Upper Toes

A249

Attlee

Burnham Ct

Retail Park

Exeter

Volante Drive

Attlee

Lane

Phillippa Ct

Regis Manor Comm. Primary

A   **B**   **36**   Quinton   **C**   **D**   **E**

5 88   89   90

Road

grid square represents 500 metres

Bobbing

F G H J K

I
2
3
4
5
6

Saxon Shore Way

Saxon Shore Way

Coldharbour Marshes

Works

Saxon Shore Way

A249

Rid
Do

Great
Grovehurst

Paper Mill

Works

The Lilies

Kemsley Down

Milton Creek

Saxon Shore Way

Menin Rd
Mons Ct
Flanders Close
The Crescent
West Gn
East Gn
Ridham
Ypres Dr
Liege Cl
Castle Rough
Coldharbour Lane
Coldharbour Lane
Marsh La
Grovehurst
Avenue
Recreation Way
Coleman
Eadred Way

PO
Godwin Cl
Ypres Dr
Grovehurst Avenue
Pavilion View

Kemsley
Celt Close
B2005
Doramowe Dr
Newman Dr
Aylwin Dr
Cheyne
Puttney
Ingleden
Colfe Way
Austin
Newman Drive
Beauvoir Dr
Newman Dr
Walsby Dr
Surgery
Vaughan
Burkeston
Chenies
Todd Crs
Yeates Dr
Miller Cl
Gregory Close

Saffron Road
St Bartholomews School
Green Porch Close
Grovehurst Rd
Trinity Road
B2005
Ashurst
Whit Cl
Tallow Cl
Turner Close

Sittingbourne & Kemsley Light Railway

Saxon Shore Way

F G H 37 J K

91 92 93

A   B   18   C   D   E

568   69   70

North Halling

I

Wingate Wood

Works

FORMBY RD

A228

65

2

Horseholders Wood

Stake

Kent Rd

Ne To

Pilgrims Road

Essex Road

Hallin Station

3

Primrose Road

Vicarage Road

Vicarage Cl

Cem

High Stree

Upper Halling

Grove Road

Bradley Rd

Street

Cemetery Rd

A228

64

Chapel Lane

The

Browndens Road

4

Medway Towns
Kent County

Meadow Crescent

Meadow Cl

Meadow

A

Pilgrims Way

5

Lad's Farm

63

Holborough

6

Ladds

Lane

Works

568   69   70

A   B   38   C   D   E

Pilgrims Way

Paddlesworth

ME6

Cemetery

1 grid square represents 500 metres

F

G

H

19

J

K

71

72

Burham Road

73

North Downs Way

I

Works

Ivy Cott

North Downs Way

ME1

Ke

2

Wouldham Road

Ringshill Place

Pilgrims Way

Hill Road

3

Marsh Road

Marsh Road

School Farm

School Lane

Hill Road

30

Halling

Meadow

Surgery

Rectory Cl

Trafalgar Rd

Nelson Rd

High Street

Wouldham

PO

Grdn Ct

Ct Dr

Olane

Pilgrims Way

4

Ferry La

Portland Rd

Scholey Cl

Hostler Cl

Herring Cl

Howlsmere Cl

Cornwall Crs

Knowle Road

Hill Road

5

Halling Primary School

Hall Road

Works

Rochester Road

Scarborough

I 63

6

River Medway

Medway Valley Walk

Scarborough Lane

Marletts Lane

Downs Vw

71

72

73

Burham Court

Burham

1 grid square represents 500 metres

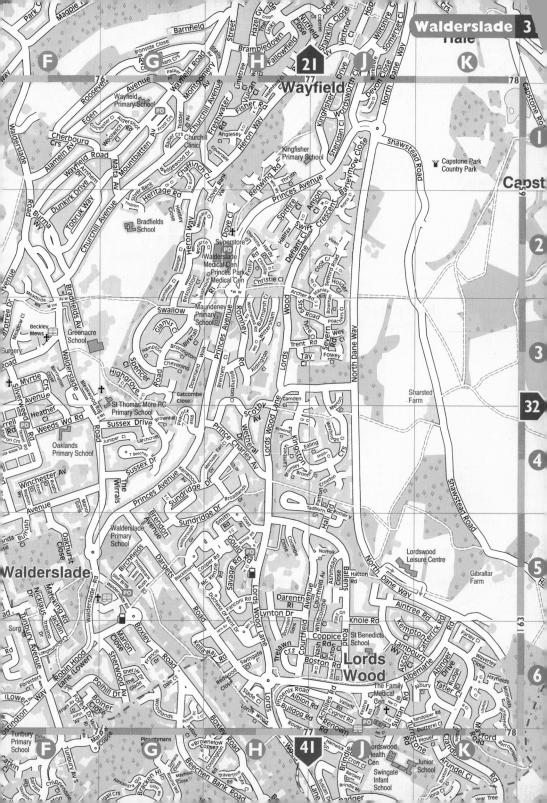

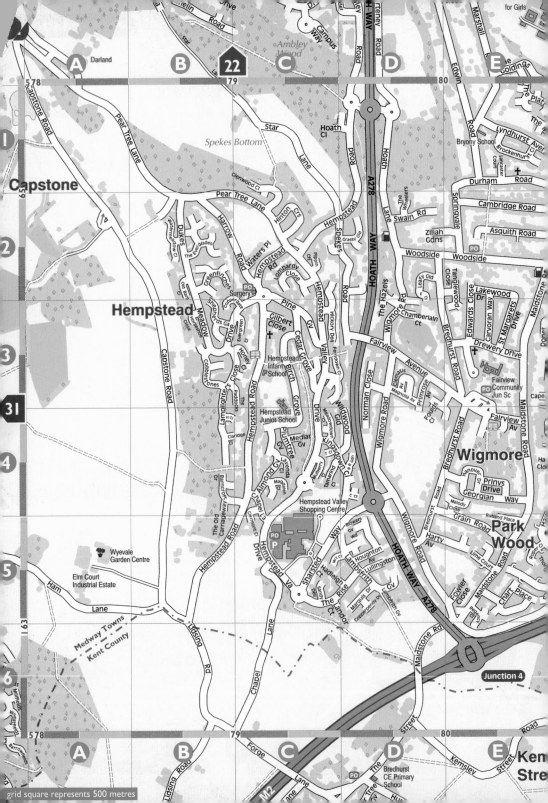

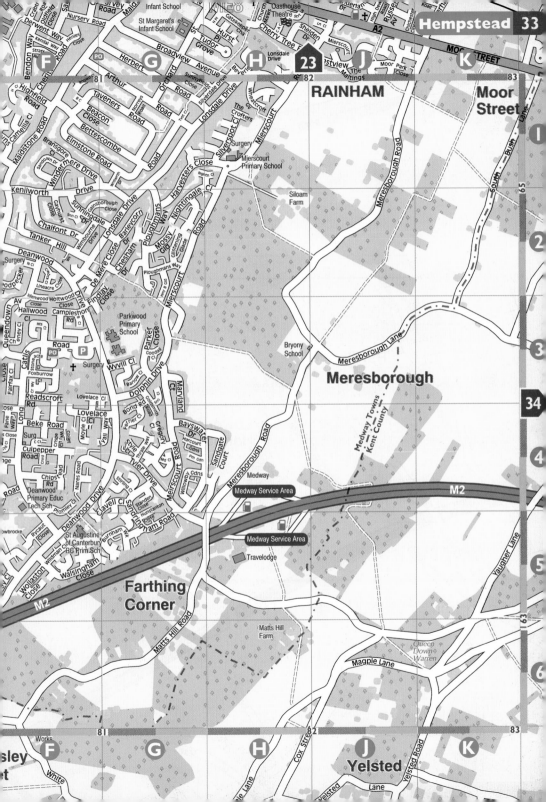

A2

MOOR STREET

F **G** **H** 23 **J** **K**

RAINHAM

Moor Street

Lonsdale Drive

I

Mierscourt Primary School

Siloam Farm

Meresborough Road

2

Meresborough Lane

Bryony School

3

Meresborough

34

Medway Towns Kent County

Parkwood Primary School

4

Medway Service Area

M2

Medway

Medway Service Area

Travelodge

Farthing Corner

M2

Matts Hill Farm

Queen Down Warren

Magpie Lane

Vaughan Lane

6

F 81 **G** **H** 82 **J** **K** 83

sley et

Works

White

Yelsted

Cox Street

Yelsted Road

Yelsted Lane

Lane

F
G
H
25
Oak Hill
J
K

Cemetery 86
87
88

Wardwell Lane
Bog Farm

School Lane

Newington CE Primary School

Denham Road
Wormley Rd
St. Mary's View
Lane

Newington Station

Cold Harbour

Cold Harbour Lane
65

Wickham Close
Church
HIGH STREET
Station Rd
PO

London Rd
Allsworth Cl
Bull Lane
The Willows
Brookes Place
Callaways Lane
The Tracies

BOYCES HILL
Keycol
A2 KEYCOL HILL
Rook Lane

Ladyfields Close
Bobbing

Newington

Newington Manor

3

36

MAIDSTONE ROAD
Chestnut Street

Works Chestnut

4

Wormdale

dale Road

Chestnut Street

Chestnut Wd La

Borden CE Primary School

School Lane

Maidstone Road

63

5

Wormdale Hill

Golf Course

A249

Sunnyhill

Sittingbourne & Milton Regis Golf Club

Munsgore Lane

Munsgore Farm

Munsgore Lane

Road

6

Woodgate

MAIDSTONE ROAD

Danaway

Lane

Eyehorn Hatch Farm

86
87
88

F
G
H
J
K

Junction 5

Oad Street

F G H J K

71 72 73

Scarborough Lane

29

I

Burham

Margetts Lane

Burham Court

Downs VW

Rochester Rd

St

Baker St

New

PH

Court Road

Old Church Road

Church Road

Church

PO

Bell Lane

Bell Crs

Court Road

River Medway

Medway Valley Walk

Nature Reserve

Tilghman Wy

Watts Cl

Church Fld

Hendy Rd

Snodland Station

A228

LC

Mill St

May St

East

Brook St

Sortmill Rd

Mid Kent Business Park

Mid Kent Business Park

Works

Reservoir

3

40

St Marks CE Primary School

Eccles RW

Leeds Rd

St Peters Cl

Jenner Southgate

Belgrave

Victoria

Jenner Ln

Skinners Cl

Mackenders Cl

4

Cork Street

PO

Hawkers

Ec

5

Larkfield Trading Estate

New Hythe Business Park

Medway Valley Walk

Rowe Place Farm

River Medway

Larkfield Trading Estate

New Hythe Lane

New Hythe Station

New Hythe

New Hythe Business Park

New Hythe Lane

Medway Valley Walk

Bull Lane

6

Way

Av

Cl

Central Road

Central Road

West Mill Road

Mill Hall Road

College Road

Perimeter Road

Belling Way

Paper Mills

F G H J K

71 72 73

46

St

ME20

AYLESFORD

40

A B **30** C D E

5 73   74   75

Common Road

Blue Bell Hill

Junction 3

Taddington

Hurst Hl

M2

A229 A2045

Lockley Robin Hood

1
Burham

Keere Cl
Robin Hood La
Robin Hood La (Upper)

Tryon Cl
Maidstone Road
Barling Cl
Laurie Gray Av
Roman rd

North Downs Way

Mill Lane

The Downs

Medway Crematorium

PO

2
Surgery

Bell Crs
Court Road

Whitehouse crs

Centenary Walk-Maidstone

Kit's Coty

Kingswood Road

North Downs Way

Chatham

A229

Warren Road

3

Little Culand

Hale Farm

Salisbury Road

Vincent Road
Beresford Road
Russell Road
Collingwood Road

Queenswood Road

Chatham Rd

39

Bull Lane

Greenfield

Centenary Walk-Maidstone

4

Skinners Cl
Mackenders Cl
Mackenders Lane

Pilgrims Way

Kit's Coty House

North Downs Way

Old Chatham Rd

A229

Warren

Lower

Warren

Rochester Road

5
Eccles

Rochester Road

Rochester Road

North Downs Way

Chatham Road

6

Medway Valley Walk

Pratling Street

Pratling Street

Gate Way
Grey Walk
Chatham Road

Tylan

Pratling Street

5 73   74   **47**   75

A B **47** C D E

Old Mill Lane

Cobtree Manor
Park Golf Club

A229

St Peters

grid square represents 500 metres

Fulston Manor
School

The M...ws
Gerrards
Drive
Shurland
Avenue

Clarendon
Close

F

SIT...NGBOURNE H

37

J

K

Norris Court

I

62

2

Rodmersham

Highsted Road

Stockers Hill

Stockers Brow

Rodmersham Green

Fruiterer's Close

PO

Browning's Orchard

Rodmersham Primary School

Green Lane

Church Street

3

Highsted

Bottles Lane

Rodmersham Squash Club

61

4

Upper Rodmersham

Bargains Hill

Dully Road

5

Bottles Lane

Cheney Pond

Bottom Road

Hill

Pitstock Farm

Penfield House

60

Dully Road

K...

6

Rawling Street

Slough Road

Penfield Lane

Pitstock Road

Kingsdown Road

F

91

G

H

92

J

K

93

Dungate

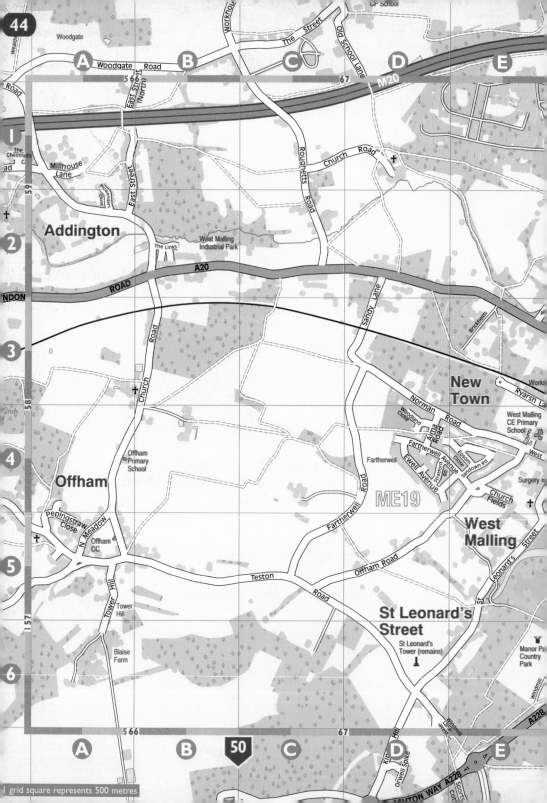

44

Woodgate

A   Woodgate   Road   B   The   Street   C   D   M20   E

CP School

Old School Lane

5 66

67

Road

The
Chestnuts

I

Church   Road

Millhouse
Lane

Roughetts
Road

Provenders
Close

East Street (North)

59

Addington

East Street

2

The Links

West Malling
Industrial Park

ROAD   A20

NDON

3

58

Church   Road

Sandy   Lane

Brickfields

**New
Town**

Ryarsh La

Works

Norman
Road

West Malling
CE Primary
School

West

4

Church

Woodland
Close

Alma Road

Epsom
Close

Offham
Primary
School

Fartherwell

Fartherwell Avenue

Stratford Rd

Sandown Rd

Surgery

Offham

Ewell   Avenue

Church
Fields

ME19

Pepingstraw
Close

N. Meadow

Fartherwell   Road

**West
Malling**

157

Offham
CC

5

Teston

Offham   Road

St Leonard's   Street

Tower Hill

Tower
Hill

Road

**St Leonard's
Street**

Blaise
Farm

St Leonard's
Tower (remains)

Manor Pa
Country
Park

6

Windmill
Lane

Windmill

A228

A   5 66   B   **50**   C   67   D   E

Kings Hill

Orwell Spike

Windmill
Lane West

Sports
Cott

ASHTON WAY A228

1 grid square represents 500 metres

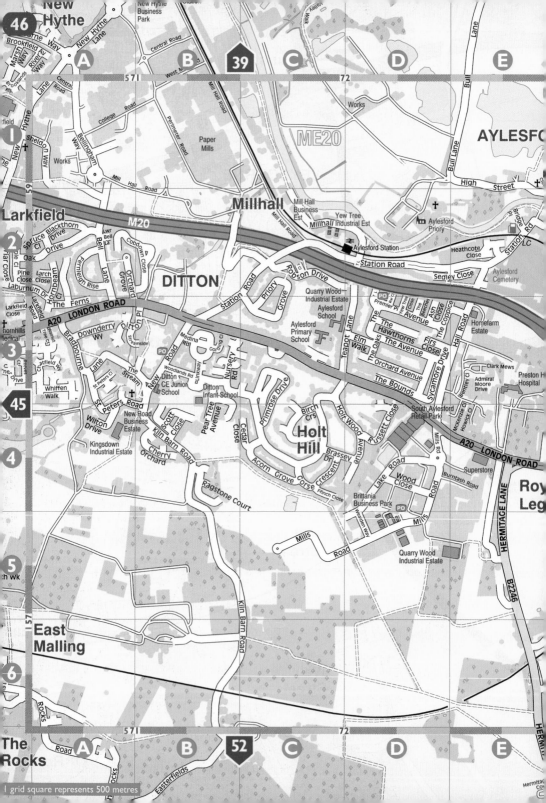

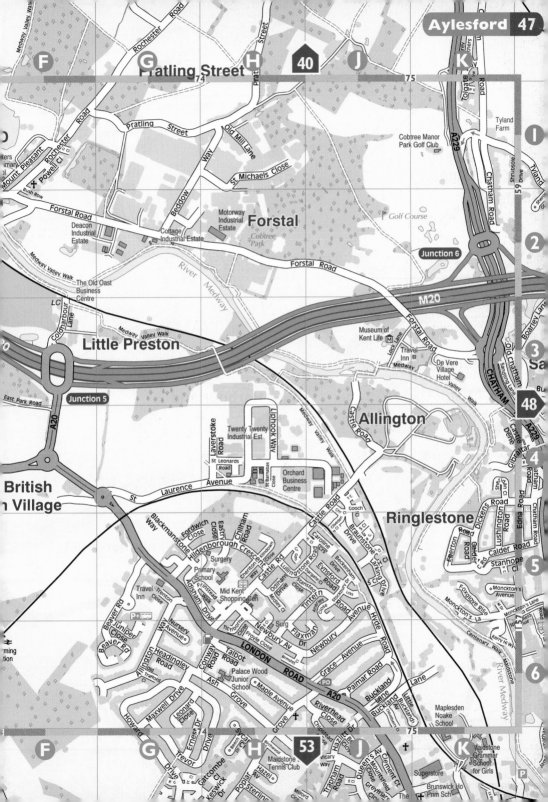

F   G   H   J   K

North Downs Way

I

Stockings Wood

79   80

Hermitage La

Mount House

North Downs Way

Pilgrims Way

Broader Lane

Scragged Oak Road

Kent County Showground

ME14

2

DETLING HILL

Pilgrims Wy

East Court

Detling CE Primary School

PO

Harpole

Harpole Lane

The Street

Princes Way

Queens Wy

Pilgrims Way

Detling

3

SITTINGBOURNE ROAD - A249

St Martin's Cl

Works

Thurnham

Orchard View

Hockers Close

4

Horish Wood

M20

Hockers Lane

Works

Court Farm

Junction 7

5

Newnham Court Farm

Honeyhills Wood

Bearsted Road

New Cut Road

Coppice View

Henley Flds

Briar Flds

Shepherds Gate Dr

Harrow Way

Exton Gdns

Golf Course

6

Grove W

Rampion Cl

Drive

Haverick Close

Greenways

Went Wk

Fulber

Birling H

Chapel Lane

Groveo

Grove Gn Rd

Weavering Street

William Ra

Ware Street

55 are Street

Bearsted Golf Club

Bearsted

79   80

F   G   H   J   K

59

58

57

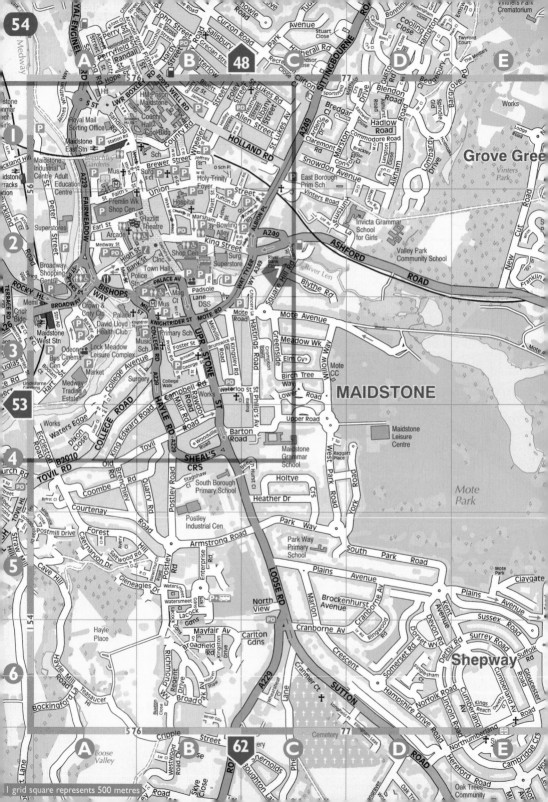

F   G   H   J   K

84   85

I

Holling
House

56

2

Hollingbourne Hill

North downs way

Allington
Farm

Pilgrims Way

Upper
Street   PH

3

Pilgrims Way

55

Hollingbourne
Station

Hollingbourne
Primary
School

Hollingbourne

orne Street

Athelstan Green

PO

Eynhorne Street

Clayvate
The
Fields

Harrods

Culpeper Close

from Road

Eynhorne Street

Greenway

4

Court   Road

Greenway
Court Rd

5

Greenway
Court

154

Oakfield

Harpswood

Hospital   Road

Warren
Wood

Court   Road

6

ASHFORD ROAD

M20

A20

Leeds Castle
Golf Club

Golf Course

bank   F   G   H   65   J   K

84   85

Greenway

Greenway
Forstal

Greenway Lan

Leeds
Castle

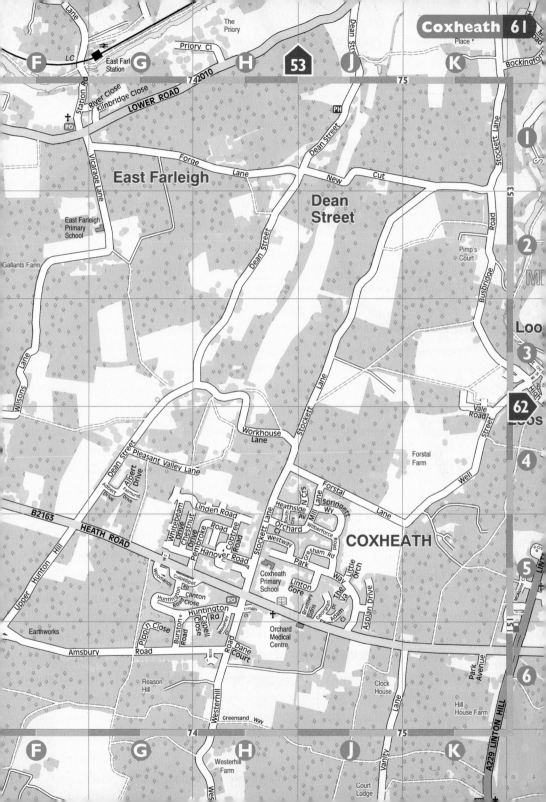

F G H 53 J K

Lane

The Priory

Priory Cl

East Farl
Station

LC

72010 75

Bockingfor

I

PO

Station Rd

Vicarage Lane

River Close
Kilnbridge Close

LOWER ROAD

Forge

Lane

New Cut

Dean Street

PH

Stockett Lane

53

East Farleigh

**Dean
Street**

East Farleigh
Primary
School

Dean Street

Pimp's
Court

2

Gallants Farm

M

Busbridge

Road

Loo

3

Wilsons

Lane

Stockett

Lane

Vale
Road

62

Loos

Workhouse
Lane

Stockett

High Street

4

Well

Forstal
Farm

Pleasant Valley Lane

Dean Street

Albert
Drive

Aldbert
Drive

Fairhurst
Drive

Linden Road

Whitebean
Drive

Chestnut
Drive

Pembroke
Road

Cobtree
Road

Stockett Lane

Heathside

N Crs

South Crs
South AV

Mill Lane

Forstal
Lane

Springett
WY

Forstal
Lane

COXHEATH

B2163

HEATH ROAD

Upper Hunton Hill

Hanover Road

Culpepper
Rd

Woodlands

Clinton
Close

Huntington Road

Burston
Road

Pippin
Close

Capell
Close

Waverley
Road

Orchard
Cl

Wilberforce
Cl

Westway

Sham Rd

Gro

Cristsin
Ct

Coxheath
Primary
School

Park

Linton
Gore

Bradley
Edns

Georgian
Dr

The
Va

Way

Little
Orch

Adam
Cl

Aspian Drive

5

PO

Orchard
Medical
Centre

Earthworks

Amsbury

Road

Dane
Court

Westerhill Road

Clock
House

Park
Avenue

6

Reason
Hill

Greensand

Way

Hill
House Farm

Hill House Farm

74 75

F G H J K

Westerhill
Farm

Vanity Lane

A229 LINTON HILL

Court
Lodge

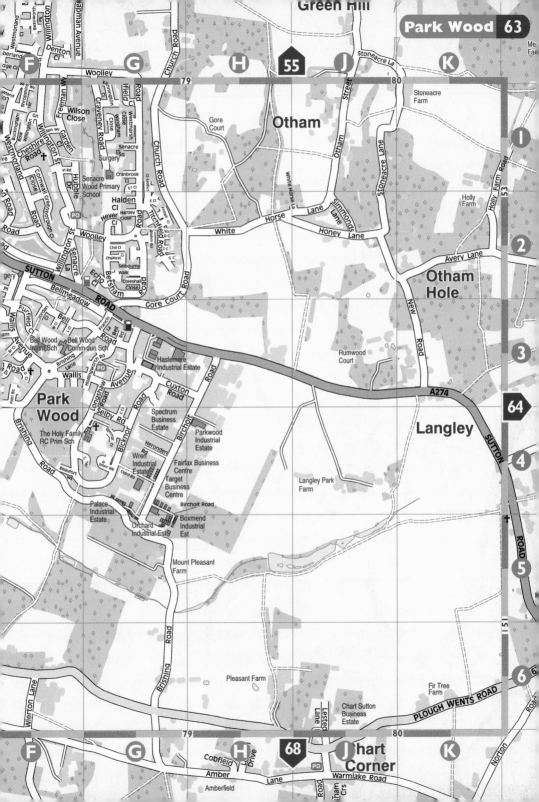

A   B   56   C   D   E

581   82

I

2

3

63

4

5

6

A   B   69   C   D   E

581   82

Merriams
Farm

Spout
Farm

Caring Lane

Street

Leeds & Broomfield
CE Primary School

LOWER STREET

Brogden

Forge Lane

Leeds

Wykeham Grove

George Lane

Holly's Farm Road

olly
arm

Lar

Arnold
Farm

Avery Lane

Back Street

Back Street

Meredith
Close

Brogden
Crescent

Burgess Hall
Drive

Farmer
Close

UPPER STREET

B2163

Burberry Lane

SUTTON ROAD

Horseshoes Lane

Gullands

Turpis
Close

Heath

Forsters

Shepherds

Close

Orchard
Close

Green Lane

LEEDS ROAD

ROAD

Copperfield Drive

Dickens Close

Heathfield

Grasslands

Langley
Heath

Ulcombe Road

151

Rectory Farm

Abbey
Wood

Gravelly Bottom

Five Wents

B2163

's ROAD

Norton Road

Apiary
Business
Park

Collingwood
Industrial
Estate

Pitt Road

Cross Drive

MAIDSTONE ROAD

Warmlake
Business
state

Warren Wood

Hospital

Leeds Castle Golf Club

Golf Course

84

57

Greenway

85

Greenway Forstal

Greenway Lane

Leeds Castle

Chegworth Road

I

53

2

Broomfield Road

Chegworth

Waterlane Farm

Broomfield

†

3

Park Barn Farm

Barn Road

Lane

66

4

Kings Wood

Chegworth Road

5

Broomfield Road

Whitehall Drive

Charlesford Avenue

Ashford Drive

Elder Close

Whitehall Drive

Bell Way

Mill Court

Bushy Grove

Kingswood Primary School

Caysey Drive

Holly Tree Close

Water Lane

Kingswood

6

Chestnut Drive

Laurel Gv

Tall Trees Close

The Witchings

Wildwood Close

51

Croft Close

Surgery

Ho Cl

Broomfield Road

PO

Lenham Road

E17

Chartway Street

84

Chartway Street

85

Hill

Hill Farm

Fairbor Heath

Chartway Street

F   **G**   **H**   **J**   **K**

F   **G**   **H**   **J**   **K**

Flint Lane

F　　**G**　　**H**　Marlow Farm　**J**　　**K**

89　　　　　　　　　　　90

Lea Farm

Marley Court

Pilgrims Way

Faversham Road

I

Works

53

North Downs Way

2

Ham Lane

Dickley Wood

Lane

Cemetery

A20　**3**

Swadelands Specialist School

Maidstone Road

Foord Road

Royton Avenue

Chilston Rd

Dale Rd

Loder Close

Ham Lane

Mitchell Close

The Square

Lime Tree Restaurant

52

Boldrewood Farm

Ham Lane

Ham Lane

Hatch Road

Beacon Road

Honywood Road

Lenham

Malthouse Close

Faversham Rd

Church Square

PO

Old Ashford Rd

Groom Wy

Glebe Gdns

Robins Avenue

Robins Close

Robins Close

High Street

Croft Gardens

School Close

Tanyard Farm

4

Lenham Station

Mill Close

Stour Valley Walk

151

Headcorn Road

Boughton Road

Leadingcross Green

Stour Valley Walk

5

Sandway

Lenham Heath Road

6

M20

Lenham Heath Road

89　　　　　　　　　　　90

F　Lewsome Farm　**G**　Boughton Road　**H**　　**J**　Lenham Heath　**K**

Chapel Farm

Back Lane

Brishing Lane

Pleasant Farm

Fir Tree Farm

PLOUGH ENTS R

t Sutton ness Estate

Lested Lane

A **B** **63** **C** **D** **E**

578 79 80

Cobfield

Laxton Drive

Amber Lane

Amberfield

PO

Chart Corner

Warmlake Road

Chart Hl Road

sham Crs

Ma

Mr H

I

50

Wierton Rd

East Hall

Wierton

Chart Hill Road

Chart Hill

Church Road

2

49

Greensand Way

Sutton Valence Preparatory School

Wierton

East Hill

Heronden

Chart Ro

3

Hermitage Lane

Lucks Lane

Chart Hill Road

Rectory Lane

4

Forge Lane

Lamb's Cross

Chart Sutton

5

48

r Farm Rd

ton

Chart Hill Road

Green Lane

Chart Bottom Farm

White House Farm

Holbrook

Moat Farm

Green Lane

6

Rabbit's Cross

Lake Farm

578 79 80

A **B** **C** **D** Devil's Den **E**

Lane

Five Wents

Collingwood Industrial Estate

B2163

Road

F Business Park

G

H

64

J

K

ME

82

83

I

MAIDSTONE ROAD

A274

Warmlake Business Estate

Pitt Road

Chartway Street

The Ridge Golf Club

Golf Course

Warmlake

NORTH STREET

A274

Workhouse Road

Church Lane

Cobtree Medical Centre

Southways

Sutton Valence School

Sutton Valence Primary School

Sutton Valence

West Drive

East Sutton Park

Greensand Way

School Lane

Broad Tumblers Hill

St

Baker Lane

East

Greensand Way

Sutton

Road

Pleasure House

High Street

PO

Rectory Lane

Lower Road

The Platt

Castle Remains

South Lane

S Bank

Stallance

Boyton Court

Boyton Court

Road

Friday Street

The Harbour

Spark's Hall

Lane

A274

HEADCORN ROAD

Brook House

Heniker Lane

Barling Farm

Heniker Lane

F

G

H

J

K

81

82

83

Lake Farm

50

49

48

I

2

3

4

5

6

Abbey Gate 48 A1
Addington 44 A2
Allington 47 J4
Ashbank 64 E1
Aylesford 46 E1
Barming Heath 52 E3
Bearsted 55 J4
Bexon 42 B6
Blue Bell Hill 10 C1
Bobbing 36 B1
Borden 36 A6
Borstal 20 B4
Boughton Green 62 B4
Boughton Monchelsea ..62 B5
Boxley 38 E2
Breach 24 D6
Bredgar 42 A5
Broad Street 10 D6
Brompton 5 F1
Broomfield 65 F3
Burham 9 H1
Burham Court 39 H1
Capstone 31 K1
Chalkwell 36 C4
Chart Corner 68 D1
Chart Hill 68 D2
Chart Sutton 68 C5
Chatham 9 K5
Chattenden 9 K5
Chegworth 65 J2
Chesley 34 E5
Chestnut Street 35 J4
Church Street 8 C1
Cliffe Woods 3 H5
Cock Street 62 E6
Cold Harbour 35 K2
Cooling Street 9 J1
Coxheath 61 J5
Cuxton 19 G4

Danaway 35 G6
Dean Street 61 J2
Detling 49 J3
Ditton 46 B2
East Barming 52 D5
East Farleigh 61 G1
East Malling 46 A6
East Malling Heath ..51 H3
Eccles 40 A5
Eyhorne Street 56 E4
Fant 6 B6
Farleigh Green 60 D2
Farthing Corner 33 G5
Five Wents 68 B6
Forstal 47 H2
Frindsbury 15 H4
Gadshill 14 B2
Gillingham 5 F1
Grange 17 J6
Green Hill 55 J6
Grove End 42 C3
Grove Green 54 E1
Hale 21 K6
Halling 29 F3
Ham Hill 38 E4
Harbourland 48 C3
The Harbour 69 G5
Harman's Corner ...36 B6
Harrietsham 66 C2
Hartlip 34 B3
Hearts Delight 42 B1
Hempstead 32 A3
Henhurst 12 B4
Herne Pound 50 B4
Higham 8 B6
Highsted 43 F3
Holborough 28 E6
Hollingbourne 57 H4
Holt Hill 46 C4

Hoo St Werburgh ...10 D4
Horn Street 38 C4
Howt Green 26 D5
Iwade 26 D2
Kemsley 27 F6
Kent Street 50 C4
Kettle Corner 52 E6
Keycol 35 J2
Key Street 36 A3
Kingsdown 43 K6
Kings Hill 50 D2
Kingswood 65 H6
Kit's Coty 40 C2
Lamb's Cross 68 B4
Langley 63 K4
Langley Heath 64 C4
Larkfield 45 K2
Leadingcross Green ..67 H5
Leeds 64 D1
Lenham 67 J3
Leybourne 45 H1
Little Preston 47 F3
Livesey Street 51 K4
Loose 62 A4
Loose Hill 62 A3
Lords Wood 31 J6
Lower Bush 18 D3
Lower Halstow 25 G3
Lower Hartlip 34 C4
Lower Higham 8 C4
Lower Rainham 23 G3
Lower Twydall 22 E1
Lower Upnor 16 A1
Lunsford 38 C6
Luton 21 H5
Maidstone 6 D6
Meresborough 33 J3
Millhall 46 B2
Mill Street 45 H5

Milton Regis 36 C3
Mockbeggar 3 F5
Moor Street 33 K1
Murston 37 J4
Nettlestead 59 F2
Nettlestead Green ..58 E6
New Hythe 39 F6
Newington 55 G2
New Town 28 E2
New Town 44 E3
New Town 9 H6
Noke Street 9 H6
North Halling 28 E1
Offham 44 A4
Otham 63 H1
Otham Hole 63 K2
Otterham Quay 24 A4
Paddlesworth 38 B1
Park Wood 32 E5
Park Wood 63 F3
Penenden Heath ...48 D5
Pizien Well 58 E1
Polihill 66 A3
Pratling Street 40 B6
Rabbit's Cross 68 A6
Rainham 33 J1
Red Hill 51 J5
Ringlestone 47 J5
Rochester 2 D3
The Rocks 51 K1
Rodmersham 43 K2
Rodmersham Green ..43 H3
Roseacre 55 H2
Royal British Legion Village ..46 E4
St Leonard's Street ..44 D5
St Mary's Island 16 B2
Sandling 48 A3
Sandway 67 G5
Sharnal Street 11 H1
Shepway 54 D6

Shorne 13 H1
Shorne Ridgeway ...13 G3
Sittingbourne 37 G6
Snipeshill 37 J5
Snodland 38 C1
Strood 2 A2
Sutton Valence 69 G3
Teston 59 K1
Thong 12 D2
Thurnham 49 K4
Tovil 53 K5
Troy Town 3 G7
Tunstall 42 D2
Twydall 22 D1
Upchurch 24 D2
Upper Bush 18 D4
Upper Halling 28 B3
Upper Rodmersham ..43 J4
Upper Upnor 15 K3
Wainscott 15 H2
Walderslade 31 F5
Ware Street 55 J1
Warmlake 69 F2
Wateringbury 59 F1
Wayfield 31 H1
Weavering Street ...55 G2
West Street 45 H6
West Farleigh 60 A2
Westfield Sole 41 J3
West Malling 44 E5
Wetham Green 24 D1
Wierton 68 B2
Wigmore 32 E4
Willington 55 G5
Windmill Hill 24 A3
Woodstock 42 E4
Wouldham 29 G3

USING THE STREET INDEX

· Street names are listed alphabetically. Each street name is followed by its postal town or area locality, the Postcode District, the page number, and the reference to the square in which the name is found.

Standard index entries are shown as follows:

Abbey Rd *RHAM* ME8 ....**22** C4

Street names and selected addresses not shown on the map due to scale restrictions are shown in the index with an asterisk:

Abbots Ct *HOO/HM* ME3 * **11** H5

GENERAL ABBREVIATIONS

ACC...........ACCESS	CTYD...........COURTYARD	HLS...........HILLS	MWY...........MOTORWAY	SE...........SOUTH EAST
ALY...........ALLEY	CUTT...........CUTTINGS	HO...........HOUSE	N...........NORTH	SER...........SERVICE AREA
AP...........APPROACH	CV...........COVE	HOL...........HOLLOW	NE...........NORTH EAST	SH...........SHORE
AR...........ARCADE	CYN...........CANYON	HOSP...........HOSPITAL	NW...........NORTH WEST	SHOP...........SHOPPING
ASS...........ASSOCIATION	DEPT...........DEPARTMENT	HRB...........HARBOUR	O/P...........OVERPASS	SKWY...........SKYWAY
AV...........AVENUE	DL...........DALE	HTH...........HEATH	OFF...........OFFICE	SMT...........SUMMIT
BCH...........BEACH	DM...........DAM	HTS...........HEIGHTS	ORCH...........ORCHARD	SOC...........SOCIETY
BLDS...........BUILDINGS	DR...........DRIVE	HVN...........HAVEN	OV...........OVAL	SP...........SPUR
BND...........BEND	DRO...........DROVE	HWY...........HIGHWAY	PAL...........PALACE	SPR...........SPRING
BNK...........BANK	DRY...........DRIVEWAY	IMP...........IMPERIAL	PAS...........PASSAGE	SQ...........SQUARE
BR...........BRIDGE	DWGS...........DWELLINGS	IN...........INLET	PAV...........PAVILION	ST...........STREET
BRK...........BROOK	E...........EAST	IND EST...........INDUSTRIAL ESTATE	PDE...........PARADE	STN...........STATION
BTM...........BOTTOM	EMB...........EMBANKMENT	INF...........INFIRMARY	PH...........PUBLIC HOUSE	STR...........STREAM
BUS...........BUSINESS	EMBY...........EMBASSY	INFO...........INFORMATION	PK...........PARK	STRD...........STRAND
BVD...........BOULEVARD	ESP...........ESPLANADE	INT...........INTERCHANGE	PKWY...........PARKWAY	SW...........SOUTH WEST
BY...........BYPASS	EST...........ESTATE	IS...........ISLAND	PL...........PLACE	TDG...........TRADING
CATH...........CATHEDRAL	EX...........EXCHANGE	JCT...........JUNCTION	PLN...........PLAIN	TER...........TERRACE
CEM...........CEMETERY	EXPY...........EXPRESSWAY	JTY...........JETTY	PLNS...........PLAINS	THWY...........THROUGHWAY
CEN...........CENTRE	EXT...........EXTENSION	KG...........KING	PLZ...........PLAZA	TNL...........TUNNEL
CFT...........CROFT	F/O...........FLYOVER	KNL...........KNOLL	POL...........POLICE STATION	TOLL...........TOLLWAY
CH...........CHURCH	FK...........FOOTBALL CLUB	L...........LAKE	PR...........PRINCE	TPK...........TURNPIKE
CHA...........CHASE	FLD...........FIELD	LA...........LANE	PREC...........PRECINCT	TR...........TRACK
CHYD...........CHURCHYARD	FLDS...........FIELDS	LDG...........LODGE	PREP...........PREPARATORY	TRL...........TRAIL
CIR...........CIRCLE	FLS...........FALLS	LGT...........LIGHT	PRIM...........PRIMARY	TWR...........TOWER
CIRC...........CIRCUS	FLTS...........FLATS	LK...........LOCK	PROM...........PROMENADE	U/P...........UNDERPASS
CL...........CLOSE	FM...........FARM	LKS...........LAKES	PRS...........PRINCESS	UNI...........UNIVERSITY
CLFS...........CLIFFS	FT...........FORT	LNDG...........LANDING	PRT...........PORT	UPR...........UPPER
CMP...........CAMP	FWY...........FREEWAY	LTL...........LITTLE	PT...........POINT	V...........VALE
CNR...........CORNER	FY...........FERRY	LWR...........LOWER	PTH...........PATH	VA...........VALLEY
CO...........COUNTY	GA...........GATE	MAG...........MAGISTRATE	PZ...........PIAZZA	VIAD...........VIADUCT
COLL...........COLLEGE	GAL...........GALLERY	MAN...........MANSIONS	QD...........QUADRANT	VIL...........VILLA
COM...........COMMON	GDN...........GARDEN	MD...........MEAD	QU...........QUEEN	VIS...........VISTA
COMM...........COMMISSION	GDNS...........GARDENS	MDW...........MEADOWS	QY...........QUAY	VLG...........VILLAGE
CON...........CONVENT	GLD...........GLADE	MEM...........MEMORIAL	R...........RIVER	VLS...........VILLAS
COT...........COTTAGE	GLN...........GLEN	MKT...........MARKET	RBT...........ROUNDABOUT	VW...........VIEW
COTS...........COTTAGES	GN...........GREEN	MKTS...........MARKETS	RD...........ROAD	W...........WEST
CP...........CAPE	GND...........GROUND	ML...........MALL	RDG...........RIDGE	WD...........WOOD
CPS...........COPSE	GRA...........GRANGE	ML...........MILL	REP...........REPUBLIC	WHF...........WHARF
CR...........CREEK	GRG...........GARAGE	MNR...........MANOR	RES...........RESERVOIR	WK...........WALK
CREM...........CREMATORIUM	GT...........GREAT	MS...........MEWS	RFC...........RUGBY FOOTBALL CLUB	WKS...........WALKS
CRS...........CRESCENT	GTWY...........GATEWAY	MSN...........MISSION	RI...........RISE	WLS...........WELLS
CSWY...........CAUSEWAY	GV...........GROVE	MT...........MOUNT	RP...........RAMP	WY...........WAY
CT...........COURT	HGR...........HIGHER	MTN...........MOUNTAIN	ROW...........ROW	YD...........YARD
CTRL...........CENTRAL	HL...........HILL	MTS...........MOUNTAINS	S...........SOUTH	YHA...........YOUTH HOSTEL
CTS...........COURTS		MUS...........MUSEUM	SCH...........SCHOOL	

POSTCODE TOWNS AND AREA ABBREVIATIONS

CHAT...........Chatham	HOO/HM ...Hoo St Werburgh/Higham	MEO...........Meopham	RTON...........Rural Tonbridge	WALD...........Walderslade
DIT/AY.....Ditton/Aylesford	IOS...........Isle of Sheppey	RHAM......Rainham (Kent)	SIT...........Sittingbourne	WBY/YAL...Wateringbury/Yalding
E/WMAL.....East & West Malling	MAID/BEAR ...Maidstone/Bearsted	RMAID.....Rural Maidstone	SNOD...........Snodland	
GILL...........Gillingham	MAID/SHEP ...Maidstone/Shepway	ROCH...........Rochester	STPH/PW...Staplehurst/Paddock Wood	
GVE...........Gravesend east	MAIDW...........Maidstone west	RSIT.....Rural Sittingbourne	STRD...........Strood	

A

Abbey Brewery Ct
E/WMAL ME19 *..............45 F4
Abbey Rd RHAM ME8..........22 C4
STRD ME2.......................14 E4
Abbey Wood Rd E/WMAL ME19 ...50 D1
Abbots Court Rd HOO/HM ME3 ..11 H5
Abbots Fld MAIDW ME16 ....60 E3
Abbott Dr RSIT ME9 *...........42 D4
Abbotts Cl ROCH ME1...........20 B3
Abigail Cl WALD ME5............41 G1
Abingdon Rd MAIDW ME16 ......52 E4
Abinger Dr WALD ME5...........31 K6
Academy Pl GILL ME7............22 B6
Achilles Rd WALD ME5..........31 J6
Acorn Cl DIT/AY ME20...........46 C4
Acorn Pl MAID/SHEP ME15 .....63 F2
Acorn Rd GILL ME7..............3 C3
Acorn Wharf Rd ROCH ME1.....5 H2
Acre Cl ROCH ME1...............20 C5
Acre Gv STRD ME2...............28 E4
Adam Cl RMAID ME12............61 J5
Adams Cl WALD ME5 *...........31 H2
Adbert Dr MAID/SHEP ME15 ...36 E5
Addington Cl SIT ME10..........36 E5
Addison Cl E/WMAL ME10 ......43 G6
Adelaide Dr SIT ME10...........36 C4
Adelaide Rd GILL ME7...........5 J5
The Adelaide HOO/HM ME3 ....10 B4
Adisham Dr MAIDW ME16........47 G5
Adisham Gn SIT ME10 *..........5 J4
Admiral Moore Dr DIT/AY ME20..46 E3
Admiralty Rd STRD ME2.........16 A3
Admiralty Ter STRD ME2........16 A3
Admiral Wy E/WMAL ME19 ......50 D5
Afghan Rd CHAT ME4............4 A5
Aintree Rd WALD ME5...........31 J5
Ajax Rd ROCH ME1..............30 C1
Alamein Av WALD ME5...........31 F1
Albany Rd CHAT ME5............4 C6
GILL ME7.......................5 H4
SIT ME10 *.....................36 E5
Albany St MAID/BEAR ME14 ....7 K1
Albany Ter MAID/BEAR ME4 ....7 K1
Albatross Av STRD ME2.........14 B6
Albemarle Rd WALD ME5.......31 J6
Albert Manor MAID/SHEP ME15..61 G4
Albert Pl STRD ME2.............2 C1
Albert Reed Gdns
MAID/SHEP ME15 ....53 K4
Albert Rd CHAT ME4 *..........4 D7
GILL ME7.......................5 H4
ROCH ME1......................20 C5
Albert St MAID/BEAR ME14 ....48 A6
Albion Pl MAID/BEAR ME14 ....7 J3
Albion Rd WALD ME5...........31 H6
Albion Ter SIT ME10 *..........36 E2
Albury Rd WALD ME5...........31 K6
Aldershot Rd WALD ME5 *......31 K6
The Alders WBY/YAL ME18 .....58 A1
Aldington Cl WALD ME5.........31 H3
Aldington Rd MAID/BEAR ME14 ..55 G2
Aldon Cl MAID/BEAR ME14 .....48 D6
Alexander Ct SIT ME10 *........9 J5
Alexander Gv E/WMAL ME19 ...50 D5
Alexandra Av GILL ME7.........22 D6
Alexandra Cl SIT ME10..........36 E1
Alexandra Gln WALD ME5.......41 G1
Alexandra St MAID/BEAR ME14 ..48 A6
Alex Hughes Cl WALD ME5......31 H2
Alfred Cl CHAT ME4.............21 J2
Alfriston Gn E/WMAL ME19 .....51 F5
Alkham Rd MAID/BEAR ME14 ...54 D1
Allen Cl WALD ME5.............31 J2
Allington St MAID/BEAR ME14 ..7 J1
Allington Dr STRD ME2..........14 C6
Allington Gdns WBY/YAL ME18...59 G1
Allington Rd RHAM ME8.........22 C3
Allington Wy MAIDW ME16......47 G6
Allison Av GILL ME7.............22 D6
Allnutt Mill Cl MAID/SHEP ME15..53 K4
All Saints Rd SIT ME10.........37 J4
Allsworth Cl RSIT ME9..........42 C5
Alma Pl STRD ME2...............2 C2
Alma Rd DIT/AY ME20 *.........39 K4
E/WMAL ME19..................44 D4
Almond Gv GILL ME7............32 C4
The Almonds MAID/SHEP ME15..36 D5
Alton Av E/WMAL ME19..........51 F5
Alton Ms GILL ME7 *............5 J5
Amanda Cl WALD ME5...........30 E5
Amber La RMAID ME17...........68 C1
Ambleside SIT ME10.............37 J5
Ambley Gn GILL ME7............22 C6
Ambley Rd GILL ME7............22 D6
Ambrose HI WALD ME5..........31 G1
Ames Av MAID/BEAR ME14 .....55 H2
Amethyst Cl MAIDW ME16.......6 C2
Amherst Cl MAIDW ME16........6 C2
Amherst HI GILL ME7............4 E2
Amherst Redoubt GILL ME7 ....4 E2
Amherst Rd ROCH ME1.........20 D3
Amsbury Rd MAID/SHEP ME15...65 F4
Anatase Cl SIT ME10............36 C1
Anchor Rd ROCH ME1...........20 C5
Andrew Broughton Wy
MAID/BEAR ME14 *............7 K3
Anerley Cl MAIDW ME16 *......7 J3
Anglesey Av MAID/SHEP ME15..62 B2
Anglesey Cl MAIDW ME16.......31 H1
Anne Figg Ct ROCH ME1 *......3 G7
Annie Rd SNOD ME6.............28 E1
Ansell Av CHAT ME4.............21 G4
Anselm Cl SIT ME10.............36 E4
Anson Av E/WMAL ME19.........50 E2
Anson Cl WALD ME5.............31 J2
Anthonys Wy STRD ME2.........3 K3
Apollo Wy CHAT ME4............16 D2
Appleby Cl ROCH ME1...........30 D1

Apple Cl SNOD ME6.............38 D4
Applecross Cl ROCH ME1 *.....20 B2
Appledore Rd RHAM ME8........22 C3
Apple Tree Cl MAIDW ME16.....52 E4
Archer Rd WALD ME5............31 H2
Archery Cl HOO/HM ME3 *......9 G3
Ardenlee Dr MAID/BEAR ME14 ..54 C1
Arden St GILL ME7 *.............5 H1
Argent Ter WALD ME5...........31 F5
Argent Wy SIT ME10.............36 C2
Argyle Cl ROCH ME1.............30 E1
Arlott Cl MAID/BEAR ME14......48 A6
Armada Ct CHAT ME4 *.........20 E5
Armada Wy CHAT ME4...........4 A5
Armstrong Rd
MAID/SHEP ME15 ....54 B5
Armytage Cl HOO/HM ME3 .....11 F6
Arnhem Dr WALD ME5...........31 F1
Arnolde Cl STRD ME2............3 K2
Arran Rd MAID/SHEP ME15.....62 B2
Arthur Rd RHAM ME8............23 G6
ROCH ME1......................20 D3
Arthur St GILL ME7..............36 E4
Arundel Av SIT ME10............42 E1
Arundel Cl MAIDW ME16 *......48 A6
Arundel St MAID/BEAR ME14...48 A6
Ascot Cl WALD ME5.............31 J6
Ashbee Cl SNOD ME6............38 E3
Ashburnham Rd
MAID/BEAR ME14 ....48 C4
Ashburn Ms GILL ME7 *.........22 A3
Ashby Cl STRD ME2 *............28 B2
Ash Cl DIT/AY ME20.............46 D5
RHAM ME8......................22 D3
WALD ME5......................21 J5
Ash Crs MAID/BEAR ME14.......14 A1
Ashcroft Cl HOO/HM ME3 ......15 G2
Ashdown Cl MAIDW ME16.......48 D5
Ashenden Cl STRD ME2 *.......15 H2
Ashford Dr RMAID ME17.........65 G6
Ashford Rd MAID/BEAR ME14...54 C2
MAID/SHEP ME15 ....7 K4
RMAID ME17....................57 G6
Ash Gv MAIDW ME16............31 H1
Ashington Cl SIT ME10..........36 C5
Ashley Rd RHAM ME8............22 E4
Ashmead Cl WALD ME5..........31 J5
Ash Rd STRD ME2...............2 A4
Ashtead Dr RSIT ME9............37 K6
Ashton Wy E/WMAL ME19 ......50 E5
Ash Tree La WALD ME5..........21 K4
Ashurst Rd MAID/BEAR ME14...54 D1
Ashwood Cl HOO/HM ME3......9 H3
Aspian Dr RMAID ME17..........61 J6
Asquith Rd RHAM ME8..........32 E2
Aster Rd HOO/HM ME3..........11 F6
Astley St MAID/BEAR ME14 *...7 J3
Aston Cl WALD ME5.............31 G6
Astra Dr GVE DA12..............12 B1
Athelstan Gn RMAID ME17......57 F4
Athelstan Rd CHAT ME4.........20 E4
Attlee Wy SIT ME10.............36 C5
Auckland Dr SIT ME10...........36 E6
Auden Rd DIT/AY ME20..........38 E6
Audley Av GILL ME7.............22 A5
Audley Cl MAIDW ME16..........53 C1
Auger Ct SIT ME10..............34 C3
Augusta Cl GILL ME7............16 E6
Austen Wy SIT ME10.............38 D6
Austin Cl SIT ME10..............27 C6
WALD ME5......................22 A4
Autumn Gld MAID/BEAR ME14..41 K2
Aveling Cl HOO/HM ME3.........10 E4
Avenue of Remembrance
SIT ME10.......................37 F5
DIT/AY ME20....................46 D3
Averenches Rd
MAID/BEAR ME14 ....55 G1
Avery Cl MAID/SHEP ME15......54 A5
Avery La MAID/SHEP ME15......63 K2
Avlemore Gdns
MAID/SHEP ME15 ....55 G2
Avington Cl MAID/SHEP ME15...54 A5
Avondale Rd GILL ME7...........5 K2
Aylesford Crs RHAM ME8........22 C3
Aylewyn Gn SIT ME10...........27 F6

B

Backfields ROCH ME1...........2 E7
Back La RMAID ME17.............62 E6
Back St RMAID ME17............64 B2
Baden Rd GILL ME7.............16 E5
Bader Crs WALD ME5............31 G1
Badger Rd WALD ME5...........41 J1
Baffin Cl CHAT ME4.............21 J2
Bailey Dr GILL ME7..............22 C6
Baker La RMAID ME17...........69 H3
Baker St ROCH ME1.............20 C3
ROCH ME1......................5 F4
Baker's Wk ROCH ME1 *.........3 F4
Balas Dr SIT ME10..............36 C2
Balfour Rd CHAT ME4............4 C6
Ballens Rd WALD ME5...........31 J5
Balmer Cl RHAM ME8............33 F1
Balmoral Rd GILL ME7...........5 K2
Bancroft La E/WMAL ME19......51 F4
Bangor Rd DIT/AY ME20.........14 C6
Bankside WALD ME5.............21 H6
Banks Rd STRD ME2.............15 H4
Bank St CHAT ME4...............5 F6
ROCH ME1......................7 G4
Banky Fields Cl RHAM ME8......23 F5
Banky Meadow MAIDW ME16...52 E5
Banning St STRD ME2............15 H4
Bannister HI RSIT ME9...........42 A3
Bannister Rd MAID/BEAR ME14..48 B5
Barberry Av WALD ME5..........30 D3
Bardell Ter ROCH ME1 *.........3 H6
Barfleur Mnr GILL ME7...........16 B6

Barfreston Cl MAID/SHEP ME15..54 A4
Bargrove Rd MAID/SHEP ME14..54 E1
Barham Cl MAID/SHEP ME15....63 F3
Barker Rd MAIDW ME16..........6 E4
Barkers St SIT ME10............36 D4
Barkis Cl ROCH ME1............30 D1
Barleycorn E/WMAL ME19.......45 H5
Barleyson Dr RHAM ME8.........33 G2
Barley Fids MAID/SHEP ME15....54 E2
Barleymow Cl WALD ME5........31 J2
Barling Cl WALD ME5............33 F1
Barlow Cl WALD ME5............33 G3
Barming Rd E/WMAL ME19......51 J4
Barnaby Ter ROCH ME1..........20 A6
Barn Cl RSIT ME9...............36 A6
Barncott Cl MAID/BEAR ME14...32 B4
Barncroft GILL ME7.............32 B4
Barned Ct RHAM ME8...........52 B5
Barnfield WALD ME5.............21 G6
Barn HI MAID/SHEP ME15.......60 D6
Barnhurst Rd MAID/BEAR ME14..48 B4
Barn Meadow STRD ME2.........28 C4
Barnsole Rd GILL ME7...........22 A2
Barnwell Pl GILL ME7............32 A3
Barnwood Cl ROCH ME1.........20 A6
Baron Cl GILL ME7..............17 F5
MAID/BEAR ME14 ....55 J1
Barrack Rd CHAT ME4...........16 C4
Barrie Dr DIT/AY ME20..........38 D6
Barrier Rd CHAT ME4............4 A5
Barrington Ct WALD ME5........31 F3
Barrowfields WALD ME5.........31 K1
Barrow Gv SIT ME10............36 D5
Bartlett Cl WALD ME5...........41 J1
Barton St MAID/SHEP ME15.....7 J7
STRD ME2.......................2 C1
Basi Cl STRD ME2...............15 H3
Basil Ter MAID/SHEP ME15 *....54 B5
Basing Cl MAID/SHEP ME15.....7 K6
Basmere Cl MAID/BEAR ME14...48 D6
Bassett Rd SIT ME10............36 A6
Batchelor St CHAT ME4..........4 C5
Bates Cl DIT/AY ME20...........45 K1
Bath Hard ROCH ME1............5 J6
Battlesmere Rd HOO/HM ME3...9 G2
Batts St GVE DA12..............12 C6
Baxter Wy E/WMAL ME19.......51 F3
Bayford Rd SIT ME10............37 C4
Bayswater Dr RHAM ME8........32 A3
Baywell E/WMAL ME19...........45 H5
Beacon Cl WALD ME5...........35 F1
Beacon HI WALD ME5............21 K4
Beacon Hill La HOO/HM ME3....10 A6
Beacon Rd RMAID ME17.........67 H3
WALD ME5......................21 J4
Beaconsfield Av GILL ME7.......5 K6
Beaconsfield Rd CHAT ME4......21 F4
SIT ME10.......................37 J5
The Beacons MAID/SHEP ME17..61 H6
The Beams MAID/SHEP ME15....55 F5
Bearsted Cl RHAM ME8..........22 D5
Bearsted Rd MAID/BEAR ME14..48 D5
Beatty Av GILL ME7.............23 G6
Beatty Rd ROCH ME1............20 B6
Beaufighter Rd E/WMAL ME19...50 B3
Beaufort Cl STRD ME2 *.........4 A1
Beaufort Rd STRD ME2..........14 D4
Beaufort Wk MAID/SHEP ME15..63 F4
Beaulieu Ri ROCH ME1..........20 D5
Beaulieu Wk MAIDW ME16 *....47 H5
Beaumont Rd MAID/BEAR ME14..53 C4
Beauvoir Dr SIT ME10...........27 C6
Beauworth Pk
MAID/SHEP ME15 ....55 F6
Beaver Rd DIT/AY ME20.........46 B3
Beckenham Dr MAIDW ME16 *..47 J5
Beckenham Pk RHAM ME8.......23 K5
Beckley Ms WALD ME5...........31 F3
Becksbourne Cl
MAID/BEAR ME14 *............7 J3
Beckworth Pl MAIDW ME16 *....53 C3
Beddow Wy DIT/AY ME20........47 C2
Bedford Av RHAM ME8...........23 F5
Bedford Pl MAIDW ME16.........6 D4
Bedgebury Cl MAID/BEAR ME14..48 D6
ROCH ME1......................20 D6
Beech Dr MAIDW ME16..........31 G1
Beechen Bank Rd WALD ME5....31 J4
The Beeches DIT/AY ME20.......46 D3
Beech Gv DIT/AY ME20..........31 H4
Beech Gv HOO/HM ME3.........14 A1

Belnor Av RSIT ME9..............25 J5
Beluncle Halt HOO/HM ME3 *...11 K2
Bendon Wy RHAM ME8..........33 G1
Benedict Ct DIT/AY ME20........29 F4
Benenden Rd STRD ME2.........15 H2
Bentlif Cl MAID/BEAR ME14.....46 E3
WALD ME5......................31 K6
Berber Rd STRD ME2............15 G4
Berengrave La RHAM ME8.......23 G5
Beresford Av MAID/BEAR ME14..20 E4
Beresford Rd DIT/AY ME20......40 C3
GILL ME7.......................5 K4
Beresfords HI RMAID ME17 *....62 E5
Bergland Pk STRD ME2 *.........15 J4
Berkeley Ct SIT ME10...........36 D5
Berkeley Mt CHAT ME4 *........4 B5
Berkshire Cl CHAT ME4..........21 J6
Berry Rd HOO/HM ME3..........17 F1
Berry St SIT ME10...............37 F4
Berwick Wy STRD ME2...........15 J3
Berwyn Gv MAID/SHEP ME15....62 B2
Best St CHAT ME4...............4 C5
Betjeman Cl DIT/AY ME20.......45 J1
Betsham Rd MAID/SHEP ME15...63 G2
Bettescombe Rd MAIDW ME16..48 E5
Beverley Cl RHAM ME8...........23 F5
Beverley Rd MAIDW ME16.......52 E4
Bexon La RSIT ME9..............42 A5
Beresfords HI MAID/SHEP ME15..55 G5
Bicclenden Cl MAID/BEAR ME14..54 D1
Bicknor Rd MAID/SHEP ME15....63 G4
Bilberry Cl MAID/BEAR ME14...55 F1
Bill Street Rd STRD ME2.........15 H3
Bilsington Cl WALD ME5.........31 H3
Bingham Rd SIT ME10...........15 H5
Bingley Cl SNOD ME6............38 D2
Bingley Gn ROCH ME1 *.........3 K7
Binland Gv WALD ME5...........31 K6
Binnacle Rd ROCH ME1..........20 C6
Birch Crs DIT/AY ME20..........46 C4
Birch Dr WALD ME5.............41 K1
Birchfield Cl MAID/SHEP ME15...62 C2
Birchington Cl
MAID/BEAR ME14 ....54 D1
Bircholt Rd MAID/BEAR ME14...54 D1
Birch Rd HOO/HM ME3..........17 F1
Birch Tree Wy MAID/SHEP ME15..55 F1
Birchwood Rd MAIDW ME16 *...48 E5
Birkdale Ct MAIDW ME16 *......6 E4
Birkhall Cl WALD ME5...........31 G3
Birling Av MAID/BEAR ME14.....55 H2
RHAM ME8......................23 F5
Birling Pk E/WMAL ME19........55 G2
Birling Rd E/WMAL ME19........38 A5
SNOD ME6......................38 E2
Birling Road Rookery HI
MAID/SHEP ME15 ....38 D3
Birnam Sq MAIDW ME16.........6 E4
Bishop Cl SIT ME10 *............15 G4
Bishops La DIT/AY ME20.........45 F2
Bishops Ter MAID/SHEP ME15 *..7 G4
Bishops Wk ROCH ME1..........20 D5
Bishops Wy MAIDW ME16.......6 C3
Blacketts E/WMAL ME19.........45 J5
Blacklands Dr E/WMAL ME19...45 J5
Blackman Cl HOO/HM ME3......10 E3
Blackmanstone Wy
DIT/AY ME20....................47 G5
Black Rock Gdns GILL ME7......32 D4
Blacksmith Dr
MAID/BEAR ME14 ....54 E1
Blackthorn Av WALD ME5........31 C5
Blackthorn Dr DIT/AY ME20......46 A2
Blackthorne Rd RHAM ME8......23 J5
Blake Dr DIT/AY ME20...........38 D6
Blakeney Cl MAID/BEAR ME14...20 E5
Blaker Av ROCH ME1............30 A1
Blandford Gdns SIT ME10........42 E1
Blatchford Cl E/WMAL ME19.....45 J3
Bleakwood Rd WALD ME5.......31 H5
Blean Rd RHAM ME8.............22 E4
Blendon Rd MAID/BEAR ME14 *..48 B5
Blendon Rd MAID/BEAR ME14...54 D1
Blenheim Av CHAT ME4..........21 F4
Blenheim Rd E/WMAL ME19.....50 C3
Bligh Wy STRD ME2.............14 B6
Blockmakers Ct CHAT ME4......21 H5
Bloomsbury Wk
MAID/BEAR ME14 *............7 J3
Bloors Ms WBY/YAL ME18 *.....59 H1
Bloors La RHAM ME8............23 G4
Bloors Wharf Rd RHAM ME8....23 J2
Blowers Grove Wd GILL ME7....32 D5
Bluebell Cl GILL ME7............17 G6
Blue Boar La ROCH ME1........3 H5
Bluett St MAID/BEAR ME14......7 K2
Blythe Rd MAID/SHEP ME15....54 C2
Boarley La MAID/BEAR ME14....48 A1
Bobbing Hl RSIT ME9............36 A1
Bockingford La
MAID/SHEP ME15 ....53 K6
Bodiam Cl MAIDW ME16.........47 H4
Bodiam Ct MAIDW ME16.........7 F6
Bodkins Cl RMAID ME17.........62 E3
Bodsham Crs MAID/SHEP ME15..55 J3
Boley Hl ROCH ME1.............3 F4
Bombay Rd E/WMAL ME19......31 F6
Bonaventure Rd E/WMAL ME19..63 H1
Bonflield Rd E/WMAL ME19......44 E3
Bonham Dr SIT ME10............37 C3
Bonnington Rd
MAID/BEAR ME14 ....48 D6
Boormans Ms WBY/YAL ME18 *..59 H1
Bossden Ct STRD ME2............19 H2
Booth Cl HOO/HM ME3..........11 G1
Booth Rd CHAT ME4.............5 F7
Borden La RSIT ME9.............36 B6
Borough Rd GILL ME7............5 K5
Borstal Rd ROCH ME1...........20 B3
Borstal St ROCH ME1...........20 A4
Boston Gdns RHAM ME8.........22 E5

Boston Rd WALD ME5............31 H6
Bottlescrew Hi RMAID ME17.....62 C4
Bottles La RSIT ME9.............43 G5
Bottom Pond Rd RSIT ME9......42 E6
Boughton La MAID/SHEP ME15..62 C1
Boughton Pde
MAID/SHEP ME15 *............62 B1
Boughton Rd RMAID ME17......62 C5
Boundary Rd ROCH ME1.........20 E5
The Bounds DIT/AY ME20........46 D3
Bourne Gv SIT ME10.............36 C3
Bourneside Ter RMAID ME17 *...57 G4
Bournewood Cl
MAID/SHEP ME15 ....55 G5
Bourville Av CHAT ME4...........21 F5
Bovarde Av E/WMAL ME19......51 F3
Bower Cl MAIDW ME16..........6 D4
Bower La MAIDW ME16..........6 C5
Bower Mount Rd MAIDW ME16..6 D5
Bower Rd MAIDW ME16.........6 C5
Bower St MAIDW ME16...........6 D4
Bower Ter MAIDW ME16.........6 E5
Bowesden La S WALD ME5......13 J3
Bowes Rd STRD ME2............15 G4
Bow HI WBY/YAL ME18..........59 H5
Bow St MAID/BEAR ME14 *.....48 A6
Bow Ter WBY/YAL ME18..........59 H1
Boxley Cl MAID/BEAR ME14.....48 C4
Boxley Rd MAID/BEAR ME14....48 B6
WALD ME5......................41 H1
Boyces HI RSIT ME9.............25 H2
Boyton Court Rd RMAID ME17...69 J5
Brabourne Av RHAM ME8........22 E2
Bracken HI WALD ME5...........41 G1
Bracken Lea WALD ME5..........21 J5
Brackley Cl MAID/SHEP ME15...54 D1
Brackwood Cl RHAM ME8........41 H1
Bradbourne La DIT/AY ME20....33 A3
Bradbourne Pkwy
DIT/AY ME20....................45 K3
Braddick Cl MAID/SHEP ME15...35 F2
Bradfields Av WALD ME5........31 F3
Bradfields Av West WALD ME5..31 F3
Bradfords Cl CHAT ME4..........16 C2
Bradley Dr SIT ME10............36 E6
Bradley Rd STRD ME2...........15 H2
Bradshaw Cl RSIT ME9..........37 K6
Braeburn Wy E/WMAL ME19.....50 E5
The Braes HOO/HM ME3.........14 B1
Brake Av WALD ME5.............30 E3
Bramble Cl MAIDW ME16........53 G3
Brambledown WALD ME5........21 H6
Bramblefield La SIT ME10.......26 E5
Brinkley St RHAM ME8...........19 K4
Braeburn St MAID/BEAR ME14..37 H4
Bramblebank Crs ROCH ME1 *..19 K4
Brambletree Whf ROCH ME1 *...19 J4
Brambling HI SIT ME10..........36 E2
Bramley Cl RHAM ME8...........23 K6
Bramley Crs MAID/SHEP ME15...15 J5
Bramley Gdns RMAID ME17......61 J5
Bramley Ri STRD ME2...........3 J2
Bramley Rd SNOD ME6..........38 E2
Bramley Wy MAIDW ME16.......50 D4
Bramshott Cl MAIDW ME16.....47 H6
Bransgore Cl RHAM ME8........33 F1
Brasenose Rd GILL ME7.........22 C4
Brassey Dr DIT/AY ME20........46 C4
Brasted Ct STRD ME2...........22 A3
Braunstone Dr MAIDW ME16....47 J5
Bray Gdns MAID/SHEP ME15....62 A3
Breach La RSIT ME9.............24 D6
Bredgar Cl MAID/BEAR ME14....54 C1
Bredgar Rd GILL ME7............22 C2
Bredhurst Rd RHAM ME8........32 A4
Brenchley Cl ROCH ME1.........20 D4
Brenchley Rd MAID/SHEP ME15..54 A4
RHAM ME8......................22 E4
SIT ME10.......................37 F6
Brendon Av WALD ME5..........31 G4
Brent Cl WALD ME5.............31 H5
Brenzett Cl WALD ME5..........31 H5
Breton Rd ROCH ME1...........20 C4
Brewer Rd HOO/HM ME3........9 G3
Brewers Rd GVE DA12...........13 F4
Brewer St MAID/BEAR ME14 *...7 H2
Brewery Rd SIT ME10............36 E2
Briar Cl DIT/AY ME20............45 K2
Briar Dr HOO/HM ME3..........14 A1
Briar Fids MAID/SHEP ME15.....55 F1
Brice Rd HOO/HM ME3..........11 G1
Brickfields E/WMAL ME19.......44 E3
Brick Field Vw STRD ME2........15 H3
Bridge House SIT ME10..........36 E2
Bridge Mill Wy
MAID/SHEP ME15 ....53 J4
Bridge Pl DIT/AY ME20...........46 C3
Bridge Rd GILL ME7.............16 D5
Bridge St MAID/SHEP ME15.....62 A3
Bridgewater Pl E/WMAL ME15...45 H2
Brier Cl WALD ME5..............21 J6
Brier Rd SIT ME10..............36 E6
Bright Rd CHAT ME4............4 D6
Brindle Wy WALD ME5...........41 J1
Brisbane Av SIT ME10...........36 C4
Brisbane Rd CHAT ME4..........4 D7
Brishing Cl MAID/SHEP ME15...55 H3
Brishing La MAID/SHEP ME15...65 G5
RMAID ME17....................62 E5
Brissenden Cl STRD ME2........16 B1
Bristol Cl STRD ME2.............29 H1
Britannia Cl DIT/AY ME20.......38 E4
STRD ME2.......................28 E4
Britannia Dr CVE DA12..........12 C1
Britton St GILL ME7.............5 H2
Broader La RMAID ME17........49 J2
Broadfield Rd
MAID/SHEP ME15 ....54 B6
Broadlands Dr WALD ME5.......31 H4
Broadmere Ter MAIDW ME16 *..6 C5
Broadoak E/WMAL ME19........50 E5
Broadoak Av MAID/SHEP ME15..54 B6
Broadoak Rd RSIT ME9..........42 D5

Broad St RMAID ME17 69 G3
Broadview Av RHAM ME8 23 G6
Broadwater Rd E/WMAL ME19 45 G6
Broadway MAIDW ME16 7 F5
RHAM ME8 22 C4
Broadwood Rd HOO/HM ME3 10 A6
Brockenhurst Av
MAID/SHEP ME15 54 C5
Brockenhurst Cl RHAM ME8 32 E1
Brogden Crs RMAID ME17 64 C1
Bromley Cl WALD ME5 31 H4
Brompton Farm Rd STRD ME2 14 E3
Brompton Hl CHAT ME4 4 C1
Brompton La STRD ME2 15 F4
Brompton Rd GILL ME7 5 F1
Bronington Cl WALD ME5 31 G3
Bronte Cl DIT/AY ME20 45 J1
Brook CHAT ME4 4 D5
Brookbank MAID/BEAR ME14 48 B4
Brooker Cl RMAID ME17 62 E3
Brookes Pl RSIT ME9 35 F2
Brookfield Av DIT/AY ME20 38 E6
Brooklands Rd DIT/AY ME20 45 K1
Brook La SNOD ME6 38 E4
Brooklyn Paddock GILL ME7 16 E6
Brookmead Rd HOO/HM ME3 9 G3
Brook Rd DIT/AY ME20 38 C6
Brookside HOO/HM ME3 11 F5
Brookside Ms MAID/SHEP ME15 53 K4
Brooks Pl MAID/BEAR ME14 7 J3
Brook St SNOD ME6 39 F2
The Brook CHAT ME4 4 D4
Broomcroft Rd RHAM ME8 23 H4
Broomfield Rd RMAID ME17 65 G6
Broom Hill Rd STRD ME2 14 E4
Broom Rd SIT ME10 37 J3
Broomshaw Rd MAIDW ME16 52 E3
Browndens Rd STRD ME2 28 C4
Brownelow Copse WALD ME5 41 G1
Brownhill Cl WALD ME5 31 G4
Browning Cl DIT/AY ME20 38 D6
Brownings Orch RSIT ME9 43 G3
Brown St RHAM ME8 23 G5
The Brucks WBY/YAL ME18 59 H1
Brunel CHAT ME4 * 16 B5
Brunel Wy CHAT ME4 16 B4
Brunswick St MAID/SHEP ME15 7 H6
Brunswick St East
MAID/SHEP ME15 7 J5
Bryant Cl WBY/YAL ME18 59 G2
Bryant Rd STRD ME2 15 F4
Bryant St CHAT ME4 4 D6
Buckingham Rd GILL ME7 * 21 K1
Buckingham Rw
MAID/SHEP ME15 63 F1
Buckland Cl WALD ME5 * 31 G6
Buckland Hl MAIDW ME16 6 D2
Buckland La MAIDW ME16 47 J6
Buckland Pl MAIDW ME16 6 E3
Buckland Rd HOO/HM ME3 8 E3
MAIDW ME16 6 D2
Bulldog Rd WALD ME5 31 H6
Buller Rd CHAT ME4 21 F4
Bull Flds SNOD ME6 38 E2
Bull La DIT/AY ME20 46 E1
HOO/HM ME3 8 C3
Bull Orch MAIDW ME16 52 E4
Bull Rd E/WMAL ME19 38 A5
Bulrush Cl WALD ME5 31 F5
Bumbles Cl ROCH ME1 20 D6
Bunny Hl GVE DA12 * 13 H2
Bunters Hill Rd HOO/HM ME3 9 F5
Burberry La RMAID ME17 64 E3
Burgess Hall Dr RMAID ME17 64 C2
Burgess Rd STRD ME2 2 E1
Burghclere Dr MAIDW ME16 53 G4
Burham Rd ROCH ME1 29 J1
Burial Ground La
MAID/SHEP ME15 53 K5
Burkeston Cl SIT ME10 27 G6
Burleigh Cl STRD ME2 14 D4
Burleigh Dr MAID/BEAR ME14 48 A3
Burley Rd SIT ME10 36 E4
Burmarsh Cl WALD ME5 31 H3
Burma Wy WALD ME5 31 F2
Burnham Cl SIT ME10 26 E6
Burnham Wk RHAM ME8 33 G5
Burn's Rd GILL ME7 16 D5
MAIDW ME16 53 H4
Burntash Rd DIT/AY ME20 46 D4
Burnt House Cl STRD ME2 15 H2
Burnt Oak Ter GILL ME7 16 E6
Burntwick Dr RSIT ME9 25 F3
The Burrs SIT ME10 37 F5
Burrstock Wy RHAM ME8 23 K4
Burston Rd RMAID ME17 61 G6
Burton Cl HOO/HM ME3 15 H1
Busbridge Rd MAID/SHEP ME15 61 K3
SNOD ME6 38 C3
Bushmeadow Rd RHAM ME8 23 H4
Bush Rd STRD ME2 18 D3
Bush Rw DIT/AY ME20 47 F2
Bushy Gv RMAID ME17 65 G6
Butcher's La WBY/YAL ME18 50 A5
Buttermere Cl GILL ME7 22 B1
Butt Haw Cl HOO/HM ME3 11 F5
Button La MAID/SHEP ME15 55 J4
The Butts SIT ME10 37 F4
Buxton Cl MAID/SHEP ME15 54 B6
WALD ME5 41 K1
Bychurch Pl MAID/SHEP ME15 * 7 J6
Byron Rd GILL ME7 5 H6
MAID/BEAR ME14 48 C5
Bythorne Ct RHAM ME8 23 K5

C

Cadnam Cl STRD ME2 14 D4
Caernarvon Dr
MAID/SHEP ME15 54 A5
Cagney Cl HOO/HM ME3 15 H1
Caldecote Cl RHAM ME8 23 K5
Calder Rd MAID/BEAR ME14 47 K5
Calderwood GVE DA12 12 B2
Caldew Av RHAM ME8 22 E5
Caldew Gv SIT ME10 37 G5
Calehill Cl MAID/BEAR ME14 48 D6
Callaways La RSIT ME9 35 F2
Callisto Ct MAIDW ME16 6 C5
Cambria Av ROCH ME1 19 K4
Cambridge Crs
MAID/SHEP ME15 62 E1
Cambridge Rd RHAM ME8 32 E2
SIT ME10 37 H6
STRD ME2 15 F4
Cambridge Ter CHAT ME4 4 B4
Camden Cl WALD ME5 31 H3
Camden Rd GILL ME7 16 E5
Camden St MAID/BEAR ME14 7 H2
Camellia Cl RHAM ME8 33 F1
Cameron Cl WALD ME5 21 H6
Campbell Rd MAID/SHEP ME15 7 H6
Campion Cl WALD ME5 30 E5
Campleshon Rd RHAM ME8 33 F3
Campus Wy GILL ME7 22 C6
Camp Wy MAID/SHEP ME15 62 D1
Canadian Av GILL ME7 22 A2
Canal Rd HOO/HM ME3 8 A2
STRD ME2 3 F2
Canberra Gdns SIT ME10 36 C4
Canning St MAID/BEAR ME14 48 B6
Canon Cl ROCH ME1 20 B4
Canon La WBY/YAL ME18 51 F5
Canterbury La RHAM ME8 24 A5
Canterbury Rd SIT ME10 37 H5
Canterbury St GILL ME7 5 H3
Capel Cl RHAM ME8 32 E3
Capell Cl RMAID ME17 61 H5
Capel Rd SIT ME10 36 E6
Capstone Rd GILL ME7 32 A1
WALD ME5 21 K5
Cardens Rd HOO/HM ME3 9 G2
Cardinal Wk E/WMAL ME19 50 E3
Cardine Cl SIT ME10 36 E1
Caring La RMAID ME17 56 B6
Caring Rd MAID/SHEP ME15 56 A5
Carisbrooke Dr MAIDW ME16 6 C2
Carisbrooke Rd STRD ME2 14 D4
Carlton Av GILL ME7 22 A2
Carlton Crs WALD ME5 21 K6
Carlton Gdns MAID/SHEP ME15 54 C6
Carnation Cl E/WMAL ME19 45 K3
Carnation Crs E/WMAL ME19 45 J4
Carnation Rd STRD ME2 14 C5
Caroline Crs MAIDW ME16 47 J5
Carpeaux Cl CHAT ME4 4 E5
Carpenters Cl ROCH ME1 20 E4
Carpinus Cl WALD ME5 41 H1
Carrington Cl GILL ME7 17 G6
Carroll Cl STRD ME2 28 E4
Carroll Gdns DIT/AY ME20 45 J1
Carton Cl ROCH ME1 20 D4
Carton Rd HOO/HM ME3 14 A1
Carver Dr RSIT ME9 * 42 D4
Carvoran Wy RHAM ME8 32 E3
Castle Av ROCH ME1 20 C2
Castle Dene MAID/BEAR ME14 47 K4
Castle Hl ROCH ME1 3 F4
Castle Hill Ct ROCH ME1 * 3 F4
Castlemaine Av GILL ME7 17 F6
Castle Rd CHAT ME4 21 G4
MAIDW ME16 47 J4
SIT ME10 37 H3
Castle Rough La SIT ME10 27 F5
Castle St ROCH ME1 29 G4
STRD ME2 15 K3
Castle View Rd STRD ME2 2 A1
Castle Wy DIT/AY ME20 38 C5
E/WMAL ME19 45 H1
Catherine Cl MAIDW ME16 53 F3
Catherine St ROCH ME1 20 D3
Catkin Cl WALD ME5 41 F1
Catlyn Cl E/WMAL ME19 45 K4
Catterick Rd WALD ME5 31 K6
Cave Hl MAID/SHEP ME15 54 A5
Cavell Wy SIT ME10 36 D3
Cavendish Av GILL ME7 17 F6
Cavendish Rd ROCH ME1 20 D3
Cavendish Wy
MAID/SHEP ME15 55 H3
Caversham Cl RHAM ME8 23 H5
Cayser Dr RMAID ME17 65 H6
Cazeneuve St ROCH ME1 3 G7
Cecil Av RHAM ME8 22 C4
STRD ME2 15 G4
Cecil Rd ROCH ME1 20 C3
Cedar Cl DIT/AY ME20 46 C4
SIT ME10 37 H6
Cedar Dr MAIDW ME16 52 D4
Cedar Gv GILL ME7 32 C3
Cedar Rd STRD ME2 2 A3
The Cedars SIT ME10 37 J3
Celestine Cl WALD ME5 41 G1
Celt Cl SIT ME10 27 F6
Cemetery Rd SNOD ME6 38 D1
STRD ME2 28 E4
Centenary Walk-Maidstone
DIT/AY ME20 40 A4
MAID/BEAR ME14 47 K6
Centenary Walk-Rochester
ROCH ME1 20 A3
Central Av SIT ME10 37 F5
Central Park Gdns ROCH ME1 20 E4
Central Rd DIT/AY ME20 39 F6
STRD ME2 2 B1
Central Ter HOO/HM ME3 10 A4
Centre Ct STRD ME2 * 3 K2
Centurion Cl GILL ME7 22 B5
Century Rd RHAM ME8 23 F6
Chada Av GILL ME7 22 A3
Chaffe's La RSIT ME9 24 C4
Chaffes Ter RSIT ME9 * 24 C4
Chaffinch Cl WALD ME5 31 G1
Chalfont Dr RHAM ME8 33 F2
Chalgrove Ms STRD ME2 * 28 E3
Chalkenden Av RHAM ME8 22 C4
Chalk Pit Hl CHAT ME4 4 D7
Chalk Rd HOO/HM ME3 8 B4
Chalkwell Rd SIT ME10 36 D4
Chalky Bank Rd RHAM ME8 23 H4
Challenger Cl SIT ME10 36 E1
Challock Wk
MAID/BEAR ME14 * 48 D6
Chalmers Wy RHAM ME8 22 C2
Chamberlain Av MAIDW ME16 53 G4
Chamberlain Ct RHAM ME8 32 D3
Chamberlain Rd CHAT ME4 21 H4
Chancery La MAID/SHEP ME15 7 K4
Chapel La GILL ME7 32 C4
MAID/BEAR ME14 55 H1
STRD ME2 28 A4
Chapel Pk SIT ME10 * 37 J2
Chapel Rd RMAID ME17 69 G3
SNOD ME6 38 E2
Chapel St E/WMAL ME19 45 K6
The Chapel MAIDW ME16 * 53 G3
Chaplin Cl HOO/HM ME3 15 H1
Chapman Av MAID/SHEP ME15 55 G5
Chapman Wy E/WMAL ME19 45 J4
Chappell Wy SIT ME10 36 D2
Chapter Rd STRD ME2 14 E5
Charing Rd RHAM ME8 22 D3
Chariot Wy STRD ME2 19 J3
Charlbury Cl MAIDW ME16 53 H3
Charles Cl SNOD ME6 38 E2
Charles Dickens Av STRD ME2 14 B2
Charles Dr STRD ME2 19 F3
Charlesford Av RMAID ME17 65 G5
Charles St CHAT ME4 4 A6
MAIDW ME16 6 E6
STRD ME2 2 C2
Charlock Cl MAIDW ME16 47 J4
Charlotte Cl WALD ME5 31 H2
Charlotte Dr RHAM ME8 22 E5
Charlotte St SIT ME10 36 E3
Charlton La MAID/SHEP ME15 60 C1
Charlton St MAIDW ME16 6 A7
Charter St CHAT ME4 21 F4
GILL ME7 16 D5
Chart Hill Rd RMAID ME17 68 C4
Chart Pl RHAM ME8 32 E5
Chart Rd RMAID ME17 68 E3
Chartway St RMAID ME17 69 H1
Chartwell Cl STRD ME2 15 G3
Chartwell Ct CHAT ME4 4 A5
Chartwell Dr MAIDW ME16 53 G2
Chartwell Gv SIT ME10 36 C5
The Chase RHAM ME8 22 C4
ROCH ME1 20 D4
Chatfield Wy DIT/AY ME20 46 A3
Chatham Gv CHAT ME4 21 F5
Chatham Hl CHAT ME4 5 F6
Chatham Rd DIT/AY ME20 40 D2
Chatsworth Dr SIT ME10 36 B3
STRD ME2 15 G3
Chatsworth Rd GILL ME7 16 D6
Chattenden Ct
MAID/BEAR ME14 48 C5
Chattenden La HOO/HM ME3 10 A6
Chaucer Cl STRD ME2 3 K1
Chaucer Rd GILL ME7 5 J6
SIT ME10 36 D5
Chaucer Wy DIT/AY ME20 38 D6
Chegwell Dr WALD ME5 31 H4
Chegworth Gdns SIT ME10 42 E1
Chegworth Rd RMAID ME17 65 J1
Cheldoc Ri CHAT ME4 16 D2
Chelmar Rd CHAT ME4 5 F5
Chelmsford Rd STRD ME2 14 C6
Cheltenham Cl
MAID/SHEP ME15 * 63 G2
Cheney Cl RHAM ME8 33 F3
Cheney Hl RSIT ME9 43 G5
Chequers Cl WALD ME5 41 G1
Chequers Ct STRD ME2 15 F3
Cherbourg Crs WALD ME5 31 F1
Cheriton Rd RHAM ME8 33 F1
Cheriton Wy MAIDW ME16 47 H5
The Cherries MAIDW ME16 52 E4
Cherry Amber Cl RHAM ME8 23 H6
Cherry Cl SIT ME10 36 D2
Cherry Flds SIT ME10 36 A3
Cherry Hill Ct RSIT ME9 * 35 G2
Cherry Orch DIT/AY ME20 46 B4
Cherry Orchard Wy
MAIDW ME16 53 G3
Cherry Rd HOO/HM ME3 * 17 F1
Cherry Tree Rd RHAM ME8 23 H6
Chervilles MAIDW ME16 53 F4
Chesham Dr RHAM ME8 33 G2
Cheshire Rd MAID/SHEP ME15 55 F4
Chester Cl STRD ME2 14 C6
Chester Rd GILL ME7 21 K4
Chesterton Rd DIT/AY ME20 38 D6
Chestfield Cl RHAM ME8 23 G4
Chestnut Av WALD ME5 30 E5
Chestnut Cl E/WMAL ME19 50 D4
Chestnut Dr RMAID ME17 61 G5
RMAID ME17 65 G6
Chestnut Rd STRD ME2 14 D6
Chestnut St RSIT ME9 35 J4
Chestnut Wood La RSIT ME9 35 J4
Chetney Cl STRD ME2 14 B5
Chetney Vw RSIT ME9 26 D2
Chevening Cl WALD ME5 31 G3
Cheviot Gdns MAID/SHEP ME15 55 H5
Cheyne Cl SIT ME10 27 F6
Chicago Av GILL ME7 22 A1
Chichester Cl RHAM ME8 23 J6
Chickfield Gdns WALD ME5 21 J4
Chiddingstone Cl
MAID/SHEP ME15 63 G2
Chieftain Cl GILL ME7 22 D5
Childscroft Rd RHAM ME8 23 H4
Chilham Cl CHAT ME4 4 A6
Chilham Rd MAIDW ME16 47 H5
RHAM ME8 22 C3
Chillington St MAID/BEAR ME14 48 A6
Chilliwack Rd HOO/HM ME3 10 A5
Chilston Rd RMAID ME17 67 J3
Chiltern Cl MAID/SHEP ME15 55 G5
Chilton Av SIT ME10 37 G5
Chilton Ct RHAM ME8 23 G5
Chilton Dr HOO/HM ME3 14 A1
Chippendale Cl WALD ME5 41 F1
Chippendayle Dr RMAID ME17 66 C2
Chipstead Cl MAIDW ME16 47 J6
Chipstead Rd RHAM ME8 33 F4
Chislehurst Cl MAID/SHEP ME15 63 G2
Chrismill La MAID/BEAR ME14 56 C2
Christie Cl WALD ME5 31 H2
Christie Dr DIT/AY ME20 38 D6
Christmas St GILL ME7 17 F5
Church Cl WBY/YAL ME18 50 A6
Church Crs RMAID ME17 66 E2
Church Farm Cl HOO/HM ME3 11 F6
Church Farm Rd RSIT ME9 24 C3
Church Fld SNOD ME6 39 F1
Church Flds E/WMAL ME19 44 E4
Churchfields Ter ROCH ME1 2 E7
Church Gn RMAID ME17 * 57 H3
STRD ME2 15 H4
Church Hl RMAID ME17 62 C6
WALD ME5 21 J4
Churchill Av WALD ME5 31 F2
Churchill Sq E/WMAL ME19 50 D3
Church La CHAT ME4 16 A6
MAID/SHEP ME15 60 C1
RMAID ME17 66 D2
RMAID ME17 69 K2
RSIT ME9 35 F2
WBY/YAL ME18 58 B3
Church Ms RHAM ME8 23 H6
Church Pth GILL ME7 17 F6
Church Rd E/WMAL ME19 44 B3
MAID/SHEP ME15 53 K4
MAID/SHEP ME15 55 G6
RMAID ME17 66 D3
RMAID ME17 68 E2
SIT ME10 37 H3
Church Sq RMAID ME17 67 J3
Church St CHAT ME4 * 4 D5
GILL ME7 17 F6
HOO/HM ME3 8 B3
HOO/HM ME3 11 F5
MAID/BEAR ME14 7 H3
MAID/SHEP ME15 53 K4
MAID/SHEP ME15 62 A3
RMAID ME17 62 C5
ROCH ME1 3 H7
ROCH ME1 39 J2
RSIT ME9 43 J3
SIT ME10 36 E4
WBY/YAL ME18 59 K1
Church Ter WALD ME5 21 J4
Church Wk E/WMAL ME19 45 K5
Chute Cl RHAM ME8 33 F4
Cinnabar Cl WALD ME5 * 41 G1
Cinnabar Dr SIT ME10 36 C2
Cirrus Crs GVE DA12 12 B1
City Wy ROCH ME1 20 D2
ROCH ME1 30 D1
Clandon Rd WALD ME5 41 K1
Clare La E/WMAL ME19 45 H4
Claremont Rd
MAID/BEAR ME14 54 C1
Claremont Wy CHAT ME4 4 C6
Clarence Ct MAID/BEAR ME14 55 F2
Clarence Rd CHAT ME4 21 H4
Clarendon Cl MAID/BEAR ME14 55 H2
SIT ME10 43 F1
Clarendon Dr STRD ME2 15 F3
Clarendon Pl MAID/SHEP ME15 * 7 J4
Clarewood Dr E/WMAL ME19 45 H4
Claridge Cl GILL ME7 32 B4
Clark Ms DIT/AY ME20 46 E3
Clavell Cl RHAM ME8 33 F5
Claygate MAID/SHEP ME15 54 E5
RMAID ME17 57 G4
Cleave Rd GILL ME7 22 A4
Cleeve Ct E/WMAL ME19 50 E4
Clematis Av RHAM ME8 32 D3
Clement Cl SIT ME10 26 E6
Clement Ct MAIDW ME16 6 C1
Clerke Dr SIT ME10 27 G6
Clermont Cl GILL ME7 32 C4
Cleveland Rd GILL ME7 16 E6
Clewson Ri MAID/BEAR ME14 48 C4
Cliffe Rd STRD ME2 15 G4
Cliff Hl RMAID ME17 62 D4
Cliff Hill Rd RMAID ME17 62 D4
Clifton Cl MAID/BEAR ME14 48 C6
STRD ME2 14 E5
Clifton Rd GILL ME7 16 D5
Clinton Av STRD ME2 14 C4
Clinton Cl RMAID ME17 61 G5
Clipper Cl STRD ME2 15 K5
Clipper Ct STRD ME2 * 15 K5
Cliveden Cl MAIDW ME16 47 J5
Clive Rd ROCH ME1 20 C3
SIT ME10 36 B3
Cloisterham Rd ROCH ME1 30 D1
Cloisters SIT ME10 * 36 E4
The Close ROCH ME1 3 F7
Cloudberry Cl MAIDW ME16 47 J6
Cloudesley Cl ROCH ME1 20 B5
Clover Bank Vw WALD ME5 31 H2
Clover Lay RHAM ME8 23 K4
Clover Rd HOO/HM ME3 17 F1
Clover St CHAT ME4 4 C5
Clover Ter MAID/SHEP ME15 * 54 E6
The Coachyard MAIDW ME16 53 G3
Cobb Cl STRD ME2 14 C4
Cobbett Cl E/WMAL ME19 45 J4
Cobblestones GILL ME7 32 B3
Cobbs Cl WBY/YAL ME18 59 H1
Cobden Rd CHAT ME4 21 H4
Cobdown Cl DIT/AY ME20 46 A2
Cobdown Gv RHAM ME8 23 J4
Cob Dr GVE DA12 13 H1
Cobfield RMAID ME17 68 C1
Cobham Av SIT ME10 42 E1
Cobham Cl MAIDW ME16 6 D3
STRD ME2 14 D5
Cobham Ri GILL ME7 22 A1
Cobtree Cl WALD ME5 21 J6
Cobtree Rd RMAID ME17 61 H5
Codrington Gdns GVE DA12 12 A1
Colchester Cl WALD ME5 31 F1
Cold Harbour La RSIT ME9 35 K2
Coldharbour La DIT/AY ME20 47 F3
SIT ME10 27 G5
Coldred Rd MAID/SHEP ME15 63 G4
Colegate Dr MAID/BEAR ME14 55 K2
Coleman Dr SIT ME10 27 F5
Coleridge Cl DIT/AY ME20 38 E6
Coleshall Cl MAID/SHEP ME15 63 G2
Cole Ter RMAID ME17 * 67 H3
Colewood Dr STRD ME2 14 A4
Colfe Wy SIT ME10 27 G6
College Av GILL ME7 5 G4
MAID/SHEP ME15 7 G6
College Ct MAID/SHEP ME15 * 7 H6
College Rd CHAT ME4 16 B5
DIT/AY ME20 46 A1
MAID/SHEP ME15 7 G7
SIT ME10 36 D6
The College ROCH ME1 * 3 G5
College Wk MAID/SHEP ME15 7 H6
College Yd ROCH ME1 3 F4
Collet Wk RHAM ME8 33 F4
Collington Ter
MAID/SHEP ME15 63 G4
Collingwood Rd DIT/AY ME20 40 C3
Collis St STRD ME2 15 F4
Colman Pde MAID/BEAR ME14 * 7 H3
Colson Dr RSIT ME9 26 D3
Coltsfoot Dr MAID/BEAR ME14 55 G2
Columbine Cl E/WMAL ME19 45 J3
STRD ME2 14 D5
Columbine Rd E/WMAL ME19 45 J3
STRD ME2 14 D5
Command Rd
MAID/BEAR ME14 48 A4
Commercial Rd STRD ME2 2 D2
Commissioners Ct CHAT ME4 4 C1
Commissioner's Rd STRD ME2 15 J4
Commodore Rd
MAID/BEAR ME14 54 D1
Common Rd HOO/HM ME3 9 G6
ROCH ME1 30 B6
The Common ROCH ME1 3 G3
Commonwealth Cl SIT ME10 37 H5
Communications Pk STRD ME2 * 2 B5
Compass Cl ROCH ME1 20 C5
Compton Cl WALD ME5 31 K6
Concord Av WALD ME5 30 E3
Conifer Dr WALD ME5 41 K1
Coniston Cl GILL ME7 17 H6
Connaught Cl MAID/SHEP ME15 63 G4
Connaught Ms WALD ME5 21 J4
Connaught Rd CHAT ME4 21 H4
GILL ME7 5 K2
SIT ME10 36 E5
Conrad Cl RHAM ME8 33 F4
Consort Cl MAID/BEAR ME14 54 C1
Constitution Hl CHAT ME4 21 H4
SNOD ME6 38 D2
Constitution Rd WALD ME5 5 G7
Conway Cl STRD ME2 14 D3
Conway Ms GILL ME7 4 D1
Conway Rd MAIDW ME16 47 H6
Cooden Cl RHAM ME8 23 J4
Cook Cl WALD ME5 31 J2
Cookham Hl ROCH ME1 20 A4
Cookham Wood Rd ROCH ME1 20 B6
Cooks La SIT ME10 36 E2
Cooks Whf ROCH ME1 3 K7
Cooling Cl MAID/BEAR ME14 48 D6
Cooling Common HOO/HM ME3 9 H2
Cooling Rd STRD ME2 15 G2
Coombe Cl SNOD ME6 38 E3
WALD ME5 31 H5
Coombe Dr SIT ME10 37 J4
Coombe Rd HOO/HM ME3 11 F5
MAID/SHEP ME15 54 A4
Cooper Rd SNOD ME6 38 D4
WALD ME5 31 G5
Copenhagen Rd GILL ME7 5 H3
Copperfield Crs STRD ME2 14 B2
Copperfield Dr RMAID ME17 64 B4
Copperfield Rd ROCH ME1 20 C4
The Copperfields ROCH ME1 * 2 D7
Coppergate GILL ME7 32 B3
Copperhouse La GILL ME7 17 J6
Copperhouse Rd STRD ME2 14 B5
Copperpenny Dr GILL ME7 32 D5
Copper Tree Ct
MAID/SHEP ME15 62 B3
Coppice Ct GILL ME7 32 D4
Coppice Rd WALD ME5 31 J6
The Coppice DIT/AY ME20 46 D3
Coppice Vw MAID/BEAR ME14 49 F6
Coppins La RSIT ME9 36 B6
Copse Cl ROCH ME1 20 E5
Copsehill DIT/AY ME20 45 H2
The Copse HOO/HM ME3 17 F1
Copsewood Wy
MAID/SHEP ME15 55 H3
Cordelia Crs ROCH ME1 19 K4
Cork St DIT/AY ME20 39 K4
Corkwell St CHAT ME4 4 A7
Cormorant Cl STRD ME2 14 B5
Cornflower Cl
MAID/BEAR ME14 55 F2
Cornforth Dr RSIT ME9 * 42 D4
Cornwall Cl MAID/SHEP ME15 63 F1
Cornwall Crs ROCH ME1 29 G4
Cornwallis Av CHAT ME4 20 E5
GILL ME7 22 B2
Cornwallis Rd MAIDW ME16 6 C4
Cornwall Rd GILL ME7 * 16 D6
ROCH ME1 20 C3
Corona Ter SNOD ME6 38 D4
Coronation Rd WALD ME5 21 J4
Corporation Rd GILL ME7 16 E6
Corporation St ROCH ME1 3 G4
Corral Cl WALD ME5 21 K4
Corrance Gn MAID/SHEP ME15 54 B6
Cortland Cl SIT ME10 36 E2
Cortland Ms SIT ME10 36 E2
Cory's Rd ROCH ME1 3 H4

Cossack St ROCH ME1................20 C3
Cossington Rd WALD ME5............41 H1
Cotswold Gdns
 MAID/SHEP ME15................55 H5
Cottage Rd CHAT ME4................16 A6
Cottall Av CHAT ME4................21 F4
Cottenham Cl E/WMAL ME19....23 J5
Coulman St GILL ME7................21 K1
Coulters Cl RMAID ME17............54 E2
County Gv E/WMAL ME19............44 E4
County Rd MAID/SHEP ME15......7 H2
Court Dr MAIDW ME16................6 B2
Courtenay Rd
 MAID/SHEP ME15................54 A4
Courtenay Rd RHAM ME8............22 D6
Courtfield Av WALD ME5............31 J5
Courtlands WBY/YAL ME18........51 K6
Court Lodge Farm
 WBY/YAL ME18........................59 H1
Court Lodge Rd GILL ME7............17 G6
Court Meadow RHAM ME8 *......22 D4
Court Rd ROCH ME1................39 H1
 SIT ME10................................36 E1
The Courtyard GILL ME7 *........22 C6
The Court Yd RHAM ME8 *........33 J3
Coventry Cl STRD ME2................14 C6
Coverdale Av MAID/SHEP ME15..62 E2
Coverdale Cl WALD ME5............31 H1
The Covert WALD ME5................41 C1
Covey Hall Rd SNOD ME6............38 E2
Cowbeck Cl RHAM ME8................38 E2
Cowden Rd MAID/BEAR ME14....54 D1
Cowdrey Cl MAIDW ME16............53 G5
 ROCH ME1................................20 B4
Cowper Rd GILL ME7................5 K6
 SIT ME10................................37 H4
Cowstead Rd RSIT ME9................14 H1
Cox Gdns RHAM ME8................24 C4
Cox's Cl SNOD ME6................38 D2
Cozenton Cl RHAM ME8................23 C5
Crabtree Cl E/WMAL ME19........50 D4
Crabtree Rd RHAM ME8................23 F6
Craddock Wy RHAM ME8............33 F3
Cranborne Av
 MAID/SHEP ME15................54 D6
Cranbrook Cl MAID/SHEP ME15..63 G1
 RHAM ME8................................22 E3
Cranbrook Dr SIT ME10............42 D1
Cranford Cl RHAM ME8................33 H2
Cranleigh Gdns MAIDW ME16....47 H5
 ROCH ME1................................20 D5
Cranmer Ct MAID/SHEP ME15....54 C6
Cranmere Ct STRD ME2............15 H4
Crawford Cl MAID/BEAR ME14....48 D6
Cremers Rd SIT ME10................37 H5
The Crescent CHAT ME4............48 A4
 MAID/BEAR ME14................48 A4
 SIT ME10................................27 F5
Crescent Wy WALD ME5............30 D3
Cressey Ct CHAT ME4................4 A5
Crest Rd ROCH ME1................20 C5
Crestway WALD ME5................21 H6
Creve Coeur Cl
 MAID/SHEP ME15................55 H1
Cricketers Cl RMAID ME17........66 C2
 SIT ME10................................27 F6
Cripple St MAID/SHEP ME15......54 E6
Crismill Rd MAID/BEAR ME14....56 B3
Crispe Cl RHAM ME8................33 F4
Crispin Ct RMAID ME17............61 H5
Crispin Rd STRD ME2................14 D4
Crispin Wy E/WMAL ME19........50 D3
Croft Cl RMAID ME17................65 G6
 WALD ME5................................31 G1
The Crofters RHAM ME8............33 H1
Croft Gdns RMAID ME17............67 J3
The Croft E/WMAL ME19............45 H2
Cromer Rd SIT ME10................42 E2
 STRD ME2................................15 G4
Crompton Gdns
 MAID/SHEP ME15................7 K2
Cromwell Rd MAID/BEAR ME14..7 J5
Cromwell Ter CHAT ME4............4 D6
Cronin Cl DIT/AY ME20............38 D6
Crosier Ct RSIT ME9................24 E3
Crosley Rd GILL ME7................21 K4
Cross Av SIT ME10................69 K1
Cross Keys MAID/BEAR ME14....55 K2
Cross La SIT ME10................36 E2
Cross St CHAT ME4................4 D4
 MAID/BEAR ME14................48 B6
 STRD ME2................................15 J3
Cross Wy WALD ME5................20 B3
Crossway WALD ME5................30 E2
Crossway SIT ME10................42 E1
Crouch Hill Ct RSIT ME9............25 C3
Crow La ROCH ME1................3 G6
Crownfields MAID/BEAR ME14....55 F2
Crown Gv GVE DA12................15 H1
Crown Quay La SIT ME10............37 F4
Crown Rd SIT ME10................36 E3
Crown St GILL ME7................5 K1
Crown Wharf STRD ME2 *........3 K1
Crowton Ct SNOD ME6............39 F5
Croydon Cl WALD ME5............31 J4
Crundale Rd RHAM ME8............22 E3
Crusader Cl GILL ME7................24 A2
Crutches La STRD ME2............14 A4
Cryalls La RSIT ME9................36 B5
Cuckowood Av
 MAID/BEAR ME14................48 A3
Cudham Cl MAID/BEAR ME14....48 D6
Culpeper Cl RMAID ME17............57 G4
 STRD ME2................................3 J3
Culpepper Rd RHAM ME8............33 F4
Cumberland Av
 MAID/SHEP ME15................54 E6
Cumberland Dr RSIT ME9............25 F3
Cumberland Rd GILL ME7............16 D5
Cunningham Crs WALD ME5........21 G6
Curlew Av RSIT ME9................25 F3
Curlew Ct SIT ME10................14 B6
Curlew Crs RHAM ME8................23 F5
Curzon Rd CHAT ME4................4 C7
 MAID/BEAR ME14................48 B6

Cutbush Cl RMAID ME17............66 C2
Cutbush & Corrali Ct
 MAID/SHEP ME15................7 K3
Cutter Cl STRD ME2................16 A1
Cuxton Rd MAID/SHEP ME15....63 G3
Cygnet Cl DIT/AY ME20............45 K2
Cygnet Rd GILL ME7................31 J6
Cypress Av GILL/HM ME3..........17 F1
Cypress Ct GILL ME7................17 G6
Cypress Ct GILL ME7 *................17 G6
Cypress Rd STRD ME2................15 H3

D

Daffodil Cl STRD ME2................14 D5
Dagmar Rd CHAT ME4................21 H4
Dale Cl WALD ME5................31 G6
Dale Rd ROCH ME1................20 C3
Dale St CHAT ME4................4 B7
Dalewood SIT ME10................37 G6
Dalison Ct STRD ME2................14 B1
Dalton St GILL ME7................5 J1
Damiem Cl CHAT ME4 *............21 G4
Damson Dr RHAM ME8................16 E1
Dane Cl RSIT ME9................34 B3
Dane Cl WALD ME5................31 J6
Dane Ct MAID/SHEP ME17........16 B6
Dane La RSIT ME9................34 B3
Danes Hl GILL ME7................17 H6
Danes Md SIT ME10................26 E4
Danns La WBY/YAL ME18..........50 D6
Danson Wy RHAM ME8................23 F5
Darby Gdns HOO/HM ME3............14 A1
Darenth Rl WALD ME5................31 H5
Dargate Cl MAIDW ME16............47 H5
Dargets Rd WALD ME5................31 G5
Darland Av GILL ME7................22 A4
Darnley Cl STRD ME2................14 D6
Darnley Rd STRD ME2................14 D6
Dart Cl STRD ME2................A2
Darwin Ct MAID/SHEP ME1 *....3 H6
Dashmonden Cl STRD ME2........15 H2
Davenport Av GILL ME7............17 J6
Davy's Pl GVE DA12................12 B2
Dawes St GILL ME7................5 H4
Deacon Cl STRD ME2................14 D4
Dean Rd SIT ME10................36 E2
 STRD ME2................................2 A2
Dean St MAID/SHEP ME15........53 J6
Deanwood Dr RHAM ME8............15 G1
Deerhurst Gdns MAIDW ME16....6 D4
Deering Cl CHAT ME4................16 C2
Defiant Cl WALD ME5................31 H2
Defoe Cl WALD ME5................31 H2
Delce Rd ROCH ME1................3 H7
Del Gdns SNOD ME6................38 E5
De Mere Ct RHAM ME8................33 F2
Denbigh Av RHAM ME8................23 F5
Denbigh Cl SIT ME10................36 E1
Denham Rd RSIT ME9................35 F1
Denning Cl MAID/BEAR ME14....53 G2
Dental Ct SIT ME10................15 F1
Denton Cl MAID/SHEP ME15......55 F6
Derby Cl SIT ME10................36 D2
Derby Rd MAID/SHEP ME15......54 D6
 WALD ME5................................22 A4
Deringwood Dr
 MAID/SHEP ME15................55 G1
Deringwood Pde
 MAID/SHEP ME15 *................55 G5
Derwent Wy RHAM ME8............23 F6
Detling Cl RHAM ME8................22 E4
Detling Hl MAID/BEAR ME14......49 H3
Devon Cl RHAM ME8................33 J1
Devon Rd MAID/SHEP ME15......54 D5
Devonshire Rd GILL ME7............16 D5
Dewbury Ct RSIT ME9................36 D5
Dhekelia Cl MAID/BEAR ME14....48 B5
Dial Cl GILL ME7................17 G6
Dial Rd GILL ME7................17 G6
Diana Rd CHAT ME4................21 G4
Dickens Cl MAID/BEAR ME17....64 B4
Dickens Dr E/WMAL ME19........45 J3
Dickens Rd MAID/BEAR ME14....47 K5
 ROCH ME1................................20 C4
Dickley La RMAID ME17............67 F3
Dignals Cl RHAM ME8................23 H4
Diligent Dr SIT ME10................37 F1
Dilly Fields Wd HOO/HM ME3....63 C2
Dillywood La HOO/HM ME3........14 D2
Discovery Dr E/WMAL ME19......50 E3
Discovery Rd MAID/SHEP ME15..55 H4
Disraeli Cl MAID/SHEP ME15....63 F5
Ditton Court Cl DIT/AY ME20 *..46 A3
Ditton Pl DIT/AY ME20..............46 A3
Dixon Cl MAID/SHEP ME15........7 F7
Dixwell Cl RHAM ME8................33 F3
Dobbie Cl SIT ME10................36 E2
Dobson Rd GVE DA12................12 B1
Dock Head Rd CHAT ME4............16 B3
Dock Rd CHAT ME4................4 C6
Doddington Ct MAIDW ME16......6 D2
Doddington Rd RHAM ME8........22 E4
Doggett's Sq STRD ME2............2 D1
Dogwood Cl WALD ME5............41 K1
Dolphin Rd MAID/SHEP ME15....38 C3
Dolphin Pk SIT ME10 *................37 H3
Dolphin Rd SIT ME10................37 H3
Dombey Cl HOO/HM ME3............14 B1
 ROCH ME1 *............................20 B4
Doncaster Cl MAID/SHEP ME15..63 G2
Donemowe Dr SIT ME10............27 F6
Donet Cl RHAM ME8................22 E4
Dongola Rd STRD ME2................15 H3
Dorchester Cl HOO/HM ME3......9 J1
Dorden Gdns WALD ME5............31 H1
Dorrit Wy ROCH ME1................20 D4
Dorset Sq RHAM ME8................23 F5
Dorset Wy MAID/SHEP ME15....54 D6

Dotterel Cl WALD ME5................41 K1
Doubleday Dr RSIT ME9............37 K6
Douglas Rd MAIDW ME16............6 E6
 MAID/BEAR ME14................7 J3
Doust Wy ROCH ME1................3 K7
Dove Cl WALD ME5................31 H2
Dover St MAIDW ME16................6 A7
 SIT ME10................................36 E4
Doves Cft RSIT ME9................36 E4
Dowling Cl MAID/SHEP ME15....38 C3
Downderry Wy DIT/AY ME20......16 E1
Downer Ct ROCH ME1................20 E6
Downlands MAID/BEAR ME14....66 E2
Dowland Wk WALD ME5............31 C3
Downs Cl MAID/SHEP ME15........48 B4
 ROCH ME1................................36 D1
Downside STRD ME2................2 B6
Downs Rd MAID/SHEP ME15......54 B4
The Downs WALD ME5................40 D1
Downs Vw ROCH ME1................39 K1
Downsview WALD ME5................21 J6
Downs View Rd
 MAID/BEAR ME14................48 B4
Drake's Av STRD ME2................14 E4
Drakes Cl RSIT ME9................24 C4
Drawbridge Cl
 MAID/SHEP ME15................55 F6
Drewery Dr RHAM ME8................32 E3
Dryland Rd SNOD ME6................38 D2
Drywall SIT ME10 *................27 H2
Duchess Cl STRD ME2................14 D4
Duchess of Kent Ct
 DIT/AY ME20 *........................16 E1
Duchess of Kent Dr GILL ME7....31 H5
Dukes Meadow Dr GILL ME7......31 H5
The Downs WALD ME5................40 D1
Dukes Wk MAID/SHEP ME15......7 J4
Dully Rd RSIT ME9................43 K6
Duncan Rd GILL ME7................5 J3
Dunedin Cl SIT ME10................36 C5
Dunera Dr MAID/BEAR ME14....48 A5
Dunkirk Dr WALD ME5................31 F2
Dunlin Dr CHAT ME4................16 D2
Dunning's La ROCH ME1 *........3 J7
The Dunnings MAIDW ME16......53 F4
Dunster Ter MAID/SHEP ME15 *..55 G1
Durham Cl MAID/SHEP ME15....54 E5
Durham Rd RHAM ME8................32 E1
Durrell Gdns WALD ME5............21 J5
Dux Ct ROCH ME1................20 E6
Dux Court Rd HOO/HM ME3........10 D2
Dyngley Cl SIT ME10................36 E1

E

Eadred Wy SIT ME10................27 G5
Eagle Cl DIT/AY ME20................45 K2
Eagles Cl SIT ME10................37 J4
Ealing Cl MAID/SHEP ME15........31 H4
Earl Cl WALD ME5................31 H4
East Cl MAID/BEAR ME14 *........7 G5
East St (North) E/WMAL ME15 *..54 B4
East Sutton Rd RMAID ME17......69 H5
Eastcourt Gn RHAM ME8............22 D3
Eastcourt La RHAM ME8............22 D4
Easterfields E/WMAL ME19........52 B1
Eastern Rd GILL ME7................17 G6
Eastgate ROCH ME1................1 H6
Eastgate Ct ROCH ME1................3 G5
Eastgate Ter ROCH ME1............3 G5
East Gn SIT ME10................3 G5
East Hall Hl MAID ME17............68 A4
East Hall La SIT ME10................37 J3
Eastling Ct RHAM ME8................23 F3
East Park Rd DIT/AY ME20........31 H4
East Rw CHAT ME4................16 B5
Eastry Ct MAIDW ME16................47 H5
East St CHAT ME4................44 A2
 E/WMAL ME19........................15 K1
 GILL ME7................................5 K1
 RMAID ME17..........................66 D3
 SIT ME10................................37 G5
 SNOD ME6................................39 F2
Eccles Rw DIT/AY ME20..............39 K4
Eccleston Rd MAIDW ME16........7 F7
Echo Cl MAID/SHEP ME15........63 G2
Eclipse Dr SIT ME10................26 E6
Eddington Cl MAID/SHEP ME15..62 C2
Eden Farm La E/WMAL ME19......45 G5
Edgeler Ct SNOD ME6................38 D3
Edinburgh Ct MAID/BEAR ME14..16 C2
Edinburgh Rd GILL ME7............21 J4
 GILL ME7................................5 J3
Edinburgh Sq
 MAID/SHEP ME15................62 D2
Edmund Cl MAIDW ME16............53 F3
Edna Rd MAID/SHEP ME15........54 D6
Edward Cl WALD ME5 *................21 J5
Edwards Cl RHAM ME8................32 E5
Edward St CHAT ME4................4 E7
 STRD ME2................................2 D1
Edward Wk E/WMAL ME19........45 J4
Edwin Rd MAID/BEAR ME14......22 E6
Edyngham Cl SIT ME10................27 H2
Egerton Rd MAID/SHEP ME15....14 E4
Egremont Rd MAID/SHEP ME15..55 G4
Elaine Av STRD ME2................14 D5
Elaine Ct STRD ME2................17 F1
 RMAID ME17..........................16 B6
Elder Ct RHAM ME8................32 D2
Eldon St CHAT ME4................16 A6
Eleanor Dr SIT ME10................27 F6
Elham Cl RHAM ME8................24 A6
Elizabeth Ct MAID/BEAR ME14..22 E5
Elizabeth Smith Ct
 E/WMAL ME19........................45 J5

Ellenswood Cl
 MAID/SHEP ME15................55 H5
Ellingham Leas
 MAID/SHEP ME15................54 D6
Ellison Wy RHAM ME8................23 J4
Elm Av CHAT ME4................20 E5
 GILL/HM ME3..........................10 B6
Elm Cl HOO/HM ME3................9 J1
Elm Ct GILL ME7 *................32 A5
Elm Crs E/WMAL ME19................45 J4
Elmfield RHAM ME8................22 C3
Elmfield Ct RMAID ME17 *........61 H5
Elmstone Cl RHAM ME8................7 K6
Elm Rd SIT ME10................37 H4
Elmhurst Gdns ROCH ME1........30 E1
Elm Rd GILL ME7................17 F6
 HOO/HM ME3..........................17 F1
Elmstone Cl MAIDW ME16........53 C4
Elmstone Rd RHAM ME8............53 F4
Elm Tree Dr WALD ME5................33 F1
Elm Wk DIT/AY ME20................46 D3
Elmwood Rd HOO/HM ME3........10 A4
Elvington Cl WALD ME5................6 B2
Elwick Rd SIT ME10................23 G4
Embassy Ct GILL ME7................22 B5
Emerald Cl ROCH ME1................20 D5
Emily Rd WALD ME5................31 H2
Emsworth Gv
 MAID/SHEP ME15................48 E6
Englefield Crs HOO/HM ME3......9 C5
Enterprise Ct STRD ME2............15 J4
Enterprise Rd
 MAID/SHEP ME15................54 B5
Epaul La ROCH ME1................3 F4
Epps Ct STRD ME2 *................15 C4
Epps Rd SIT ME10................36 E5
Epsom Cl E/WMAL ME19............44 E4
 MAID/SHEP ME15................62 E2
Erith Cl MAID/BEAR ME14..........48 B4
Ernest Dr MAIDW ME16............53 C1
Ernest Rd CHAT ME4................4 D7
Eshcol Rd HOO/HM ME3............11 K4
Esplanade ROCH ME1................2 E5
The Esplanade ROCH ME1..........2 E5
Essex Rd MAID/SHEP ME15........63 F2
 STRD ME2................................28 E3
Estelle Ct ROCH ME1................30 D1
Esther Ct SIT ME10................26 E6
Ethelbert Rd ROCH ME1............20 C2
Ethel Maud Ct GILL ME7 *........16 D5
Eton Cl WALD ME5................31 F4
Euroreik Wy SIT ME10................37 G4
Eva Rd GILL ME7................K7
Evelyn Cl STRD ME2................15 H4
Evelyn Rd MAIDW ME16............16 B5
Everest Dr HOO/HM ME3............11 F6
Everest La STRD ME2................15 C3
Everest Ms HOO/HM ME3............11 F6
The Everglades GILL ME7............32 B2
Evergreen Cl E/WMAL ME19......45 H2
 MAID/SHEP ME15................32 C3
 HOO/HM ME3..........................28 D2
 RSIT ME9................................26 D2
Eversley Cl MAIDW ME16............47 H6
Ewart Rd CHAT ME4................20 E5
Ewell Av E/WMAL ME19............44 D4
Ewell La MAID/SHEP ME15........60 C3
Exmouth Rd GILL ME7................16 D6
Exton Cl WALD ME5................31 J6
Exton Gdns MAID/BEAR ME14....55 C1
Eyhorne St RMAID ME17............57 F5
Eynsford Rd MAIDW ME16..........47 J5

F

Fagus Cl WALD ME5................41 H1
Fairbourne La RMAID ME17........66 E3
Fairfax Cl RHAM ME8................33 F3
Fairfield GVE DA12................12 B1
Fairhurst Dr MAID/SHEP ME15..61 C4
Fairlawn Cl WBY/YAL ME18........51 K6
Fairlead Rd ROCH ME1................20 D5
Fairleas SIT ME10................42 C4
Fairmeadow MAID/SHEP ME15..7 C5
Fairview Av RHAM ME8................32 E4
Fairview Dr HOO/HM ME3............8 A6
Fairview Rd SIT ME10................37 C5
Fairway Cl ROCH ME1................20 C5
The Fairway SIT ME10................42 E1
Falkland Pl WALD ME5................40 E1
Fallowfield SIT ME10................37 G6
 WALD ME5................................21 H6
Fallowfield Cl MAID/BEAR ME14..55 H5
Fanconn Rd WALD ME5................31 H5
Fane Wy RHAM ME8................33 F4
Fans La RSIT ME9................26 D2
Fant La MAIDW ME16................53 C4
Faraday Rd MAID/SHEP ME15....48 D5
Farleigh Hl MAID/SHEP ME15....53 K5
Farleigh La MAIDW ME16............53 J6
Farley Cl WALD ME5................31 G6
Farm Crs SIT ME10................27 G6
Farmdale Rd CHAT ME4............19 K4
Farmdale Av ROCH ME1............19 K4
Farmer Cl MAID/BEAR ME14......55 G2
Farm Hill Av STRD ME2................14 E3
Farm Rd WALD ME5................30 E5
Farnborough Cl MAID/SHEP ME15 *..53 H4
Farne Cl MAID/SHEP ME15........62 B2
Farnham Cl RHAM ME8................23 H5
Farningham Cl
 MAID/BEAR ME14................48 D6
Farraday Cl ROCH ME1................20 D6
Farrier Cl MAID/BEAR ME14......54 E1
Farriers Ct RHAM ME8................24 A6
Fartherwell Av E/WMAL ME19....44 D4
Fartherwell Rd E/WMAL ME19....44 C5
Fauchon's Cl MAID/SHEP ME15..55 C3
Fauchon's La MAID/SHEP ME15..55 C3

Faversham Rd RMAID ME17........67 J3
Fawley Cl MAID/BEAR ME14......47 K5
Featherbed La RSIT ME9............26 E4
Featherby Rd RHAM ME8............22 C3
Felderland Cl RMAID ME17........63 F3
Felderland Dr RMAID ME17........63 F3
Felderland Rd RMAID ME17........63 F3
Feldspar Ct SIT ME10................36 D2
 WALD ME5................................41 F1
Fennel Cl MAIDW ME16................53 C3
 ROCH ME1................................30 E1
Fernbank Cl WALD ME5................40 E1
Ferndale Rd GILL ME7................22 A1
Ferndown Ct GILL ME7................22 E3
Fernhill Rd MAIDW ME16............53 F4
Fernleigh Ri DIT/AY ME20............46 A2
Fernleigh Ter SIT ME10 *............34 D6
The Ferns DIT/AY ME20..............46 A3
Ferrier Cl RHAM ME8................33 C4
Ferry La ROCH ME1................20 E2
Ferry Rd RSIT ME9................26 E2
 STRD ME2................................28 E4
Ffinch Cl DIT/AY ME20................46 B3
Field Cl WALD ME5................30 E2
Fielding Dr DIT/AY ME20............45 K1
The Fieldings SIT ME10................42 B3
Fields La WBY/YAL ME18............59 H1
Fieldworks Rd CHAT ME4............16 B3
Fiji Ter MAID/BEAR ME14............48 B5
The Finches SIT ME10 *................42 A3
Findlay Cl RHAM ME8................33 F3
Finglesham Ct
 MAID/SHEP ME15................54 D6
Fintonagh Dr MAID/BEAR ME14..48 A4
Finwell Rd RHAM ME8................23 J4
Firethorn Cl GILL ME7................31 F2
Firmin Av RMAID ME17................62 E3
Firs Cl DIT/AY ME20................46 B3
First Av CHAT ME4................21 J4
 SIT ME10................................22 A4
First La MAID/SHEP ME15..........56 B4
Fir Tree Gv WALD ME5................41 J1
Fisher Rd WALD ME5................31 H1
Fisher St MAID/BEAR ME14........7 C5
Fitzwilliam Rd
 MAID/SHEP ME15................55 G1
Five Bells La ROCH ME1 *..........3 J7
Five Ways Ct CHAT ME4............4 E6
Flack Gdns HOO/HM ME3............11 F5
Flamingo Cl WALD ME5..............41 H1
Flanders Ct SIT ME10................27 F5
Flaxman Dr MAIDW ME16..........47 H6
Flaxmans Ct GILL ME7................16 B6
Fleet Rd ROCH ME1................20 D5
Flint Cl SIT ME10................37 J6
Flint Cl WALD ME5................41 F1
Flood Hatch MAID/SHEP ME15...53 J4
Florence Rd MAIDW ME16..........6 E6
Florence St STRD ME2................15 C4
Florin Dr ROCH ME1................20 B2
Flume End MAIDW ME16............53 J4
Foley St MAID/BEAR ME14..........7 J1
Fontwell Cl MAID/SHEP ME15....63 G2
Foord Rd RMAID ME17................67 J3
Foord St ROCH ME1................3 G7
Fordcombe Cl
 MAID/SHEP ME15................63 G1
Fordingbridge Cl MAIDW ME16..53 G1
Fordwich Cl MAIDW ME16..........47 C5
Fordwich Dr HOO/HM ME3........15 F2
Foremans Barn Rd
 MAID/SHEP ME15................60 E5
Forestdale Rd WALD ME5............41 G2
Forest La SIT ME10................37 G6
Foresters Cl WALD ME5................31 F1
Forest Hill MAID/SHEP ME15......54 D5
Forest Wy E/WMAL ME19..........50 D3
Forge Ct RMAID ME17................23 J3
Forge La GILL ME7................17 F6
 GVE DA12................................13 H1
 HOO/HM ME3..........................14 B1
 MAID/BEAR ME14................48 D1
 MAID/SHEP ME15................61 C1
 RMAID ME17..........................68 B5
Forge Meadow RMAID ME17......60 E5
Forge Rd SIT ME10................36 E2
Formby Rd STRD ME2................28 E4
Forsham La RMAID ME17............61 J4
Forstal La MAID/BEAR ME14......7 J1
Forstal Rd DIT/AY ME20..............39 G1
Forsters RMAID ME17................64 B4
Forsyth Cl E/WMAL ME19..........45 K3
Fort Bridgewood ROCH ME1 *....30 B3
Fort Pitt Hl ROCH ME1................4 B1
Fort Pitt St CHAT ME4................4 A2
Fort St ROCH ME1................20 D5
Fortune Wy E/WMAL ME19........50 D3
Forward Wy ROCH ME1................20 C3
Foster Clarke Dr
 MAID/SHEP ME15................55 J1
Foster St MAID/SHEP ME15........7 H5
Fostington Wy WALD ME5..........41 H1
Foulds Cl RHAM ME8................32 D4
Foundry Whrf ROCH ME1............15 J1
Fountain La MAID/SHEP ME15....53 C4
Fountain Rd STRD ME2................14 D3
Fountain St SIT ME10................36 E2
Four Elms Hl HOO/HM ME3........15 K1
Fourwents Rd HOO/HM ME3......10 A4
Fowey Cl WALD ME5................31 J3
Fowler Cl RHAM ME8................32 E5
Foxburrow Cl RHAM ME8............33 H2
Foxden Dr MAID/SHEP ME15......55 G5
Foxglove Cl WALD ME5................30 E1
Foxglove Ri MAID/BEAR ME14....49 K3
Foxglove Rw STRD ME2 *............28 E1
Foxgrove Cl GILL ME7................31 F2
Fox Hl WALD ME5................31 F1
Fox St GILL ME7................5 H1
Foxwood Cl RHAM ME8................33 H1
Francis La MAID/SHEP ME15......63 G3
Frankapps Cl RSIT ME9................13 J6

Franklin Dr MAID/BEAR ME14 ......54 E2
Franklin Rd GILL ME7 ....5 K3
GVE DA12 ....12 A1
Franks Ct RHAM ME8 ....25 F5
Frederick Rd GILL ME7 ....5 H5
Frederick St SIT ME10 ....36 E4
Freelands Rd SNOD ME6 ....38 C2
Freeman Gdns CHAT ME4 ....21 F5
Freeman Wy MAID/SHEP ME15 .....63 F1
Freesia Cl GILL ME7 * 5 K3
Fremlins Rd MAID/BEAR ME14 ....54 C2
Frensham St SIT ME10 ....37 H4
Frensham Wk WALD ME5 ....41 F1
Freshland Rd MAIDW ME16 ....53 G2
Freshwater Rd WALD ME5 ....31 H1
Friars Av WALD ME5 ....41 F1
Friars Ct MAID/BEAR ME14 * 7 K3
Friary Pl STRD ME2 ....2 D1
Friday St RMAID ME17 ....69 K3
Frindsbury Hl STRD ME2 ....15 H5
Frindsbury Rd STRD ME2 ....15 G5
Frinstead Wk MAIDW ME16 ....47 G5
Frinsted Cl RHAM ME8 ....22 E3
Friston Wy ROCH ME1 ....20 D6
Frithwood Cl MAID/SHEP ME15 .....55 G5
Frittenden Cl STRD ME2 ....15 J3
Frobisher Cl SIT ME10 ....36 E1
Frobisher Gdns ROCH ME1 ....20 D3
Frobisher Wy GVE DA12 ....12 B1
Frog La E/WMAL ME19 ....45 F4
Frost Crs WALD ME5 ....31 G1
Froyle Cl MAIDW ME16 ....47 H6
Fruiterer's Cl RSIT ME9 * 43 G3
Fulbert Dr MAID/BEAR ME14 ....54 D2
Fullers Cl MAID/BEAR ME14 ....55 H2
Fulmar Rd STRD ME2 ....19 H1
Fulston Pl SIT ME10 ....37 G5
Furfield Cl MAID/SHEP ME15 ....63 F5
Furrell's Rd ROCH ME1 ....3 H6
Future Ct STRD ME2 * 15 K4

G

Gabriel Gdns GVE DA12 ....12 B1
Gabriel's Hl MAID/BEAR ME14 ....7 H3
Gadby Rd SIT ME10 ....36 C3
Gads Hill Pl HOO/HM ME3 * 14 A1
Gagetown Ter
MAID/BEAR ME14 ....48 A5
Gainsborough Cl RHAM ME8 ....33 F2
SIT ME10 ....36 B3
Gainsborough Dr
MAIDW ME16 * 53 G2
Galahad Av SIT ME10 ....14 C6
Galena Ct SIT ME10 ....16 A4
WALD ME5 ....41 G1
Gallants La MAID/SHEP ME15 ....60 E2
Galleon Cl ROCH ME1 ....20 C6
Galleon Wy STRD ME2 ....16 A1
Galley Dr RSIT ME9 * 42 D4
Gandy's La RMAID ME17 ....62 D6
Garden Cl MAID/SHEP ME15 ....6 B1
Garden Ct ROCH ME1 ....29 G3
Gardenia Cl STRD ME2 ....15 G3
Garden of England Pk
RMAID ME17 * 66 A1
The Gardens RMAID ME17 * 61 G1
Garden St GILL ME7 ....6 C4
Garden Wy E/WMAL ME19 ....50 C4
Gardiner St GILL ME7 ....5 J1
Garfield Rd GILL ME7 ....16 E6
Garner Dr E/WMAL ME19 ....45 F4
Garrington Cl MAID/BEAR ME14 ...48 A6
Gascoyne Cl MAID/SHEP ME15 ......55 J4
Gas House Rd ROCH ME1 ....3 G4
Gas Rd SIT ME10 ....37 F3
Gassons Rd SNOD ME6 ....38 C2
Gatcombe Cl MAIDW ME16 ....53 G1
WALD ME5 ....31 G3
Gatekeeper Cha RMAID ME8 ....23 H6
Gatland La MAIDW ME16 ....53 G4
Gault Cl MAID/SHEP ME15 ....55 H4
Gayhurst Cl RHAM ME8 ....33 F2
Gayhurst Dr SIT ME10 ....36 C3
Gaze Hill Av SIT ME10 ....37 G5
Gazelle Gld GVE DA12 ....12 C1
Gean Cl WALD ME5 ....41 G1
Genesta Cl SIT ME10 ....36 E1
Genesta Gld SIT ME10 ....12 D1
Geneva Av RHAM ME8 ....22 C4
Gentian Cl MAID/BEAR ME14 ....55 F1
George La RMAID ME17 ....62 C6
ROCH ME1 ....3 G4
George St MAID/SHEP ME15 * 7 H6
SIT ME10 ....37 H5
George Summers Cl STRD ME2 ......15 K4
Georgian Dr MAID/BEAR ME14 * ...61 J5
Georgian Wy RHAM ME8 ....33 F2
Gerald Av CHAT ME4 ....21 F4
Gerrard Av ROCH ME1 ....20 D6
Gerrards Dr SIT ME10 ....37 F6
Gibbons Rd SIT ME10 ....36 B3
Gibbs Hl WBY/YAL ME18 ....58 C3
Gibraltar Av GILL ME7 ....16 B5
Gibraltar Hl CHAT ME4 ....4 B5
Gibraltar La MAID/BEAR ME14 ....47 K4
Gibson Dr E/WMAL ME19 ....50 C2
Gibson St SIT ME10 ....36 E4
Giddyhorn La MAIDW ME16 ....53 F1
Gifford Cl GILL ME7 ....22 E2
Gighill Rd DIT/AY ME20 ....45 J1
Gilbert Cl STRD ME2 ....32 C3
Giles Young Ct SIT ME10 * 5 H6
Gill Av WALD ME5 ....15 J1
Gilletts La E/WMAL ME19 ....45 K6
Gillingham Gn GILL ME7 ....5 F4
Gillingham Rd GILL ME7 ....5 J1
Gills Ct STRD ME2 ....15 K4
Ginsbury Cl STRD ME2 ....3 K4
The Glades GVE DA12 ....12 A2
The Glade MAID/SHEP ME15 ....31 G6
Gladstone Dr SIT ME10 ....37 J5

Gladstone Rd CHAT ME4 ....20 E4
MAID/BEAR ME14 ....48 B6
Gladwyn Cl RHAM ME8 ....33 F4
Glamford Rd SIT ME10 ....19 H1
Glamis Cl WALD ME5 ....31 G3
Glanville Rd GILL ME7 ....21 K1
STRD ME2 ....2 C1
Gleaming Wood Dr
MAID/BEAR ME14 ....41 K2
Gleaners Cl MAID/BEAR ME14 ....55 F2
Gleanings Ms ROCH ME1 * 3 F6
Glebe Gdns RMAID ME17 ....67 K3
Glebe La MAIDW ME16 ....52 E5
SIT ME10 ....57 H6
Glebe Meadow WBY/YAL ME18 ....59 G1
Glebe Rd GILL ME7 ....22 A5
The Glebe STRD ME2 ....19 G4
Glenbrook Gv SIT ME10 ....36 E1
Glencoe Rd CHAT ME4 ....21 G4
Gleneagles Dr
MAID/SHEP ME15 ....54 A5
Glenrosa Gdns GVE DA12 ....12 C1
Glenwood Cl GILL ME7 ....32 B1
MAIDW ME16 ....53 H1
WALD ME5 ....31 J2
Glistening Gld RHAM ME8 ....33 G2
Globe La CHAT ME4 ....4 B5
Gloucester Cl RHAM ME8 ....23 J6
Gloucester Rd
MAID/BEAR ME14 ....54 E6
Glover Cl SIT ME10 ....27 F5
Glovers Crs SIT ME10 * 37 F5
Goad Av WALD ME5 ....31 H5
Godden Rd SNOD ME6 ....38 D2
Godden Wy RHAM ME8 ....22 C2
Goddings Dr ROCH ME1 ....20 A3
Goddington La RMAID ME17 ....66 B1
Goddington Rd STRD ME2 ....15 G4
Godwin Cl SIT ME10 ....37 F5
Goldcrest Dr CHAT ME4 ....16 C2
Golden Wood Cl WALD ME5 ....41 K2
Goldfinch Cl DIT/AY ME20 ....25 K2
Golding Cl DIT/AY ME20 ....46 B5
ROCH ME1 ....20 D4
Goldings Cl E/WMAL ME19 ....50 D4
The Goldings RHAM ME8 ....22 E6
Goldsmith Rd RHAM ME8 ....33 G3
Goldstone Wk WALD ME5 ....41 G1
Goldsworth Dr RHAM ME8 ....31 H1
Goldthorne Cl
MAID/BEAR ME14 ....54 D2
Gooch Cl MAIDW ME16 ....47 J4
Goodall Cl RHAM ME8 ....33 G3
Goodnestone Rd SIT ME10 ....37 H5
Goodwin Dr MAID/BEAR ME14 ......48 C4
Goodwin Rd HOO/HM ME3 ....9 G3
Goodwood Cl MAID/SHEP ME15 ....63 G2
Goose Cl WALD ME5 ....31 G1
Gordon Cl SIT ME10 ....37 J4
Gordon Rd CHAT ME4 ....21 G4
GILL ME7 ....16 B6
STRD ME2 ....2 A1
SIT ME10 ....37 J5
STRD ME2 ....15 F4
Gordon Ter ROCH ME1 ....3 F7
Gore Court Rd
MAID/SHEP ME15 ....63 G3
SIT ME10 ....36 E6
Gore Green Rd HOO/HM ME3 ....8 C4
Gorham Cl SNOD ME6 ....38 D3
Gorham Dr MAID/SHEP ME15 ....55 H5
Gorse Av WALD ME5 ....30 E4
Gorse Crs DIT/AY ME20 ....46 C4
Gorse Rd SIT ME10 ....37 J5
STRD ME2 ....14 E4
Gorst St GILL ME7 ....16 A5
Goudhurst Cl MAIDW ME16 ....6 E3
Goudhurst Rd RHAM ME8 ....22 D3
Gould Rd WALD ME5 ....31 H5
Grace Av MAIDW ME16 ....47 J6
Grafton Av ROCH ME1 ....20 E6
Grafton Rd SIT ME10 ....37 J5
Grainey Fld RSIT ME9 ....34 C4
Grain Rd RHAM ME8 ....32 E5
Grampian Wy
MAID/SHEP ME15 ....55 H5
Granada St MAID/SHEP ME15 * 7 H4
Granary Cl MAID/BEAR ME14 * 8 A5
RHAM ME8 ....23 H5
Grandsire Gdns HOO/HM ME3 ....11 F4
Grange Cl E/WMAL ME19 ....45 F2
Grange Hl WALD ME5 ....31 J2
Grange La MAID/BEAR ME14 ....48 A5
Grange Rd GILL ME7 ....2 E1
STRD ME2 ....2 E1
The Grange E/WMAL ME19 ....45 K5
Grange Wy ROCH ME1 ....20 C3
Grant Cl GILL ME7 ....22 D5
Grant Dr MAID/SHEP ME15 ....62 E2
Grant Rd HOO/HM ME3 ....11 F4
Granville Rd GILL ME7 ....22 A1
MAID/BEAR ME14 ....48 B6
Grapple Rd MAID/BEAR ME14 ....48 B5
Crasmere Gv WALD ME5 ....31 H2
Grasslands RMAID ME17 ....64 B4
Grassmere DIT/AY ME20 ....45 H5
Grassy Gld GILL ME7 * 32 D2
Gravelly Bottom Rd
RMAID ME17 ....64 E6
Gravel Wk ROCH ME1 ....3 G6
Graveney Cl HOO/HM ME3 ....9 H5
Graveney Rd MAID/SHEP ME15 .....63 G1
Gravesend Rd HOO/HM ME3 ....14 B2
Graylings Ct SIT ME10 ....36 C6
The Graylings ROCH ME1 ....20 B3
Grayshott Cl SIT ME10 ....37 F5
Great Lines GILL ME7 ....4 E2
Great South Av CHAT ME4 ....21 F5
Grecian St MAID/BEAR ME14 ....48 B6
Greenacre Cl WALD ME5 ....31 G3
Greenbank WALD ME5 ....21 H6
Green Bank GILL ME7 * 32 C3
Greenborough Cl
MAID/SHEP ME15 ....63 F2
Green Cl ROCH ME1 ....20 D4

Greenfield Cl DIT/AY ME20 ....40 A4
Greenfield Rd SIT ME10 ....16 E6
Greenfields MAID/SHEP ME15 ....55 F6
Greenfields Cl HOO/HM ME3 ....15 J1
Greenfinches GILL ME7 ....32 B2
Green Hl MAID/SHEP ME15 ....55 J5
Greenhithe CHAT ME4 * 7 G4
Green La RMAID ME17 ....62 D5
RMAID ME17 ....68 A6
RMAID ME17 ....68 B5
RSIT ME9 ....43 H5
Greenside MAID/SHEP ME15 * 7 H1
Greensand Rd
MAID/SHEP ME15 ....60 D6
RMAID ME17 ....68 B2
WBY/YAL ME18 ....58 D5
Greensleeves Wy
E/WMAL ME19 ....51 F3
Green St GILL ME7 ....22 A1
The Green RSIT ME9 * 25 F3
Greenvale Gdns RHAM ME8 ....22 D4
Green Wy MAIDW ME16 ....53 G3
Greenway Court Rd
RMAID ME17 ....57 H4
Greenway La RMAID ME17 ....65 K1
SIT ME10 * 25 F5
Greenwich Cl MAIDW ME16 ....6 B5
WALD ME5 ....31 H4
Gregory Cl RHAM ME8 ....30 C6
SIT ME10 ....27 G6
Grenadier Cl RHAM ME8 ....23 H5
Gresham Cl RHAM ME8 ....23 H5
Gresham Rd MAID/SHEP ME15 ......53 K6
Greyfriars Cl MAIDW ME16 ....6 C2
Greystones Rd
MAID/SHEP ME15 ....55 H4
Grey Wethers
MAID/BEAR ME14 ....40 E6
Griffin Ct GILL ME7 ....17 G4
Grizedale Cl RHAM ME8 ....20 D6
Groombridge Dr GILL ME7 ....23 E4
Groombridge Sq
MAID/BEAR ME14 * 63 G2
Groom Wy RMAID ME17 ....37 F5
Grosvenor Av RHAM ME8 ....20 E6
Grosvenor Rd GILL ME7 ....22 B5
Grove Green La
MAID/BEAR ME14 ....55 F1
Grove Green Rd
MAID/BEAR ME14 ....55 F1
Grovehurst Av SIT ME10 ....27 F6
Grovehurst Rd RSIT ME9 ....26 E6
Grovelands RMAID ME17 ....67 K3
Grove Park Av SIT ME10 ....36 A3
Grove Rd CHAT ME4 ....21 H4
GILL ME7 * 21 K4
MAID/SHEP ME15 ....7 G4
STRD ME2 ....15 G4
SIT ME10 ....36 E2
The Groves SNOD ME6 ....38 D5
The Grove MAID/BEAR ME14 ....48 B5
Grovewood Dr
MAID/BEAR ME14 ....54 E2
Guardian Ct RHAM ME8 ....23 H5
Guildford Gdns STRD ME2 ....14 B6
Guillat Av RSIT ME9 * 42 D4
Guiness Dr DIT/AY ME20 ....15 G2
Guilands RMAID ME17 ....64 B4
Gundulph Rd CHAT ME4 ....3 K7
Gundulph Sq ROCH ME1 * 3 F4
Gun La STRD ME2 ....2 E4
Gunnis Cl RHAM ME8 ....32 E4
Gun Tower Ms ROCH ME1 ....3 H4
Guston Rd MAID/BEAR ME14 ....54 D1

H

Hackney Rd MAIDW ME16 ....53 H4
Hadleigh Ct GILL ME7 ....32 C5
Hackville Rd MAID/BEAR ME14 ......34 D1
Haig Av CHAT ME4 ....21 G4
GILL ME7 ....22 A2
ROCH ME1 ....20 D4
Halden Cl MAID/SHEP ME15 ....63 G2
Hale Rd HOO/HM ME3 ....9 J5
Hales Rd SIT ME10 ....42 D1
Haleys Pl ROCH ME1 ....40 A2
Halfpence La GVE DA12 ....12 E6
Halfpenny Cl MAIDW ME16 ....53 F4
Half Yoke MAIDW ME16 * 53 C6
Halifax Cl WALD ME5 ....31 H2
Hall Rd DIT/AY ME20 ....45 J6
ROCH ME1 ....29 G5
WALD ME5 ....31 J5
Hallsfield Rd WALD ME5 ....30 D5
Hallwood Cl RHAM ME8 ....33 F5
Halstow Cl MAID/SHEP ME15 ....62 C5
Hambledon Cl MAIDW ME16 ....53 G4
Hambrook Wk SIT ME10 ....27 F6
Hamelin Rd GILL ME7 ....22 B6
Hamilton Ct ROCH ME1 * 20 B2
Hamilton Crs SIT ME10 ....36 C5
Hamilton Rd GILL ME7 ....16 A6
Ham La GILL ME7 ....32 A5
RMAID ME17 ....67 H3
Hammonds Sq SNOD ME6 ....38 E2
Hammond Hl CHAT ME4 ....4 A4
Hampshire Ct WALD ME5 ....31 J1
Hampshire Drive Rd
MAID/SHEP ME15 ....54 D6
Hampson Wy MAID/BEAR ME14 ....55 H2
Hampton Cl WALD ME5 ....31 G3
Hampton Rd MAID/BEAR ME14 .....48 D6
Ham River Hl HOO/HM ME3 ....9 F4

Hamwick Gn WALD ME5 ....41 J1
Hanbury Ct WBY/YAL ME18 ....59 H1
Hancock Cl SIT ME10 ....16 D1
Hanover Cl SIT ME10 ....36 E6
Hanover Dr RHAM ME8 ....32 E4
Hanover Gn DIT/AY ME20 ....45 J1
Hanover Rd RMAID ME17 ....61 H5
Hanway RHAM ME8 ....22 C4
Harbourland Cl
MAID/BEAR ME14 ....48 C4
The Harbour RMAID ME17 ....69 G5
Harcourt Gdns RHAM ME8 ....33 G4
Hardie Cl E/WMAL ME19 * 45 J3
Hardres Ter MAID/BEAR ME14 ....4 E5
Hards Town CHAT ME4 ....4 A5
Hardy Cl WALD ME5 ....31 H2
Hardy St MAID/BEAR ME14 ....48 B6
Harebell Cl MAID/BEAR ME14 ....55 F1
Haredale Cl ROCH ME1 ....30 D1
Harlech Cl STRD ME2 ....15 J3
Harold Av GILL ME7 ....22 A2
Harold Rd SIT ME10 ....37 H4
STRD ME2 ....19 F3
Harp Farm Rd
MAID/BEAR ME14 ....41 J3
Harple La MAID/BEAR ME14 ....49 G3
Harptree Dr WALD ME5 ....15 F3
Harrier Dr SIT ME10 ....37 G6
Harriet Cl ROCH ME1 ....20 A3
Harris Ct GILL ME7 ....22 B4
Harrison Dr RMAID ME17 ....66 D2
Harrow Rd GILL ME7 ....32 B2
Harrow Wy MAID/BEAR ME14 ....55 G1
Hartington St CHAT ME4 ....4 D6
Hartley Cl MAID/SHEP ME15 ....63 G2
Hartley Ms RHAM ME8 ....22 D4
Hartlip Hl RSIT ME9 ....34 C1
Hartnup St MAIDW ME16 ....53 H4
Hartpiece Cl RHAM ME8 ....23 H4
Hart St MAIDW ME16 ....7 F2
Harty Av RHAM ME8 ....32 D5
Harvel Av STRD ME2 ....14 D5
Harvesters Cl MAID/BEAR ME14 ....33 G2
Harvesters Wy
MAID/BEAR ME14 ....54 E2
Harvest Rdg E/WMAL ME19 ....45 G2
Harvey Dr SIT ME10 ....37 G6
Harvey Rd RHAM ME8 ....23 G6
Harwood Rd RHAM ME8 ....23 K5
Hasted Rd HOO/HM ME3 ....15 F2
RSIT ME9 ....34 D1
Hasteds RMAID ME17 ....57 F4
Haste Hill Cl MAID/SHEP ME15 ......62 B5
Haste Hill Rd MAID/SHEP ME15 .....62 B5
Hastings Rd MAID/BEAR ME14 ....7 K5
Hatch Rd RMAID ME17 ....67 H3
Hatfield Rd STRD ME2 ....15 H4
Hathaway Ct ROCH ME1 ....2 E6
Hatheralh Rd MAID/BEAR ME14 ....48 C6
Hatton Rd WALD ME5 ....31 J5
Haven Cl ROCH ME1 ....20 C4
Haven St HOO/HM ME3 ....10 A5
Havisham Cl ROCH ME1 * 20 D4
Hawbeck Rd RHAM ME8 ....32 E5
Hawkenbury Rd HOO/HM ME3 ......15 G2
Hawkes Dr DIT/AY ME20 ....39 K5
Hawkhurst Rd RHAM ME8 ....22 C3
Hawkins Cl CHAT ME4 ....16 B3
SIT ME10 ....36 E2
Hawks Hill La RSIT ME9 ....42 C6
Hawkwood Cl MAID/BEAR ME14 ...53 J1
Hawkwood Cl ROCH ME1 ....3 J6
Hawser Rd ROCH ME1 ....20 C5
Hawthorne Av RHAM ME8 ....33 F4
Hawthorn Rd SIT ME10 ....36 E4
STRD ME2 ....2 A3
Hawthorns WALD ME5 * 41 F1
The Hawthorns DIT/AY ME20 ....46 D5
Haydon Cl MAIDW ME16 ....53 C2
Hayes Cl HOO/HM ME3 ....13 H1
Hayes Ter GVE DA12 * 13 H1
Hayfield E/WMAL ME19 ....45 G2
Hayfields WALD ME5 ....31 K6
Hayle Mill Rd MAID/SHEP ME15 ....54 A6
Hayle Pl MAID/SHEP ME15 * 54 A6
Hayley's Cl SIT ME10 ....19 G4
Hayman Wk DIT/AY ME20 * 39 K4
Haymen St CHAT ME4 ....4 A7
Hayrick Cl MAID/BEAR ME14 ....55 F1
Haysel SIT ME10 ....37 G6
Hays Rd SNOD ME6 ....38 D4
Haywain Cl MAID/BEAR ME14 ....55 G2
Hayward Av STRD ME2 ....15 G4
Hazel Av HOO/HM ME3 ....17 F1
ROCH ME1 ....6 A1
Hazel Gv WALD ME5 ....21 H6
Hazelmere Dr SIT ME10 ....55 F4
Hazelwood Dr MAIDW ME16 ....55 C2
Hazen Rd E/WMAL ME19 ....50 E3
Haziemere Dr GILL ME7 ....22 C1
Hazlitt Dr MAIDW ME16 ....6 B1
Headcorn Rd RHAM ME8 ....22 D2
RMAID ME17 ....69 G5
Headingley Rd MAIDW ME16 ....47 G6
The Head Race MAIDW ME16 ....53 J4
Heaf Gdns DIT/AY ME20 * 46 E3
Heard Wy SIT ME10 ....37 H3
Hearts Delight Rd RSIT ME9 ....42 E1
Heathcote Cl DIT/AY ME20 * 46 E2
Heather Cl SIT ME10 ....37 G5
WALD ME5 ....31 H4
Heather Dr MAID/SHEP ME15 ....54 C4
Heatherwood Cl RMAID ME17 ....65 H6
Heathfield RMAID ME17 ....64 B4
Heathfield Av
MAID/BEAR ME14 ....48 C5
Heathfield Cl MAID/BEAR ME14 ....48 C5
MAIDW ME16 ....31 H1
Heathfield Rd
MAID/SHEP ME15 ....54 D6
Heath Gv MAIDW ME16 ....53 F4
Heathorn St MAID/BEAR ME14 ....7 K1

Heath Rd MAID/SHEP ME15 ....60 D4
MAIDW ME16 ....52 E5
RMAID ME17 ....64 B4
Heathside Av RMAID ME17 ....61 H4
The Heath PI MAID/SHEP ME19 .....51 H1
The Hedgerow
MAID/BEAR ME14 ....55 F1
The Hedges MAID/BEAR ME14 ......48 B5
Hedley St MAID/BEAR ME14 ....7 J2
Heeley Cl RSIT ME9 * 42 D4
Helen Thompson Cl RSIT ME9 ....26 E2
Hellyar Ct ROCH ME1 ....3 G7
Hempstead Rd SIT ME10 ....32 B5
Hempstead Valley Dr GILL ME7 .....32 C2
Henbane Cl MAID/BEAR ME14 ....55 F1
Hendy Rd SNOD ME6 ....38 F2
Hengist Ct MAID/BEAR ME14 * 7 J3
Henhurst Rd MEO DA13 ....12 A5
Heniker La RMAID ME17 ....61 H4
Henley Av SIT ME10 ....23 F6
WALD ME5 ....31 G2
Henley Flds MAID/BEAR ME14 ....54 D2
Henry St CHAT ME4 ....23 H5
RHAM ME8 ....23 J3
Herbert Rd CHAT ME4 ....4 D7
GILL ME7 ....22 B5
Herdsdown HOO/HM ME3 ....10 C5
Hereford Rd MAID/SHEP ME15 ......62 D1
Heritage Dr GILL ME7 ....32 C3
Heritage Rd MAID/BEAR ME14 ....51 G2
Herman Ter CHAT ME4 ....4 D6
Hermitage La MAIDW ME16 ....52 E1
Hermitage La DIT/AY ME20 ....49 J1
MAID/BEAR ME14 ....49 J1
RMAID ME17 ....61 K1
Hermitage Rd HOO/HM ME3 ....14 B1
Herne Rd RHAM ME8 ....22 E4
Heron Cl RSIT ME9 ....25 F3
Heronden Rd MAID/SHEP ME15 .....63 G4
Heron Rd DIT/AY ME20 ....45 J1
Heron Wy WALD ME5 ....31 G2
Herts Crs MAID/SHEP ME15 ....63 G3
Herying Ct STRD ME2 ....29 F4
Hever Cl MAID/SHEP ME15 ....63 G2
Hever CfR STRD ME2 ....19 K1
Hever Gdns MAIDW ME16 ....6 D6
Hever Pl SIT ME10 ....36 C5
Hewitt Cl SIT ME10 ....17 C6
MAIDW ME16 ....47 J5
Hextable Cl MAIDW ME16 ....47 H5
Hickory Dell GILL ME7 ....32 C3
Higham Cl MAID/SHEP ME15 ....53 J4
Higham Rd HOO/HM ME3 ....15 J1
Higham Vw MAID/BEAR ME14 ....40 E6
High Bank ROCH ME1 ....20 D4
High Banks MAID/SHEP ME15 ....62 A5
Highberry E/WMAL ME19 ....45 H2
High Dewar Rd RHAM ME8 ....23 J5
High Elms RHAM ME8 ....23 G4
Highfield Cl RHAM ME8 ....33 J1
Highfield Rd RHAM ME8 ....23 J4
Highgrove Rd WALD ME5 ....31 G3
Highland Rd MAID/SHEP ME15 ......63 F1
Highlands Cl STRD ME2 ....14 C6
High Oak Hl RSIT ME9 ....22 B5
Highridge GILL ME7 ....22 B5
Highridge Cl MAID/BEAR ME14 .....55 G2
Highsted Rd RSIT ME9 ....43 F5
High St CHAT ME4 ....4 D5
DIT/AY ME20 ....46 E1
E/WMAL ME19 ....44 E4
E/WMAL ME19 ....45 K6
GILL ME7 ....5 J1
MAID/BEAR ME14 ....7 H3
RHAM ME8 ....23 H6
RMAID ME17 ....67 J4
ROCH ME1 ....3 G4
RSIT ME9 ....35 F2
SIT ME10 ....36 E2
SNOD ME6 ....38 C2
STRD ME2 ....2 A1
STRD ME2 ....16 A2
STRD ME2 ....28 B6
High Vw HOO/HM ME3 ....10 D5
Highview Dr WALD ME5 ....30 D5
Highwoods Cl HOO/HM ME3 ....8 A6
Hilary Gdns ROCH ME1 ....29 F4
Hilda Rd CHAT ME4 ....4 B7
Hildenborough Crs
MAID/BEAR ME14 ....47 G5
Hillary Rd MAID/SHEP ME15 ....48 B5
Hillborough Gv WALD ME5 ....31 C5
Hill Brow MAID/BEAR ME14 ....55 H1
Hill Cha WALD ME5 ....30 E5
Hill Ct HOO/HM ME3 ....10 C6
Hillcrest Dr STRD ME2 ....14 B4
Hillcrest Rd CHAT ME4 ....21 F4
Hillden Shaw MAID/SHEP ME15 .....54 B6
Hill Rd ROCH ME1 ....20 A4
ROCH ME1 ....29 F4
Hillshaw Crs STRD ME2 ....19 H1
Hillside Av STRD ME2 ....15 H2
Hillside Cl STRD ME2 * 3 H1
Hillside Rd CHAT ME4 ....4 C5
Hills Pl STRD ME2 * 2 E8
Hill's Ter CHAT ME4 ....4 C5
Hilltop Rd STRD ME2 ....15 H5
Hill View Wy WALD ME5 ....30 E5
Hillyfield Cl STRD ME2 ....15 H2
Hilton Dr SIT ME10 ....36 B2
Hilton Rd HOO/HM ME3 ....14 E1
Hinckley Cl MAID/BEAR ME14 ....53 J1
Hinde Cl MAID/BEAR ME14 ....55 F1
Hines Ter WALD ME5 * 7 F1
Hinton Crs GILL ME7 ....32 C1
Hoath Cl GILL ME7 ....32 C1
Hoath La RHAM ME8 ....22 D6
Hoath Wy RHAM ME8 ....32 D6
Hobart Gdns SIT ME10 ....37 J4
Hockers Cl MAID/BEAR ME14 ....49 H4
Hockers La MAID/BEAR ME14 ....49 G4

Hodgson Crs SNOD ME6 38 E2
Hog Hl MAID/BEAR ME14 55 J2
Holborn La CHAT ME4 4 B3
Holborough Rd SNOD ME6 38 E2
Holcombe Rd CHAT ME4 21 F4
ROCH ME1 20 C3
Holder Cl WALD ME5 31 J2
Holding St RHAM ME8 23 G5
Holland Rd MAID/BEAR ME14 7 J2
WALD ME5 30 E4
Hollands Cl GVE DA12 13 H1
The Hollies GVE DA12 12 A2
Hollingbourne Hl RMAID ME17 57 J2
Hollingbourne Rd RHAM ME8 22 E3
Hollingworth Rd
MAID/SHEP ME15 63 G3
Hollow La RSIT ME9 34 B3
SNOD ME6 38 D3
The Hollow MAID/SHEP ME15 * 60 D2
Holly Cl GILL ME7 17 F6
WALD ME5 21 J5
Holly Farm Rd
MAID/SHEP ME15 63 K2
Holly Gdns MAID/BEAR ME14 * 7 G1
Holly Rd STRD ME2 14 D6
STRD ME2 15 J2
Holly Tree Cl RMAID ME17 65 H6
Hollytree Dr HOO/HM ME3 14 A1
Holly Vls MAID/SHEP ME15 * 60 D2
Hollywood La STRD ME2 15 J1
Holmesdale Cl
MAID/SHEP ME15 62 A5
Holm Mill La RMAID ME17 66 A2
Holmoaks MAID/BEAR ME14 54 D1
RHAM ME8 23 G4
Holmside GILL ME7 22 A4
Holt Wood Av DIT/AY ME20 46 C4
Holtwood Cl RHAM ME8 33 F3
Holtye Crs MAID/SHEP ME15 54 C4
Holywell La RSIT ME9 24 D4
Homefield Dr RHAM ME8 23 K4
The Homestead RHAM ME8 * 23 K6
Homestead Vw RSIT ME9 36 B6
Homeview SIT ME10 37 H4
Homewood Av SIT ME10 36 D5
Honduras Ter
MAID/BEAR ME14 48 B5
Hone St STRD ME2 15 G4
Honey Bee Gld RHAM ME8 33 K2
Honey Cl GILL ME7 32 C3
Honey La MAID/SHEP ME15 63 J2
Honeypot Cl STRD ME2 15 G4
Honeysuckle Cl GILL ME7 32 B4
Honywood Rd RMAID ME17 67 H3
Hoo Common HOO/HM ME3 10 B6
Hook Cl WALD ME5 30 E3
Hook La RMAID ME17 66 B2
Hook Rd SNOD ME6 38 D2
Hoo Marina Pk HOO/HM ME3 * 17 F1
Hooper's Pl ROCH ME1 * 3 G7
Hoopers Rd ROCH ME1 3 G7
Hope St CHAT ME4 4 E7
Hope Ter HOO/HM ME3 * 8 C3
Hopewell Dr GVE DA12 12 C1
WALD ME5 21 J6
Horatio Pl ROCH ME1 * 20 B2
Hornbeam Av WALD ME5 31 H6
Hornbeam Cl DIT/AY ME20 46 A3
Horns La WBY/YAL ME18 50 A4
Horseshoe Cl GILL ME7 32 B3
MAID/BEAR ME14 55 F1
Horseshoes La RMAID ME17 64 A4
Horsewash La ROCH ME1 3 F3
Horsham La RHAM ME8 24 B3
Horsley Rd ROCH ME1 2 E7
Horsted Av CHAT ME4 20 E5
Horsted Wy ROCH ME1 30 D1
Horton Downs
MAID/SHEP ME15 55 G5
Horwood Cl ROCH ME1 20 B6
Hospital La ROCH ME1 * 3 K7
Hospital Rd RMAID ME17 57 H6
Hostier Cl STRD ME2 29 F4
Hotel Rd RHAM ME8 22 C4
Hothfield Rd RHAM ME8 23 H5
Houghton Av GILL ME7 32 D5
Howard Av ROCH ME1 20 D5
SIT ME10 36 D2
Howard Dr MAIDW ME16 47 G6
Howard Rd E/WMAL ME19 45 J4
Howick Cl DIT/AY ME20 46 E4
Howlsmere Cl STRD ME2 29 F5
Howt Gn SIT ME10 * 26 D5
Hubbard's La
MAID/SHEP ME15 62 B5
Hubble Dr MAID/SHEP ME15 63 F1
Huckleberry Cl WALD ME5 31 H5
Hudson Cl RHAM ME8 22 E5
Hughes Dr STRD ME2 15 J2
Hugh Price Cl SIT ME10 37 J3
Hulkes La ROCH ME1 3 K7
Humber Crs STRD ME2 2 A2
Hunstanton Cl RHAM ME8 33 G5
Huntersfield Cl WALD ME5 41 J1
Hunters Wy GILL ME7 22 A5
Hunters Wy West WALD ME5 21 K4
Huntingdon Wk
MAID/SHEP ME15 * 63 F1
Huntington Rd RMAID ME17 61 G5
Huntsman La MAID/BEAR ME14 54 C2
Huntsmans Cl ROCH ME1 20 D5
Hunt St WBY/YAL ME18 59 H4
Hurricane Rd E/WMAL ME19 50 C3
Hurst Cl WALD ME5 30 E2
Hurst Hl WALD ME5 30 E6
The Hurstings MAIDW ME16 6 C7
Hurst La SIT ME10 27 F5
Hurst Pl RHAM ME8 23 H6
Hurst Wy MAIDW ME16 52 E4
Hurstwood WALD ME5 30 E4
Hutsford Cl RHAM ME8 33 F3
Huxley Ct ROCH ME1 * 3 H7
Hyacinth Rd STRD ME2 14 C6
Hybrid Cl ROCH ME1 20 D5
Hyde Rd MAIDW ME16 47 J5
Hyperion Dr STRD ME2 14 E3
Hythe Rd SIT ME10 36 D3

I

Iden Rd STRD ME2 15 H3
Idenwood Cl RHAM ME8 33 F2
Ifield Cl MAID/SHEP ME15 55 G6
Ifield Wy GVE DA12 12 A2
Illustrious Cl WALD ME5 31 G3
Imperial Dr GVE DA12 12 C1
Imperial Rd GILL ME7 5 H7
Impton La WALD ME5 41 F2
Ingleden Cl SIT ME10 27 F6
Ingle Rd CHAT ME4 21 F4
Ingram Rd GILL ME7 22 A1
Inner Lines GILL ME7 16 B6
Institute Rd CHAT ME4 4 E5
Invicta Ct SIT ME10 37 F1
Iona Cl WALD ME5 41 K1
Iona Rd MAID/SHEP ME15 62 B1
Iris Cl WALD ME5 41 G2
Ironside Cl WALD ME5 21 G6
Irvine Rd HOO/HM ME3 14 A1
Island Wy East CHAT ME4 16 C3
Island Wy West CHAT ME4 16 C2
Islingham Farm Rd
HOO/HM ME3 15 H1
Ivens Wy RMAID ME17 66 C2
Iversgate Cl RHAM ME8 23 H4
Ivy Cl RMAID ME17 65 G6
Ivy Pl ROCH ME1 * 20 A4
Ivy St RHAM ME8 23 H6

J

Jacinth Dr SIT ME10 36 C2
Jacklin Cl WALD ME5 31 F5
Jackson Av ROCH ME1 20 E6
Jackson Cl RHAM ME8 22 E5
Jacob's La HOO/HM ME3 11 K4
Jade Cl SIT ME10 36 C1
Jamaica Ter MAID/BEAR ME14 48 B5
James Rd STRD ME2 19 F4
James St CHAT ME4 4 C5
GILL ME7 5 J1
MAID/BEAR ME14 7 H1
ROCH ME1 3 G7
James Whathan Wy
MAID/BEAR ME14 7 F1
James Whatman Ct
MAID/SHEP ME15 * 54 D3
Japonica Cl WALD ME5 31 J6
Jarrett Av STRD ME2 15 J2
Jasmine Cl E/WMAL ME19 45 J4
Jasmine Rd E/WMAL ME19 45 J4
Jasper Av ROCH ME1 20 C4
Javelin Rd E/WMAL ME19 50 C3
Jefferson Dr RHAM ME8 22 E5
Jeffery St GILL ME7 5 H1
Jeffrey St MAID/BEAR ME14 7 J2
Jenkins' Dl CHAT ME4 4 C7
Jenkins Dr MAID/SHEP ME15 63 F3
Jenner Rd ROCH ME1 20 C2
Jenner Wy DIT/AY ME20 39 K4
Jennifer Ct HOO/HM ME3 * 11 F5
Jerome Rd DIT/AY ME20 38 D6
Jersey Rd STRD ME2 15 F4
Jeskyns Rd MEO DA13 12 A5
Jessica Ms SIT ME10 36 E1
Jeyes Rd GILL ME7 5 H5
Jezreels Rd GILL ME7 5 K7
Jiniwin Rd ROCH ME1 30 D1
Johnson Av GILL ME7 16 D5
Johnson Rd SIT ME10 36 D4
John St MAID/BEAR ME14 48 B6
ROCH ME1 3 G7
Joiners Ct CHAT ME4 21 H4
Jordan Cl MAID/SHEP ME15 63 F3
Joy Wd RMAID ME17 62 E3
Jubilee St SIT ME10 36 E3
Jubilee Ter GILL ME7 16 D6
Judeth Gdns GVE DA12 12 B1
Judkins Cl WALD ME5 31 J2
Junction Rd GILL ME7 21 K2
Juniper Cl MAIDW ME16 47 G6
WALD ME5 31 G4

K

Karloff Wy HOO/HM ME3 15 G2
Katherine Ct WALD ME5 31 H6
Keating Cl ROCH ME1 20 A3
Keats Rd DIT/AY ME20 45 J1
Keefe Cl WALD ME5 40 D1
Keeley Ms GILL ME7 * 22 A3
Kellaway Rd WALD ME5 31 G6
Kelly Dr GILL ME7 16 D5
Kemp Cl WALD ME5 30 E4
Kempton Cl WALD ME5 31 J5
Kendall Av E/WMAL ME19 51 F3
Kendal Wy RHAM ME8 23 F6
Kenilworth Ct SIT ME10 36 C3
Kenilworth Dr RHAM ME8 33 F2
Kennard Cl ROCH ME1 19 K4
Kennington Cl
MAID/SHEP ME15 55 G6
RHAM ME8 22 D2
Kent Av MAID/SHEP ME15 54 D5
SIT ME10 36 D5
Kent Cl ROCH ME1 20 C6
Kent Rd SNOD ME6 38 E4
STRD ME2 28 E2
Kent St WBY/YAL ME18 50 B4
Kent Ter HOO/HM ME3 * 8 C3
RHAM ME8 24 A4
Kenward Rd MAIDW ME16 53 H1
WBY/YAL ME18 59 H5
Kenwood Av WALD ME5 31 G4
Kenya Ter MAID/BEAR ME14 48 B5
Kerry Hill Wy MAID/BEAR ME14 47 K6
Kesteven Cl STRD ME2 28 E3
Keston Ct RHAM ME8 * 22 C4
Kestrel Cl SIT ME10 37 G6
Kestrel Rd WALD ME5 31 J6
Keswick Dr MAIDW ME16 53 H1
Keswick Rd SIT ME10 37 J5
Ketridge La WBY/YAL ME18 51 G4
Kettle La MAID/SHEP ME15 60 D1
Kewlands MAID/BEAR ME14 48 D6
Keycol Hl RSIT ME9 35 J3
Keyes Av CHAT ME4 21 F4
Key St SIT ME10 36 A3
Khartoum Rd CHAT ME4 4 D1
Khyber Rd GILL ME7 16 C5
Killick Rd HOO/HM ME3 10 E5
Kiln Barn Rd DIT/AY ME20 46 B4
Kilnbridge Cl MAID/SHEP ME15 61 G1
Kiln Cl SIT ME10 37 G5
Kilndown Cl MAIDW ME16 47 H5
Kimberley Rd GILL ME7 5 K6
King Arthur's Dr STRD ME2 15 F3
King Edward Rd CHAT ME4 21 F4
GILL ME7 17 G6
MAID/SHEP ME15 7 G7
ROCH ME1 3 F6
Kingfisher Cl RSIT ME9 26 E2
Kingfisher Dr WALD ME5 31 J1
Kingfisher Rd DIT/AY ME20 45 J2
King George Rd WALD ME5 30 E4
King Hl E/WMAL ME19 50 D2
Kings Acre MAID/SHEP ME15 55 H5
King's Av ROCH ME1 20 C3
King's Bastion GILL ME7 4 E3
Kingsdown Cl GILL ME7 32 C4
MAIDW ME16 6 D3
Kingsgate Cl MAIDW ME16 53 H2
Kings Hill Av E/WMAL ME19 50 D2
Kingshill Dr HOO/HM ME3 10 E4
Kingsley Rd MAID/SHEP ME15 7 J5
Kings Mill Cl SIT ME10 36 E3
Kingsnorth Rd RHAM ME8 22 E2
Kingsoak Ms WALD ME5 31 F4
King's Orch ROCH ME1 3 G5
King's Reach MAID/SHEP ME15 54 E6
King's Rd WALD ME5 21 K5
Kings Rw MAID/SHEP ME15 * 54 B5
Kingston Crs WALD ME5 31 H4
Kingston Dr MAID/SHEP ME15 54 B6
King St CHAT ME4 4 D4
E/WMAL ME19 44 E4
GILL ME7 5 J2
MAID/BEAR ME14 7 J3
ROCH ME1 3 G7
SIT ME10 36 E3
Kings Wk MAID/BEAR ME14 7 K2
Kingsway GILL ME7 22 A5
WALD ME5 21 K5
Kingswear Gdns STRD ME2 2 E2
Kingswood Av CHAT ME4 20 E4
Kingswood Rd GILL ME7 5 K1
ROCH ME1 40 D2
King William Rd GILL ME7 16 D5
Kinross Cl WALD ME5 31 H1
Kipling Dr DIT/AY ME20 38 D6
Kirby Rd HOO/HM ME3 9 K5
Kirkdale MAID/SHEP ME15 62 A3
Kirkdale Cl WALD ME5 41 K1
Kirkdale Rd MAID/SHEP ME15 62 A2
Kirk La HOO/HM ME3 * 9 J1
Kitchener Av CHAT ME4 21 F5
Kitchener Rd HOO/HM ME3 10 A6
STRD ME2 15 F4
Kit Hill Av WALD ME5 30 E5
Knight Av GILL ME7 16 E6
Knightrider Ct MAID/SHEP ME15 7 H5
Knightrider St MAID/SHEP ME15 7 H5
Knight Rd STRD ME2 2 B5
Knights Cl HOO/HM ME3 11 F5
Knightsfield Rd SIT ME10 36 D1
Knights Rd HOO/HM ME3 10 E4
Knole Rd WALD ME5 31 J6
Knott Ct MAID/BEAR ME14 48 B6
Knowle Rd MAID/BEAR ME14 48 B6
ROCH ME1 29 G4
Knowlton Gdns MAIDW ME16 53 G4
Kyetop Wk RHAM ME8 33 F2

L

Laburnum Dr DIT/AY ME20 45 K2
Laburnum Pl SIT ME10 36 E4
Laburnum Rd STRD ME2 19 J1
Lacey Cl RMAID ME17 64 B4
Lacock Gdns MAID/SHEP ME15 54 B5
Lacy Cl MAIDW ME16 47 J5
Ladds La SNOD ME6 28 E6
Ladyclose Av HOO/HM ME3 9 F3
Ladyfields WALD ME5 31 K6
Ladyfields Cl RSIT ME9 35 K3
Ladywood Rd STRD ME2 19 F4
Lake Dr HOO/HM ME3 8 B4
Lakelands MAID/SHEP ME15 62 B1
RMAID ME17 66 D2
Lake Rd DIT/AY ME20 46 D4
Laker Rd ROCH ME1 30 C2
Lakeside SNOD ME6 38 D4
Lakeview Cl SNOD ME6 38 E4
Lakewood Dr RHAM ME8 32 E2
Lambarde Cl STRD ME2 * 28 E4
Lamberhurst Gn RHAM ME8 22 D4
Lambert Ms SNOD ME6 38 E2
Lambeth Cl WALD ME5 31 H4
Lambfrith Gv GILL ME7 32 D5
Lambourne Dr E/WMAL ME19 50 C4
Lambourne Pl RHAM ME8 23 J4
Lambourne Rd
MAID/SHEP ME15 55 G4
Lambourn Wy WALD ME5 31 J6
Lambsfrith Gv GILL ME7 32 D5
Lammas Dr SIT ME10 36 E2
Lamplighters Cl GILL ME7 32 B4
Lancashire Rd
MAID/SHEP ME15 63 F1
Lancaster Ct RHAM ME8 32 E1
Lancaster Wy E/WMAL ME19 50 C3
Lance Cl SIT ME10 27 F6
Lancelot Av STRD ME2 14 D5
Lancelot Cl STRD ME2 14 D6
Lancet La MAID/SHEP ME15 62 A2
Landor Ct GILL ME7 32 C5
Landrail Rd RSIT ME9 25 F3
Land Wy HOO/HM ME3 8 C5
The Landway MAID/BEAR ME14 55 H3
Langdale Cl RHAM ME8 23 F5
Langdale Ri MAIDW ME16 6 A2
Langham Gv MAIDW ME16 53 H2
Langley Rd SIT ME10 37 F2
Langton Cl MAID/BEAR ME14 54 D1
Lankester Parker Rd
ROCH ME1 30 C2
Lansdowne Av
MAID/SHEP ME15 62 E2
Lansdowne Rd CHAT ME4 20 E4
Lansdown Rd SIT ME10 37 J4
Lapins La E/WMAL ME19 50 C4
La Providence ROCH ME1 3 G5
Lapwing Dr RSIT ME9 25 F3
Larch Cl DIT/AY ME20 46 A2
Larch Crs HOO/HM ME3 17 F1
Larchcroft WALD ME5 31 G4
The Larches HOO/HM ME3 14 B1
Larch Wood Cl WALD ME5 41 K1
Larkfield Av GILL ME7 22 A2
SIT ME10 36 E2
Larkfield Cl DIT/AY ME20 45 K3
Larkfield Rd DIT/AY ME20 45 K3
Larkin Cl STRD ME2 15 G2
Larking Dr MAIDW ME16 47 J5
Larkspur Cl E/WMAL ME19 45 K3
Larkspur Rd E/WMAL ME19 45 J3
WALD ME5 30 E4
Laser Quay STRD ME2 3 K3
Latimer Pl GILL ME7 16 D5
Latona Dr GVE DA12 12 C1
Launder Wy MAID/SHEP ME15 6 D7
Laura Pl ROCH ME1 19 K4
Laurel Gv RMAID ME17 65 G6
Laurel Rd GILL ME7 16 D5
The Laurels MAIDW ME16 53 H4
Laurie Gray Av WALD ME5 40 D1
Lavenda Cl GILL ME7 32 C4
Lavender Cl E/WMAL ME19 45 J4
Lavender Ct SIT ME10 37 G5
Lavender Rd E/WMAL ME19 45 J4
Lavenders Rd E/WMAL ME19 45 F5
Laverstoke Rd MAIDW ME16 47 H4
Lawn Cl CHAT ME4 21 H4
Lawrence Cl MAID/SHEP ME15 62 B1
Lawrence St GILL ME7 5 H3
Lawson Ct GILL ME7 * 17 G6
The Laxey MAID/SHEP ME15 53 K5
Laxton Cl MAID/SHEP ME15 55 G3
Laxton Dr RMAID ME17 68 C1
Laxton Wy SIT ME10 36 D2
Layfield Rd GILL ME7 17 G5
Leafy Gld RHAM ME8 32 D2
Leander Rd ROCH ME1 30 C1
Leeds Rd RMAID ME17 64 B5
Leeds Sq RHAM ME8 22 D3
Lee Green Rd HOO/HM ME3 9 J6
Lee Rd SNOD ME6 38 E2
Leet Cl GILL ME7 17 F6
Leeward Rd ROCH ME1 20 C5
Legge La E/WMAL ME19 38 B3
Leicester Rd MAID/SHEP ME15 62 E1
Leigh Av MAID/SHEP ME15 62 C2
Leigh Rd HOO/HM ME3 15 H1
Lendrim Cl GILL ME7 * 16 A6
Leney Rd WBY/YAL ME18 59 H1
Lenfield Av MAID/BEAR ME14 54 C2
Lenham Heath Rd RMAID ME17 67 G5
Lenham Rd RMAID ME17 65 J6
Lenside Dr MAID/SHEP ME15 55 H4
Leonard Cl MAIDW ME16 47 G6
Leonard Rd CHAT ME4 21 H4
Leopold Rd CHAT ME4 4 D7
Lesley Pl MAIDW ME16 6 E2
Leslie Rd GILL ME7 16 E5
Lested La RMAID ME17 63 J6
Lester Rd CHAT ME4 4 E6
Letchworth Av CHAT ME4 21 F5
Leviathan Wy CHAT ME4 16 B4
Lewis Av RHAM ME8 22 D6
Lewis Court Dr RMAID ME17 62 C5
Lewis Ms SNOD ME6 38 D4
Leybourne Cl WALD ME5 31 G6
Leybourne Rd STRD ME2 14 E4
Leybourne Wy DIT/AY ME20 38 E6
Leyton Av GILL ME7 22 A5
Libya Ter MAID/BEAR ME14 48 B5
Lidsing Rd GILL ME7 32 B6
MAID/BEAR ME14 41 K5
Liege Cl SIT ME10 27 F5
Lilac Crs STRD ME2 14 D6
Lilac Gn E/WMAL ME19 45 K4
Lilac Rd STRD ME2 19 J1
Lillechurch Rd HOO/HM ME3 8 E3
Lillieburn E/WMAL ME19 45 G2
Lime Ct RHAM ME8 32 E5
Lime Crs E/WMAL ME19 45 K5
Lime Gv SIT ME10 37 G4
Limehouse Whf ROCH ME1 * 3 H2
Limetree Cl WALD ME5 31 H1
Lincoln Rd MAID/SHEP ME15 54 D6
Lincon Rd GILL ME7 16 E5
Linden Cl SIT ME10 36 D5
Linden Rd GILL ME7 22 A1
RMAID ME17 61 H4
The Lindens DIT/AY ME20 46 D3
Lindisfarne Gdns MAIDW ME16 6 E6
Lineacre Cl RHAM ME8 33 F2
Lines Ter CHAT ME4 4 D4
Lingley Dr STRD ME2 15 H2
The Links E/WMAL ME19 44 B2
WALD ME5 21 H6
Linkway DIT/AY ME20 46 B3
RSIT ME9 26 D2
Linton Dann Cl HOO/HM ME3 10 E4
Linton Gore RMAID ME17 61 H5
Linton Rd MAID/SHEP ME15 62 A5
Linwood Av STRD ME2 14 D4
Liphook Wy MAIDW ME16 47 H4
Lismore Cl MAID/SHEP ME15 62 B1
Lister Cl E/WMAL ME19 45 J4
Listmas Rd CHAT ME4 5 F7
Littlebourne Av RHAM ME8 22 D2
Littlebourne Rd
MAID/BEAR ME14 48 D6
Little Buckland Av
MAIDW ME16 47 J6
Littlefield Rd RHAM ME8 23 K4
Little Glovers SIT ME10 37 F5
Little John Av WALD ME5 31 F6
Little Market Rw
E/WMAL ME19 45 H2
Little Orch RMAID ME17 61 J5
Little Oxley DIT/AY ME20 45 H2
Livesey St WBY/YAL ME18 51 K5
Livingstone Buildings
GILL ME7 * 21 K1
Livingstone Circ GILL ME7 21 K1
Livingstone Gdns GVE DA12 12 A1
Livingstone Rd GILL ME7 22 A1
GVE DA12 12 A1
Lobelia Cl GILL ME7 22 A1
Locarno Av RHAM ME8 22 C4
Lochat Rd HOO/HM ME3 9 K4
Lockham Farm Av
MAID/SHEP ME15 62 E3
Lockington Gv ROCH ME1 3 F6
Lock La MAIDW ME16 47 J3
Locksley Cl WALD ME5 30 E6
Lock St GILL ME7 5 H2
Lockswood MAIDW ME16 47 J5
Loder Cl RMAID ME17 67 G3
Lodge Cl WBY/YAL ME18 51 G6
Lodge Ct GVE DA12 13 H2
Lodge Hl HOO/HM ME3 10 A4
Lodge Hill La HOO/HM ME3 10 A2
Lodge Rd MAID/BEAR ME14 54 E1
Lomas Rd SIT ME10 37 K4
Lombardy Cl GILL ME7 32 C2
Lombardy Dr MAID/BEAR ME14 54 D1
London Rd DIT/AY ME20 46 A3
E/WMAL ME19 45 J3
MAIDW ME16 6 C2
RHAM ME8 34 A1
SIT ME10 36 C3
STRD ME2 2 B1
London Road Rocky Hl
MAIDW ME16 6 E4
Long Catlis Rd RHAM ME8 33 F4
Longfellow Rd GILL ME7 5 H7
Longfield Pl MAID/SHEP ME15 54 C6
Longfields Dr MAID/BEAR ME14 55 H1
Longford Cl RHAM ME8 23 J6
Longham Copse
MAID/SHEP ME15 55 G5
Longhill Av GILL ME7 5 F6
Longhurst Dr WALD ME5 31 F6
Longley Rd RHAM ME8 23 H5
ROCH ME1 20 C3
Longparish Cl
MAID/SHEP ME15 63 G1
Long Rede La MAIDW ME16 52 E3
Longridge SIT ME10 37 H6
Longshaw Rd
MAID/SHEP ME15 63 G4
Longwood WALD ME5 41 H2
Lonsdale Dr RHAM ME8 33 G2
SIT ME10 36 C3
Loose Rd MAID/SHEP ME15 54 C5
MAID/SHEP ME15 62 B3
Lords Wood Cl WALD ME5 31 H6
Lords Wood La WALD ME5 31 H3
Lorimar Ct SIT ME10 36 C1
Louisville Av GILL ME7 21 K2
Lovelace Cl RHAM ME8 33 F4
Love La ROCH ME1 3 F5
WBY/YAL ME18 59 G1
Lower Bell La DIT/AY ME20 46 A2
Lower Bloors La RHAM ME8 23 G4
Lower Boxley Rd
MAID/BEAR ME14 7 G1
Lower Fant Rd MAIDW ME16 6 D6
Lower Hartlip Rd RSIT ME9 34 C3
Lower Rainham Rd GILL ME7 17 J6
RHAM ME8 23 K3
Lower Rd GVE DA12 8 A4
MAID/SHEP ME15 7 K7
MAID/SHEP ME15 60 C1
RMAID ME17 69 G3
Lower Rochester Rd
HOO/HM ME3 8 C4
HOO/HM ME3 9 F6
Lower Stone St
MAID/SHEP ME15 7 H4
Lower St RMAID ME17 64 D1
Lower Tovil MAID/SHEP ME15 53 K4
Lower Twydall La GILL ME7 22 E2
Lower Warren Rd WALD ME5 40 E4
Lower Woodlands Rd GILL ME7 17 G6
Low Meadow STRD ME2 28 E3
Lubbock Cl MAID/SHEP ME15 63 F3
Lucas Rd SNOD ME6 38 C3
Lucerne St MAID/BEAR ME14 7 J2
Lucks Hl E/WMAL ME19 45 G4
Lucks La RMAID ME17 68 B4
Luddenham Cl
MAID/BEAR ME14 48 D6
Lughorse La WBY/YAL ME18 59 K6
Lullingstone Cl GILL ME7 32 D5
Lullingstone Rd MAIDW ME16 47 H5
Lumsden Ter CHAT ME4 4 A5
Lunsford La DIT/AY ME20 38 D5
Lushington Rd
MAID/BEAR ME14 47 K5

Luton High St WALD ME5 .....21 J4
Luton Rd CHAT ME4 .....5 F6
Lyall Wy RHAM ME8 .....33 F4
Lychfield Dr STRD ME2 .....15 F5
Lydbrook Ct SIT ME10 .....36 C4
Lydd Rd MAID ME5 .....31 H3
Lyle Cl MAIDW ME16 .....53 H1
Lyminge Cl RHAM ME8 .....22 E4
Lymington Ct
 MAID/SHEP ME15 .....63 G4
Lyndhurst Av RHAM ME8 .....32 E1
Lyndhurst Gv SIT ME10 .....36 C3
Lyndhurst Rd MAID/SHEP ME15 ....54 D6
Lynette Av STRD ME2 .....15 F3
Lynors Av STRD ME2 .....15 J2
Lynsted Rd RHAM ME8 .....22 D3
Lynton Dr MAID ME5 .....31 F4
Lysander Rd E/WMAL ME19 .....50 C3

M

Macaulay Cl DIT/AY ME20 .....38 E6
Macdonald Rd SIT ME10 .....16 E6
Mackenders Cl DIT/AY ME20 .....39 G4
Mackenders La DIT/AY ME20 .....40 A4
Mackenzie Wy GVE DA12 .....12 B2
Macklands Wy RHAM ME8 .....23 J4
Madden Av WALD ME5 .....30 E1
Madginford Cl
 MAID/SHEP ME15 .....55 H4
Madginford Rd
 MAID/SHEP ME15 .....55 G4
Mafeking Rd WALD ME5 .....31 F5
Magdalen Cl GILL ME7 .....32 C4
Magnolia Av RHAM ME8 .....32 D3
Magpie Cl DIT/AY ME20 .....45 K3
Magpie Hall Rd CHAT ME4 .....21 F6
Magwitch Cl ROCH ME1 .....20 B2
Maida Rd CHAT ME4 .....21 H4
Maidstone Rd CHAT ME4 .....4 C1
 CHAT ME4 .....32 D6
 GILL ME7 .....64 B6
 RMAID ME17 .....67 H3
 RSIT ME9 .....51 J5
 SIT ME10 .....36 A2
 WBY/YAL ME18 .....58 E6
The Malfrys RHAM ME8 .....32 E1
Main Gate Rd CHAT ME4 .....16 A5
Main Rd HOO/HM ME3 .....10 A6
Main St CHAT ME4 .....16 C2
Malden Dr MAID/BEAR ME14 .....48 A4
Mallards Wy MAID/SHEP ME15 .....55 H4
Mallingdene Cl HOO/HM ME3 .....9 G2
Malling Rd DIT/AY ME20 .....38 C5
 WBY/YAL ME18 .....50 B5
 WBY/YAL ME18 .....58 D1
Mallings Dr MAID/BEAR ME14 .....55 K2
Mallings La MAID/BEAR ME14 .....55 K2
Mallings Ter MAIDW ME16 .....53 H2
The Mall GILL ME7 .....5 H1
Malta Av WALD ME5 .....31 J5
Malta Ter RHAM ME8 .....48 B5
Malthouse Cl RMAID ME17 .....67 J3
Malthouse Hl MAID/SHEP ME15 ....62 A4
Malthouse La GVE DA12 .....13 H3
The Maltings MAID/BEAR ME14 ....48 B4
 RHAM ME8 .....23 J6
 RMAID ME17 .....62 C4
Malt Ms ROCH ME1 .....3 F5
Malus Cl WALD ME5 .....41 G1
Malvern Rd GILL ME7 .....5 J5
Mamignot Cl MAID/BEAR ME14 ....55 G1
Manchester Cl WALD ME5 .....31 J2
Mangravet Av
 MAID/SHEP ME15 .....55 J3
Manor Cl MAID/BEAR ME14 .....55 J3
Manor Ct MAID/BEAR ME14 .....55 J3
Manor Fld GVE DA12 .....13 H1
Manor Gdns WALD ME5 .....31 F4
Manor Gv SIT ME10 .....36 E5
Manor House Dr MAIDW ME16 .....6 B5
Manor La ROCH ME1 .....19 K3
Manor Rd MAID/BEAR ME14 .....55 J3
Manor Rd CHAT ME4 .....4 B4
Manor St GILL ME7 .....7 J6
Mansel Dr ROCH ME1 .....20 A4
Mansfield Wk MAIDW ME16 .....6 C7
Mansion Rw GILL ME7 .....6 B6
Manwood St SIT ME10 .....37 F6
Maple Av GILL ME7 .....47 H6
Maple Cl DIT/AY ME20 .....45 K2
 MAIDW ME16 .....47 H6
Maple Rd HOO/HM ME3 .....17 F1
 STRD ME2 .....14 E6
Maplesden Cl MAIDW ME16 .....52 E3
Maplins Cl RHAM ME8 .....23 H5
Mara Ct CHAT ME4 .....21 F5
Marathon Paddock GILL ME7 .....21 K2
Marconi Wy ROCH ME1 .....19 J2
Mardale Cl RHAM ME8 .....23 J5
Marden Rd STRD ME2 .....15 H4
Margate Cl GILL ME7 .....17 F6
Margetts La ROCH ME1 .....39 H1
Margetts Pl STRD ME2 .....14 A5
Marine Dr HOO/HM ME3 .....17 F1
The Mariners ROCH ME1 * 2 E7
Marine Vw SIT ME10 .....37 H4
Marion Cl WALD ME5 .....31 G6
Marion Crs MAID/SHEP ME15 .....54 C6
Maritime Cl STRD ME2 .....15 J4
Maritime Wy CHAT ME4 .....7 G3
Market Buildings
 MAID/BEAR ME14 .....7 G3
Mark St CHAT ME4 .....21 G4
Marlborough Pde
 MAIDW ME16 * 52 E4
Marlborough Rd GILL ME7 .....5 G3
Marley Rd HOO/HM ME3 .....10 E4
 RMAID ME17 .....66 E2
Marley Wy ROCH ME1 .....20 C4

Marling Wy GVE DA12 .....12 B1
Marlow Copse WALD ME5 .....41 F1
Marlowe Rd DIT/AY ME20 .....45 K1
Marquis Dr GILL ME7 .....32 D5
Marshall Rd RHAM ME8 .....22 E5
Marsham Crs MAIDW ME17 .....68 D1
Marsham St MAID/BEAR ME14 .....7 J3
Marsham Wy MAID/BEAR ME14 .....28 E5
Marsh Ri STRD ME2 .....29 F3
Marsh Rd STRD ME2 .....29 F3
Marsh St STRD ME2 .....2 E1
Marsh Wy DIT/AY ME20 .....38 E6
Marstan Cl RSIT ME9 .....24 C4
Marston Cl MAID/SHEP ME15 .....30 E5
Marston Dr MAID/BEAR ME14 ....54 C1
Martin Cl GILL ME7 .....22 C2
Martin Rd STRD ME2 * 15 G4
Martins Cl MAID/BEAR ME14 .....8 C4
Martins La STPH/PW TN12 .....58 B6
Martin Sq DIT/AY ME20 .....45 K3
Mary Dukes Pl
 MAID/SHEP ME15 * 7 K5
Maryland Cl RHAM ME8 .....33 G3
Maryland Dr MAIDW ME16 .....52 E4
Mary Last Cl SNOD ME6 .....38 C3
Masefield Dr HOO/HM ME3 .....9 G2
Matfield Crs MAID/BEAR ME14 ....54 D1
Matilda Cl GILL ME7 .....33 G2
Matterdale Gdns MAIDW ME16 ....52 D4
Matthews Ct GILL ME7 * 5 K3
Matts Hill Rd RSIT ME9 .....33 G6
Maunders Cl WALD ME5 .....21 J6
Maximilian Dr STRD ME2 .....29 F4
Maxton Cl MAID/BEAR ME14 .....55 G1
Maxwell Dr MAIDW ME16 .....47 C6
Maxwell Rd GILL ME7 .....4 D2
Mayfair STRD ME2 * 15 H4
Mayfair Av MAID/SHEP ME15 .....54 B6
Mayfield Ct RHAM ME8 .....23 G4
 WALD ME5 .....21 J6
Mayford Rd WALD ME5 .....31 K6
Maylam Gdns RSIT ME9 .....36 B4
Maynard Pl WALD ME5 .....21 K4
Maypole Dr MAID/BEAR ME14 .....51 F3
May Rd GILL ME7 .....5 J4
 ROCH ME1 * 20 C3
May St SNOD ME6 .....39 F2
 STRD ME2 .....19 F4
May Ter GILL ME7 .....16 B5
Maywood Av WALD ME5 .....30 E4
McAlpine Crs MAID/SHEP ME15 ....62 A5
McCudden Rw GILL ME7 * 5 J6
McKenzie Cl DIT/AY ME20 .....46 E4
Mc Kenzie Rd WALD ME5 .....31 G5
Meadow Bank E/WMAL ME19 .....45 F4
Meadowbank Rd CHAT ME4 .....4 E5
Meadow Cl RSIT ME9 .....26 D2
 STRD ME2 * 15 H2
 WALD ME5 .....31 F5
Meadow Ct RHAM ME8 .....22 D4
Meadow Crs STRD ME2 .....28 C4
Meadowdown
 MAID/BEAR ME14 .....55 F2
Meadowdown Cl GILL ME7 .....31 K4
Meadow Ri STRD ME2 .....26 D2
The Meadows
 MAID/SHEP ME15 .....53 K4
 SIT ME10 .....37 F6
Meadowsweet Vw CHAT ME4 .....21 H1
Meadow Vw STRD ME2 * 25 F3
 WALD ME5 .....31 K1
Meadow View Rd RMAID ME17 ....62 C5
Meadow Wk MAID/BEAR ME14 .....7 K5
 SNOD ME6 .....38 D3
The Meads Av SIT ME10 .....36 D1
Meadside Wk WALD ME5 .....31 G1
Medina Rd DIT/AY ME20 .....46 B3
Medlar Cl RSIT ME9 .....42 A4
Medlar Cl RHAM ME8 .....32 C4
The Medlars MAID/BEAR ME14 ....48 E6
Medway Br STRD ME2 .....19 J3
Medway Ct SIT ME10 .....36 D4
Medway Gdns CHAT ME4 .....16 A5
Medway Rd GILL ME7 .....16 D5
Medway St CHAT ME4 .....4 B3
Medway Ter WBY/YAL ME18 * 59 G2
Medway Valley Wk
 DIT/AY ME20 .....39 H6
 MAIDW ME16 .....47 J3
 ROCH ME1 .....2 E5
 WBY/YAL ME18 .....58 E6
Meers Court La SIT ME10 .....37 J3
Meeting House La CHAT ME4 .....4 C4
Meirscourt Rd RHAM ME8 .....33 G4
Melbourne Rd CHAT ME4 .....4 E7
Melford Dr MAIDW ME16 .....53 H2
Mellor Rw SIT ME10 .....27 F5
Melody Cl RHAM ME8 .....32 E4
Melrose Cl MAID/SHEP ME15 .....63 B1
Melville Ct CHAT ME4 .....16 A6
Melville Rd MAID/SHEP ME15 .....7 J5
Menin Rd SIT ME10 .....27 F5
Mercer Dr RMAID ME17 .....66 E2
Mercers Pl E/WMAL ME19 .....50 C3
Mercer Wy RMAID ME17 .....68 D1
Mercury Cl ROCH ME1 .....20 A4
Meredith Rd CHAT ME4 .....64 C1
Meresborough La RHAM ME8 ....33 J3
Meresborough Rd RHAM ME8 ....33 H4
Mereworth Cl RHAM ME8 .....22 C5
Meridian Pk STRD ME2 .....15 K6
Merivale Gv WALD ME5 .....31 H4
Merleburgh Dr SIT ME10 .....37 F6
Merlin Av DIT/AY ME20 .....45 J3
Merlin Cl GILL ME7 .....22 B1
Mermaid Cl WALD ME5 .....31 J4
Merrals Wood Ct STRD ME2 * 19 H1
Merrals Wood Rd STRD ME2 .....19 H1
Merrimans Vw WALD ME5 * 21 J4
Merry Boys Rd HOO/HM ME3 .....9 G2
Merryfields STRD ME2 .....15 F3
Merton Cl WALD ME5 .....31 J4
Merton Rd MAID/SHEP ME15 .....15 G4

Meteor Cl SIT ME10 .....26 E6
Meteor Rd E/WMAL ME19 .....50 C3
Mews Ct GILL ME7 .....22 B4
The Mews MAIDW ME16 * 7 F5
 SIT ME10 .....37 F5
 STRD ME2 .....2 A2
Micawber Cl WALD ME5 .....41 G1
Michael Gdns CHAT ME4 .....12 B2
Middlefields RHAM ME8 .....23 J6
Middle Mill Rd E/WMAL ME19 ....45 J5
Middle Rw MAID/BEAR ME14 .....7 F5
Middlesex Rd MAID/SHEP ME15 ....62 E1
Middle St GILL ME7 .....16 B6
Middleton Cl RHAM ME8 .....33 C4
Middletune Av SIT ME10 .....36 E1
Middle Wy SIT ME10 .....37 H5
Midley Cl MAIDW ME16 .....47 H5
Midsummer Rd SNOD ME6 .....38 C2
Mierscourt Cl RHAM ME8 .....23 J6
Mierscourt Rd RHAM ME8 .....33 G3
Milbourne Gv SIT ME10 .....36 E1
Milburn Rd GILL ME7 .....16 D5
Miles Pl ROCH ME1 .....20 D3
Milford Cl MAIDW ME16 .....6 A2
Military Rd CHAT ME4 .....4 C3
Millbrook E/WMAL ME19 .....45 F4
Millbrook La MAID/SHEP ME15 ....55 A4
Mill Cl RMAID ME17 .....67 H4
 STRD ME2 .....15 G3
Millen Rd SIT ME10 .....27 G6
Miller Cl SIT ME10 .....27 C6
Millers Whf MAIDW ME16 .....6 D7
Mill Wy STRD ME2 .....15 H2
Millfield SIT ME10 .....37 F5
Millfields MAID/BEAR ME14 .....55 H1
Millfordhope Rd STRD ME2 .....14 B5
Millhall DIT/AY ME20 .....46 A4
Mill Hall Rd DIT/AY ME20 .....46 B1
Mill Hill La GVE DA12 .....13 G1
Millhouse La E/WMAL ME19 .....44 A1
Mill La RMAID ME17 .....61 J5
 RSIT ME9 .....34 C2
 SNOD ME6 .....39 F2
 WALD ME5 .....31 J6
 WALD ME5 .....40 D1
 WBY/YAL ME18 .....51 G6
Mill Meadow Yd MAIDW ME16 * 7 F2
Millpond Cl STRD ME2 .....15 H2
Mill Rd GILL ME7 .....16 D6
 STRD ME2 .....15 C4
Mill St DIT/AY ME20 .....46 D6
 SNOD ME6 .....39 F2
Mill Wk MAIDW ME16 .....55 F3
Mill Wy SIT ME10 .....36 E3
Millwood Ct CHAT ME4 * 4 B4
Miners RMAID ME17 * 64 C2
Milstead Cl MAID/BEAR ME14 ....54 D1
Milsted Rd RHAM ME8 .....22 E4
Milton Av HOO/HM ME3 .....9 G2
Milton La E/WMAL ME19 .....50 E3
Milton Rd GILL ME7 .....5 G6
Milton St MAIDW ME16 .....6 A7
Mincers Cl WALD ME5 .....31 J6
Minerva Rd STRD ME2 .....15 F4
Minor Canon Rw ROCH ME1 * 3 F5
Minster Rd MAID/SHEP ME15 ....62 E3
Minterne Av SIT ME10 .....36 C6
Miskin Rd MAID ME5 .....10 E5
Miskin Wy GVE DA12 .....12 A2
Mitchell Av CHAT ME4 .....21 J6
Mitchell Rd RMAID ME17 .....67 H3
Mitchell Rd E/WMAL ME19 .....45 F4
Mitre Rd ROCH ME1 .....2 E7
Mollison Ri GVE DA12 .....12 B1
Monarch Cl MAID ME5 .....31 G2
Monckton's Av
 MAID/BEAR ME14 .....47 K5
Monckton's Dr
 MAID/BEAR ME14 .....47 K5
Monckton's La
 MAID/BEAR ME14 .....47 K5
Moncrif Cl MAID/BEAR ME14 .....55 J2
Monkdown MAID/SHEP ME15 ....55 H5
Monkwood Cl ROCH ME1 .....20 B6
Monmouth Cl RHAM ME8 .....33 G4
Mons SIT ME10 .....27 F5
Montfort Dr MAID/SHEP ME19 ....50 D4
Montfort Rd STRD ME2 .....2 C1
 WALD ME5 .....30 E6
Montgomery Av WALD ME5 .....31 G1
Montgomery Rd GILL ME7 .....5 H6
Montpelier Ga MAIDW ME16 * 55 J3
Montrose Av WALD ME5 .....22 A4
Moonstone Dr WALD ME5 .....31 J6
Moore St STRD ME2 .....15 F4
Mooring Rd ROCH ME1 .....20 D5
The Moorings
 MAID/SHEP ME15 * 7 H4
Moor Park Cl RHAM ME8 .....23 J6
Moor St RHAM ME8 .....23 K6
Morden St ROCH ME1 .....3 J1
Morement Rd HOO/HM ME3 .....10 E4
Morgan Rd STRD ME2 .....15 F4
Morhen Cl SNOD ME6 .....38 C2
Morland Dr STRD ME2 .....15 F3
Morris Cl E/WMAL ME19 .....45 J3
Morris Ct GILL ME7 .....22 B1
Morris Court Cl RSIT ME9 .....37 K6
Mortimers Av RHAM ME8 .....33 H4
Mosquito Rd E/WMAL ME19 ....50 C3
Mossbank WALD ME5 .....31 G5
Mossy Gld RHAM ME8 .....33 G2
Mostyn Rd MAID/BEAR ME14 ....54 D2
Mote Av MAID/SHEP ME15 .....55 H4
Mote Pk MAID/SHEP ME15 .....54 E5
Mote Rd MAID/SHEP ME15 .....7 J5

Motney Hill Rd RHAM ME8 .....23 J2
Mountbatten Av HOO/HM ME3 ....8 B6
 WALD ME5 .....31 G1
Mount Dr MAID/BEAR ME14 .....55 J2
Mount La MAID/BEAR ME14 .....55 J2
Mount Lodge Ter ROCH ME1 * 20 B5
Mount Pleasant CHAT ME4 .....5 F6
Mount Pleasant Dr
 DIT/AY ME20 .....47 F1
Mount Pleasant Dr
 MAID/BEAR ME14 .....55 H1
Mount Rd CHAT ME4 .....4 C7
 ROCH ME1 .....20 A4
Mountsfield Cl MAIDW ME16 .....6 C1
The Mount CHAT ME4 .....4 C7
Mountview RSIT ME9 .....36 B6
Mount View Ct CHAT ME4 * 4 C7
Moyle Ct RHAM ME8 .....33 F4
Mozart Ct CHAT ME4 .....4 A7
Muir Rd MAID/SHEP ME15 .....7 H6
Mulberry Cl GILL ME7 .....32 C4
Mungo Park Rd GVE DA12 .....12 A1
Munn's La GILL ME7 .....34 C2
Munsgore La RSIT ME9 .....35 J6
Murrain Dr MAID/SHEP ME15 ....55 H5
Murston Rd SIT ME10 .....37 F2
Murston Rd SIT ME10 .....15 H4
Musgrave Rd SIT ME10 .....37 F2
Musket La RMAID ME17 .....56 E4
Mustang Rd E/WMAL ME19 .....50 C3
Mynn Crs MAID/SHEP ME15 .....55 H2
Myrtle Crs WALD ME5 .....31 F3

N

Nags Head La ROCH ME1 .....3 J7
Napier Cl SIT ME10 .....36 C4
Napier Rd GILL ME7 .....5 K6
Napwood Cl RHAM ME8 .....33 F2
Nares Rd RHAM ME8 .....33 F4
Nashenden Farm La ROCH ME1 ....19 H4
Nashenden La ROCH ME1 .....19 K4
Natal Rd CHAT ME4 .....21 G4
Nativity Cl SIT ME10 .....36 E4
Neale St CHAT ME4 .....21 F4
Neath Ct MAID/SHEP ME15 * 55 F4
Nelson Rd GILL ME7 .....5 H1
 ROCH ME1 .....29 G4
Nelson Ter WALD ME5 .....21 J5
Neptune Cl STRD ME2 .....15 K5
Neptune Ter RSIT ME9 .....25 C3
Neptune Wy STRD ME2 .....15 K6
Nestor Ct WBY/YAL ME18 .....51 H3
Netley Cl MAID/BEAR ME14 .....48 E6
Nettlestead La WBY/YAL ME18 ...58 D2
Nevill Ct E/WMAL ME19 .....45 F4
Neville Cl MAID/BEAR ME14 .....48 E6
Neville Rd CHAT ME4 .....5 G6
Nevill Pl SNOD ME6 .....38 E3
Nevill Rd SNOD ME6 .....38 E3
Newark Yd STRD ME2 .....2 D1
New Barns Rd
 MAID/BEAR ME14 .....48 B4
Newbridge Av SIT ME10 .....36 E1
Newbury Av MAIDW ME16 .....47 J6
Newbury Cl HOO/HM ME3 .....9 G2
Newchurch Rd
 MAID/SHEP ME15 .....54 B5
New Covenant Pl ROCH ME1 * 3 F6
New Cut CHAT ME4 .....4 A4
 ROCH ME1 .....4 A4
New Cut Rd MAID/BEAR ME14 ...54 D2
Newenden Cl MAID/BEAR ME14 ...48 D6
Newenden Rd STRD ME2 .....15 J6
New Hythe La DIT/AY ME20 .....45 K2
Newington Wk
 MAID/BEAR ME14 * 48 D6
Newitt Rd HOO/HM ME3 .....10 E5
Newlands Av SIT ME10 .....36 E1
Newman Dr SIT ME10 .....27 G6
Newnham Ct MAID/BEAR ME14 ...28 E4
Newnham St CHAT ME4 .....4 A5
New Rd CHAT ME4 .....4 A6
 DIT/AY ME20 .....45 K2
 RMAID ME17 .....63 K3
 ROCH ME1 * 3 G5
 ROCH ME1 .....39 K2
New Road Av CHAT ME4 .....4 E5
New Stairs CHAT ME4 .....4 A4
New St CHAT ME4 .....4 A6
Newton Cl MAIDW ME16 .....6 D6
 WALD ME5 .....31 J6
Nicholas Cl MAIDW ME16 .....53 F3
Nicklaus Dr WALD ME5 .....31 F5
Nickleby Cl ROCH ME1 .....20 C4
Nightingale Cl DIT/AY ME20 .....45 J2
 RHAM ME8 .....32 D3
Nightingale Ct STRD ME2 * 14 B6
Nile Rd GILL ME7 .....6 A5
Nine Acres Rd STRD ME2 .....18 E3
Noakes Av SIT ME10 .....37 F1
The Nook WBY/YAL ME18 .....59 J6
Norah La HOO/HM ME3 .....1 A6
Nore Cl GILL ME7 .....22 A5
Norfolk Cl WALD ME5 .....31 J5
Norfolk Rd
 MAID/SHEP ME15 .....54 D6
Norman Cl MAID/BEAR ME14 ....48 C6
 RHAM ME8 .....33 F4
 STRD ME2 .....15 H4
Norman Rd E/WMAL ME19 .....44 D3
 SNOD ME6 .....38 C3
Normead Rd RHAM ME8 .....33 C1
Norrington Rd
 MAID/SHEP ME15 .....62 B2
North Bank Cl STRD ME2 .....2 A5
Northbourne Rd RHAM ME8 .....22 D3
Northcote Rd STRD ME2 .....2 B2
North Crs MAID/SHEP ME15 .....54 C5
North Crs RMAID ME17 .....61 J4
North Dane Wy WALD ME5 .....31 J3

Northdown Cl
 MAID/BEAR ME14 .....48 C5
North Downs Wy RMAID ME17 ...67 J1
 SIT ME10 .....18 D5
Northdown Vw RMAID ME17 .....66 E2
Northfields MAID/BEAR ME14 ....52 E4
Northfleet Cl MAID/SHEP ME15 ...54 D1
North Foills Rd
 MAID/SHEP ME15 .....60 C5
Northgate ROCH ME1 .....3 G4
Northleigh Cl MAID/SHEP ME15 ...62 B2
North Lockside CHAT ME4 * 16 C4
North Meadow E/WMAL ME19 ....44 A5
North Pasley Rd CHAT ME4 .....16 C5
North Pole Rd WALD ME5 .....52 A4
North Pondside CHAT ME4 * 16 B4
North Pondside Rd CHAT ME4 ....16 B4
North Rd CHAT ME4 .....16 B4
Northside Three CHAT ME4 * 16 D4
North St MAIDW ME16 .....54 D4
 RMAID ME17 .....69 C5
 SIT ME10 .....36 E1
 STRD ME2 .....2 D1
Northumberland Av
 RHAM ME8 .....23 C5
Northumberland Ct
 MAID/SHEP ME15 * 62 E1
Northumberland Rd
 MAID/SHEP ME15 .....54 C5
North Vw MAID/SHEP ME15 .....54 C5
North Wy MAID/BEAR ME14 .....48 C5
Northwood Dr SIT ME10 .....16 E1
Norton Cl WALD ME5 .....30 E4
Norton Rd RMAID ME17 .....68 E1
Norway Ter MAID/BEAR ME14 ...48 A5
Norwich Cl STRD ME2 .....14 C6
Nottingham Av
 MAID/SHEP ME15 .....62 E2
Nursery Av MAID/BEAR ME14 ....55 J5
 RHAM ME8 .....47 G6
Nursery Gdns HOO/HM ME3 .....11 F5
Nursery Rd DIT/AY ME20 .....46 B3
 RHAM ME8 .....23 F6
Nutfield Cl WALD ME5 .....21 H6
Nutfields SIT ME10 .....37 H5
Nutwood Cl MAID/BEAR ME14 ....55 F2

O

Oakapple La MAIDW ME16 .....53 F3
Oak Av GILL ME7 .....17 F6
Oak Cl HOO/HM ME3 .....17 F1
Oak Dr DIT/AY ME20 .....45 K2
 HOO/HM ME3 .....1 A6
Oakfields SIT ME10 .....36 C5
Oakhurst Cl WALD ME5 .....31 F5
Oak La RSIT ME9 .....24 B5
Oakleigh Cl WALD ME5 .....30 E6
Oak Rd HOO/HM ME3 .....17 F1
 SIT ME10 .....37 J5
Oaks Dene WALD ME5 .....41 F1
The Oaks DIT/AY ME20 .....46 D3
Oak Ter WALD ME5 .....31 G6
Oak Tree Av MAID/SHEP ME15 ...62 D1
Oakum Ct CHAT ME4 .....21 H4
Oakwood Cl MAIDW ME16 .....6 A5
Oakwood Pk MAIDW ME16 .....6 A5
Oakwood Rd MAIDW ME16 .....6 A5
Oakwood Ter SIT ME10 * 37 J4
Oast Ct SIT ME10 .....36 E6
Oastview RMAID ME8 .....23 J4
Ocelot Ct WALD ME5 .....31 J6
Octavia Cl WALD ME5 * 31 H5
Odiham Dr MAIDW ME16 .....47 H1
Offham Rd E/WMAL ME19 .....44 D5
Officers Ter CHAT ME4 .....16 A4
Old Ashford Rd RMAID ME17 ....66 D2
The Old Bailey RMAID ME17 .....66 D2
Old Barn Cl GILL ME7 .....32 B2
Old Barn Rd E/WMAL ME19 .....45 C2
The Old Brewery MAIDW ME16 * ...7 F4
The Old Carriageway GILL ME7 ...32 B5
Old Chatham Rd DIT/AY ME20 ....40 C4
 MAID/BEAR ME14 .....47 K3
Old Church Rd WBY/YAL ME18 ...58 B4
Old Church Rd ROCH ME1 .....39 H1
 WBY/YAL ME18 .....58 A3
The Old Courthouse CHAT ME4 * ...4 A4
Oldfield Cl MAID/SHEP ME15 .....55 F3
 RHAM ME8 .....23 F6
Oldfield Dr ROCH ME1 .....29 C3
Old George St HOO/HM ME3 * 10 A6
Old Ham La RMAID ME17 .....67 G4
Old House Rd RSIT ME9 .....34 C6
Old Lain RMAID ME17 .....66 B4
Old Loose Hl MAID/SHEP ME15 ...62 A4
Old Mill La DIT/AY ME20 .....47 H3
Old Mill Rd RMAID ME17 .....56 C6
Old Orchard La E/WMAL ME19 ....45 C5
The Old Orch RHAM ME8 .....23 H6
Old Pattens La ROCH ME1 .....4 D2
 WBY/YAL ME18 .....51 J6
Old School Cl WBY/YAL ME18 ....58 B4
Old School Cl HOO/HM ME3 .....8 E1
Old School Pl MAID/SHEP ME15 ...54 E6
Old Tovil Rd MAID/SHEP ME15 ...54 A4
Old Trafford Cl MAIDW ME16 ....47 G6
Old Tree La RMAID ME17 .....62 B3
Old Watling St STRD ME2 .....14 A4
Oliver Cl CHAT ME4 .....4 B3
Oliver Twist Cl ROCH ME1 .....20 C4
Olivine Cl SIT ME10 .....36 E6
 WALD ME5 .....41 G1
Olliffe Cl WALD ME5 .....31 H6
Onslow Rd ROCH ME1 .....20 D5
Orache Dr MAID/BEAR ME14 .....54 A4
Orange Ter ROCH ME1 .....3 H3
Orbit Cl WALD ME5 .....41 F1
Orchard Av DIT/AY ME20 .....46 D5

STRD ME2 ......14 E4
Orchard Cl MAID/SHEP ME15 * 7 H6
  RMAID ME17 ......61 H5
Orchard St MAID ME7 ......64 D4
Orchard Gv RSIT ME9 ......43 C6
Orchard Gv DIT/AY ME20 ......46 A2
Orchard Pl MAIDW ME16 ......6 E5
  SIT ME10 ......37 G5
Orchard Rd RSIT ME9 ......55 F3
Orchard St MAID/SHEP ME15 ......63 J1
  RHAM ME8
The Orchard MAID/BEAR ME14 ......55 J2
Orchard Vw MAID/BEAR ME14 ......49 H4
Orchard Wy SNOD ME6 ......38 D5
Orchid Cl STRD ME2 ......14 B6
Ordnance St CHAT ME4 ......4 A5
Ordnance Ter CHAT ME4 ......4 A7
Oriole Wy DIT/AY ME20 ......45 J4
Orion Rd ROCH ME1 ......30 C1
The Orpines WBY/YAL ME18 ......59 J1
Orwell Cl DIT/AY ME20 ......45 J4
Orwell Spike E/WMAL ME19 ......50 D1
Osborne Dr MAID/BEAR ME14 * 48 A7
Osborne Rd GILL ME7 ......5 J3
Osprey Av E/WMAL ME19 ......22 A4
Osprey Ct SIT ME10 ......37 G5
Osprey Wk DIT/AY ME20 ......45 J3
Ostlers Ct HOO/HM ME3 *
  SNOD ME6 ......38 E2
Otham La MAID/SHEP ME15 ......55 H5
Otham St MAID/SHEP ME15 ......63 J1
Otterbourne Pl
  MAID/SHEP ME15
Otterham Quay La RHAM ME8 ......23 K6
Otteridge Rd MAID/BEAR ME14 ......55 H5
Ottway St CHAT ME4 ......4 D7
Ottway Ter CHAT ME4
Owen Cl E/WMAL ME19 ......45 J4
Owens Wy GILL ME7 ......17 H6
Owletts Cl MAID/SHEP ME15 ......54 E6
Oxford Rd GILL ME7
Oxford St SIT ME10 ......54 E5
Oxford St SNOD ME6 ......38 E2
Oxley Shaw La E/WMAL ME19 ......45 K4
Oyster Cl SIT ME10 * 36 E2

P

Packer Pl WALD ME5 ......21 C6
Paddlesworth Rd SNOD ME6 ......38 A1
The Paddocks CHAT ME4 ......32 C3
The Paddock CHAT ME4 ......4 B5
  SIT ME10 * 36 D6
Pad's Hl MAID/SHEP ME15 ......7 J4
Padsole La MAID/SHEP ME15 ......7 J4
Paget St GILL ME7 ......5 G2
Pagitt St CHAT ME4 ......20 E4
Palace Av MAID/SHEP ME15 ......7 H4
Palmar Rd MAIDW ME16 ......47 J6
Palmerston Rd CHAT ME4 ......21 F5
Pankhurst Rd HOO/HM ME3
Panton Cl WALD ME5 ......31 J4
Papion Gv WALD ME5 ......30 E6
The Parade SIT ME10 * 37 F6
Parham Rd CHAT ME4 ......14 D4
Park Av GILL ME7 ......21 H4
  MAID/BEAR ME14 ......48 C6
  RMAID ME17 ......61 K6
Park Barn Rd RMAID ME17 ......36 E6
Park Crs CHAT ME4 ......64 E3
Park Dr SIT ME10 ......21 F6
Parker Cl RHAM ME8 ......33 C3
Parkfield Rd RHAM ME8 ......23 H4
Parkfields STRD ME2 ......14 B5
Park La MAID/BEAR ME14 ......48 A5
  RMAID ME17 ......62 E6
Park Rd E/WMAL ME19 ......36 E5
  WBY/YAL ME18 ......58 C3
Parkside HOO/HM ME3 ......9 G3
Park Wy MAID/SHEP ME15 ......54 C5
Parr Rd RMAID ME17 ......61 H5
Parrs Haed Ms ROCH ME1 * 3 G3
Parsonage La RSIT ME9 ......26 A6
  STRD ME2 ......14 H4
Partridge Av DIT/AY ME20 ......45 J1
Partridge Dr CHAT ME4 ......16 C3
Pasley Rd GILL ME7
Pasley Rd East CHAT ME4 ......16 B5
Pastime Ct SIT ME10 ......26 E6
Patrixbourne Av RHAM ME8 ......22 E4
Pattens Cl CHAT ME4 ......20 E6
Pattens La CHAT ME4 ......20 E6
Pavilion Dr SIT ME10 ......27 F5
Pavilion La WBY/YAL ME18 ......50 D6
Payne's La MAID/SHEP ME15 ......62 B1
Peacock Ms MAIDW ME16 * 7 H4
Peacock Rd WALD ME5 ......31 C4
Peal Ct HOO/HM ME3 ......11 F5
Pearl Wy E/WMAL ME19 ......11 F3
Pearman Ct RHAM ME8 ......23 J5
Pear Tree Av DIT/AY ME20 ......46 B4
Pear Tree La GILL ME7 ......32 A1
Peartree La STRD ME2 ......13 K2
Peartree Pl HOO/HM ME3 * 11 F3
Peckham Ct STRD ME2 ......15 H4
Peel Dr SIT ME10 ......37 J4
Peel St MAID/BEAR ME14 ......48 B6
Peggotty Cl HOO/HM ME3 ......14 A1
Pelican Cl STRD ME2 ......14 B6
Pemberton Sq STRD ME2 ......15 H4
Pembroke CHAT ME4
Pembroke Gdns RHAM ME8 ......33 C4
Pembroke Rd CHAT ME4 * 16 B4
  RMAID ME17 ......61 H5
Pembury Gdns MAIDW ME16 ......6 C5
Pembury St SIT ME10 ......36 E4

Pembury Wy RHAM ME8 ......23 G4
Penenden Heath Rd
  MAID/BEAR ME14 ......48 C5
Penenden St MAID/BEAR ME14 ......48 B6
Penfield La RSIT ME9 ......43 G6
Penfold Cl MAID/SHEP ME15 ......63 F2
  WALD ME5 * 31 H1
Penfold Hl RMAID ME17 ......56 E6
Penfold Wy MAID/SHEP ME15 ......62 A2
Penguin Cl STRD ME2 ......14 B6
Penhurst Cl MAID/BEAR ME14 ......55 C1
Pennant Rd ROCH ME1 ......30 C1
Penn Cl SIT ME10 ......37 H6
Pennine Wy MAID/SHEP ME15 ......55 H5
Penny Cress Gdns MAIDW ME16 ......6 A6
Penshurst Ct RHAM ME8 ......23 F4
The Penstocks MAIDW ME16 ......53 J4
The Pentagon CHAT ME4 * 4 C4
Pepingstraw Cl E/WMAL ME19 ......44 A5
Pepy's Wy STRD ME2 ......14 E4
Peregrine Dr SIT ME10 ......37 G5
Peregrine Rd E/WMAL ME19 ......50 D4
Perie Rd GILL ME7 * 16 B6
Perimeter Rd MAID/BEAR ME14 ......46 B1
Periwinkle Cl SIT ME10 ......36 E3
Perryfield St MAID/BEAR ME14 ......48 A6
Perry Hl HOO/HM ME3 ......9 H1
Perry St CHAT ME4 ......20 E3
  MAID/BEAR ME14 ......48 A6
Perth Gdns SIT ME10 ......36 C4
Pested Bars Rd MAID/SHEP ME15 ......62 C1
Petchart Cl STRD ME2 ......19 G3
Petham Gn RHAM ME8 ......22 E4
Pettenden Dr SIT ME10 ......27 F6
Peverel Dr MAID/BEAR ME14 ......55 C1
Pheasant La MAID/SHEP ME15 ......62 C1
Pheasant Rd CHAT ME4 * 21 J4
Phillippa Ct SIT ME10 ......36 E1
Phillips Ct RHAM ME8 ......22 D4
Phoenix Dr WBY/YAL ME18 ......59 H2
Phoenix Pk MAID/SHEP ME15 * 23 G4
Phoenix Rd WALD ME5 ......31 H6
Pickering St MAID/SHEP ME15 ......62 B2
Pickwick Ct ROCH ME1 ......20 C4
Pier Approach Rd GILL ME7 ......16 E5
Pier Rd CHAT ME4 ......16 E6
Pikey La E/WMAL ME19 ......51 C1
Pilgrims Lakes RMAID ME17 ......66 C1
Pilgrims Rd DIT/AY ME20 ......28 D2
Pilgrims Vw MAID/SHEP ME15 * 47 K1
Pilgrims Wy DIT/AY ME20 ......40 B4
  MAID/BEAR ME14 ......49 J3
  RMAID ME17 ......57 J5
  RMAID ME17 ......66 E1
  ROCH ME1 ......29 J4
  STRD ME2 ......19 G3
  STRD ME2 ......18 C3
Pilot Rd ROCH ME1 ......20 C6
Pimpernel Cl MAID/BEAR ME14 ......55 J2
Pimpernel Wy WALD ME5 ......30 E4
Pine Cl DIT/AY ME20 ......45 K2
Pine Gv GILL ME7 ......32 C5
  MAID/BEAR ME14 ......48 C6
Pine Rd MAID/SHEP ME15 ......55 H5
Pine Rd STRD ME2 ......2 A4
Pinewood Dr MAID/BEAR ME14 ......41 K2
The Pinnacles CHAT ME4 ......26 E3
Pintail Dr STRD ME2 ......18 E3
The Pintails CHAT ME4 ......16 C3
Pippin Cl RMAID ME17 ......61 G6
Pippin Cft GILL ME7 ......36 D2
Pippin St WALD ME5 ......50 D4
Pippin Wy E/WMAL ME19 ......50 D4
Pirbright Cl WALD ME5 ......31 K6
Pittstock Rd RSIT ME9 ......43 H6
Pitt Rd MAIDW ME16 ......58 D2
  RMAID ME17 * 64 D6
Pizien Well Rd WBY/YAL ME18 ......58 D2
Place La RSIT ME9 ......54 B5
Plains Av MAID/SHEP ME15 ......54 C5
Plaistow Sq MAID/SHEP ME15 * 48 D6
Plantation La MAID/BEAR ME14 ......55 H2
Plantation Rd GILL ME7 ......17 H6
The Platters RHAM ME8 ......69 G3
The Platt RMAID ME17 ......69 G3
Playstool Cl RSIT ME9 ......34 E2
Playstool Rd RSIT ME9 ......34 E2
Pleasant Valley La
  RMAID ME17 ......69 J2
Pleasure House La
  RMAID ME17 ......61 G4
Plomley Cl RHAM ME8 ......33 H4
Ploughmans Wy RHAM ME8 ......33 C2
  MAID/SHEP ME15 ......41 C1
Plough Wents Rd RMAID ME17 ......63 H5
Plover Cl WALD ME5 ......41 K1
Plover Rd DIT/AY ME20 ......45 J2
Plowenders Cl E/WMAL ME19 ......44 A4
Pluckley St MAID/SHEP ME15 ......22 E3
Plumtree Gv GILL ME7 ......32 C4
Plumtrees MAID/BEAR ME14 ......53 F4
Poachers Cl WALD ME5 ......31 J5
Podkin Wd WALD ME5 ......41 F2
The Poles RHAM ME8 ......24 C2
Polhill Dr WALD ME5 ......30 E6
Police Station Rd
  MAID/SHEP ME15 ......45 F4
Pond Dr SIT ME10 ......37 G6
Pondfield La GVE DA12 ......13 H3
Pope St MAIDW ME16 ......6 A7
Popjak Rd RSIT ME9 * 42 D4
Poplar Cl HOO/HM ME3 ......17 F1
  STRD ME2 ......19 K1
Poplar Gv MAIDW ME16 ......53 G1
Poplar Rd STRD ME2 ......19 F3
Poplicans Rd STRD ME2 ......19 F3
Poppy Cl GILL ME7 ......36 C4
  RHAM ME8 ......6 C6
Porchester Cl MAID/SHEP ME15 ......62 B2
Port Cl MAID/SHEP ME15 ......31 G2
  WALD ME5 ......31 H5
Porters Wk RMAID ME17 ......64 B4
Portland Av STRD ME2 ......37 J4
Portland Pl SNOD ME6 ......38 E2

Portland Rd GILL ME7 ......17 F6
  ROCH ME1 ......29 G4
Portland St CHAT ME4 ......21 H4
Portree Ms GILL ME7 * 22 A3
Port Rd CHAT ME4
Portsdown Cl MAIDW ME16 ......53 G4
Portsmouth Cl STRD ME2 ......14 C6
Postley Rd MAID/SHEP ME15 ......7 H7
Postmill Dr MAID/SHEP ME15 ......54 A5
Pottery Rd HOO/HM ME3 ......10 C5
Pout Rd SNOD ME6 ......38 D3
Povey Av STRD ME2 ......15 H7
Powell Cl DIT/AY ME20 ......47 F1
Powlett Rd STRD ME2 ......15 H5
Pratling St DIT/AY ME20 ......47 C1
The Precincts ROCH ME1 ......3 F5
Premier Pl DIT/AY ME20 ......46 D3
Prentis Cl SIT ME10 ......36 C3
Prentis Quay SIT ME10 ......37 F5
Preston Av GILL ME7 ......22 A5
Pretoria Rd CHAT ME4 ......21 F4
  GILL ME7 ......5 K6
Pridmore Rd SNOD ME6 ......38 D2
Priestfield Rd GILL ME7 ......22 A1
Priestfields ROCH ME1 ......20 B4
Priestley Dr DIT/AY ME20 ......38 D6
Primrose Av CHAT ME4 ......32 D5
Primrose Cl CHAT ME4 ......30 E7
Primrose Dr DIT/AY ME20 ......46 C4
Primrose La RSIT ME9 ......42 A4
Primrose Rd STRD ME2 ......28 C3
Prince Arthur Rd GILL ME7 ......16 C6
Prince Charles Av GILL ME7 ......31 H4
  WALD ME5 ......31 H4
Princes Av WALD ME5 ......31 H4
Princess Mary Av CHAT ME4 ......16 C5
Princes St MAID/BEAR ME14 ......49 H5
  ROCH ME1 ......20 C3
Princes Wy MAID/SHEP ME15 ......49 H5
Prinys Dr RHAM ME8 ......22 D5
Priorsdean Cl MAIDW ME16 ......52 D5
Priory Cl MAID/SHEP ME15 ......53 C6
Priory Ga MAID/SHEP ME15 ......7 H2
Priory Gv DIT/AY ME20 ......46 C3
Priory Pk DIT/AY ME20 * 46 C3
Priory Rd GILL ME7 ......5 H5
  RHAM ME8 ......2 B3
  STRD ME2
The Progress Est
  MAID/SHEP ME15 * 63 H4
Prospect Av STRD ME2 ......15 C4
Prospect Pl MAIDW ME16 ......6 C6
  ROCH ME1 ......20 A4
Prospect Rw CHAT ME4 ......4 D1
Provender Wy
  MAID/BEAR ME14 ......55 F2
Pudding La MAID/SHEP ME15 ......7 G4
Pudding Rd RHAM ME8 ......33 G4
Pump Cl E/WMAL ME19 ......45 G3
Pump La RHAM ME8 ......22 E4
Purbeck Rd CHAT ME4 ......20 E4
Purser Wy GILL ME7 ......16 D5
Puttney Dr SIT ME10 ......27 C6
Pyrus Cl WALD ME5 ......41 G2

Q

The Quarries RMAID ME17 ......62 D4
Quarry Rd MAID/SHEP ME15 ......54 B4
Quarry Sq MAID/BEAR ME14 ......7 H1
Quayside CHAT ME4 ......16 C4
Queen Anne Rd
  MAID/BEAR ME14 ......7 K3
Queendown Av RHAM ME8 ......33 F5
Queen Elizabeth Sq
  MAID/SHEP ME15 ......62 D2
The Queen Mother Ct
  SNOD ME6 ......20 B2
Queen's Av MAIDW ME16 ......6 C1
  SNOD ME6 ......38 E2
Queens House MAIDW ME16 ......53 F5
Queen's Rd GILL ME7 ......5 J4
  MAE Naed Ms RHAM ME8
  SNOD ME6 ......38 E2
  WALD ME5 ......31 K5
Queen St CHAT ME4 ......4 D4
  E/WMAL ME19 ......50 D3
  ROCH ME1 ......3 G7
Queens Wy MAID/SHEP ME15 ......49 H3
Queenswood Rd DIT/AY ME20 ......45 G5
The Quern MAID/SHEP ME15 ......53 K5
Quested Wy MAID/SHEP ME17 ......66 B2
Quickstep Cl SIT ME10 ......27 F6
Quickthorn Crs WALD ME5 ......30 C5
Quinion Cl WALD ME5 ......41 F2
Quinnell St RHAM ME8 ......33 C4
Quinton Rd RSIT ME9 ......36 C1
Quixote Crs STRD ME2 ......15 G3

R

Racefield Cl GVE DA12 ......13 H2
Radleigh Gdns CHAT ME4 ......20 E5
Raggatt Pl MAID/SHEP ME15 ......54 C4
Ragstone Ct DIT/AY ME20 ......46 B4
Ragstone Rd MAID/SHEP ME15 ......55 H4
Railway St CHAT ME4 ......3 F5
  GILL ME7 ......5 K2
Rainham Cl MAID/SHEP ME15 ......54 B5
Rainham Rd GILL ME7 ......5 H7
Raleigh Cl WALD ME5 ......31 G2
Ramillies Cl WALD ME5 ......41 C4
Rampion Cl MAID/SHEP ME15 ......55 F1
Randall Rd CHAT ME4 ......20 E5
Randall St MAID/BEAR ME14 ......48 A6
Randolph Cl GILL ME7 ......5 J3

Ranscombe Cl STRD ME2 ......19 H1
Ratcliffe Hwy HOO/HM ME3 ......10 C5
Raven Cl DIT/AY ME20 ......45 K3
Ravens Dane Cl
  MAID/SHEP ME15 ......55 H5
Ravenswood Av STRD ME2 ......15 C4
Rawdon Rd MAID/SHEP ME15 ......7 J6
Rawling St RSIT ME9 ......43 F6
Rayfield Ct SNOD ME6 ......38 E1
Rayleigh Cl MAIDW ME16 ......47 J5
Raymer Rd MAID/BEAR ME14 ......48 C4
Readscroft Rd RHAM ME8 ......33 F5
Read Wy GVE DA12 ......12 A1
Recreation Av SNOD ME6 ......38 E2
Recreation Cl MAID/BEAR ME14 ......48 C6
Recreation Wy SIT ME10 ......27 F5
Rectory Cl ROCH ME1 ......20 C4
  SNOD ME6 ......38 E2
Rectory Gra ROCH ME1 ......20 C4
Rectory La MAID/SHEP ME15 ......53 F5
  RMAID ME17 ......66 D3
  RMAID ME17 ......68 A4
Rectory La North
  E/WMAL ME19 ......45 G2
Rectory La South
  E/WMAL ME19 ......45 H2
Redbank E/WMAL ME19 ......45 H2
Redbridge Cl MAID/SHEP ME15 ......31 H3
Redcliffe La MAID/BEAR ME14 ......48 C4
Rede Court Rd STRD ME2 ......14 D4
Rede Wood Rd MAIDW ME16 ......52 D3
Redfern Av GILL ME7 ......22 A1
Red Hl WBY/YAL ME18 ......51 H6
Red House Gdns
  WBY/YAL ME18 ......59 C1
Redland Shaw ROCH ME1 ......20 E5
Redsells Cl MAID/SHEP ME15 ......55 H5
Redshank Rd CHAT ME4 ......16 B3
Redvers Rd CHAT ME4 ......21 C4
Redwell Gv E/WMAL ME19 ......51 F4
Redwing Rd MAID/SHEP ME15 ......31 H3
Redwood Cl WALD ME5 ......31 H6
Reedham Crs HOO/HM ME3 ......9 H3
Reeves Ct DIT/AY ME20 ......45 K3
Reform Rd CHAT ME4 ......4 F7
Regency Ct RHAM ME8 ......32 E5
Regency Ct SIT ME10 ......36 D6
Regent Dr MAID/SHEP ME15 ......54 B6
Regent Rd GILL ME7 ......5 C4
Regent Wy E/WMAL ME19 ......51 F3
Reginald Av STRD ME2 ......19 G3
Reginald Rd MAIDW ME16 ......6 E6
Regis Crs SIT ME10 ......27 F6
Reinden Gv MAID/SHEP ME15 ......55 G5
Renown Rd WALD ME5 ......31 J6
Repton Wy WALD ME5 ......31 K4
Resolution Cl WALD ME5 ......31 G3
Restharrow Rd
  MAID/BEAR ME14 ......55 F2
Restharrow Wy CHAT ME4 ......16 D3
Rettenden Dr SIT ME10 ......27 F6
Revenge Rd MAID/BEAR ME14 ......41 J2
Reynolds Flds HOO/HM ME3 ......8 B4
Rhode St CHAT ME4 ......4 D5
Rhodewood Cl
  MAID/SHEP ME15 ......55 H5
Richard St CHAT ME4 ......4 C3
  ROCH ME1 ......20 C3
Richard Watts Ct CHAT ME4 * 4 B3
Richborough Dr STRD ME2 ......15 F3
Richmond Cl STRD ME2 ......15 H4
  WALD ME5 ......31 H4
Richmond Dr SIT ME10 ......36 E1
Richmond Rd GILL ME7 ......16 D6
Richmond Wy
  MAID/SHEP ME15 ......54 B6
  WALD ME5 ......31 H4
Riddles Rd SIT ME10 ......27 F6
The Ridgeway CHAT ME4 ......30 E1
  GILL ME7 * 16 D5
  GVE DA12 ......13 H3
Ridgway MAIDW ME16 ......53 G4
Ridham Av SIT ME10 ......27 C5
Ridley Rd ROCH ME1 ......2 E7
Ringlestone Crs
  MAID/BEAR ME14 ......48 A4
Ringlet Rd CHAT ME4 ......16 C2
Ringwood Cl RHAM ME8 ......33 F1
Ringwood Rd
  MAID/SHEP ME15 ......54 D6
Ripon Cl RHAM ME8 ......23 F5
The Rise GILL ME7 ......32 C5
  ROCH ME1 ......36 B6
Ritch Rd SNOD ME6 ......38 C2
River Bank Cl MAID/SHEP ME15 ......7 H4
River Cl MAID/SHEP ME15 ......61 C1
River Dr STRD ME2 ......14 D5
Riverhead Cl MAIDW ME16 ......47 J6
  SIT ME10 ......36 C5
Rivermead CHAT ME4 ......16 D2
Rivers Cl WBY/YAL ME18 ......59 H1
Riverside CHAT ME4 ......4 B3
Riverside Est STRD ME2 * 15 K6
River St GILL ME7 ......16 B6
River Vw GILL ME7 ......23 F3
River Vw MAID/SHEP ME15
Roach St STRD ME2 ......2 D2
Roan Ct STRD ME2 ......14 E4
Roberts Cl SIT ME10 ......36 D1
Roberts Orchard Rd
  MAID/BEAR ME14 ......55 D5
Roberts Rd RHAM ME8 ......22 D5
  SNOD ME6 ......38 D2
Robin Hood La MAID/SHEP ME15 ......40 D1
Robin Hood La (Lower)
  WALD ME5 ......40 E1
Robin Hood La (Upper)
  WALD ME5 ......40 E1
Robins Av RMAID ME17 ......67 H4
Robins Cl RMAID ME17 ......67 H4
Robson Dr DIT/AY ME20 ......46 E5
  HOO/HM ME3 ......10 E5
Rocfort Rd SNOD ME6 ......38 E2

Rochester Av ROCH ME1 ......20 C2
Rochester Br ROCH ME1 ......3 F3
Rochester Ct STRD ME2 ......15 K4
Rochester Crs HOO/HM ME3 ......10 E4
Rochester Ga ROCH ME1 * 3 H6
  DIT/AY ME20 ......47 F1
  ROCH ME1 ......29 J5
  STRD ME2 ......19 H3
  WALD ME5 ......30 C4
Rochester St CHAT ME4 ......20 D4
Rock Av GILL ME7 ......5 J6
Rock Rd MAID/BEAR ME14 ......48 B5
  SIT ME10 ......36 E5
Rocks Cl E/WMAL ME19 ......45 K6
The Rocks Rd E/WMAL ME19 ......45 K6
Rocky Hill Ter MAIDW ME16 * 6 E4
Roebuck Rd ROCH ME1 ......3 F6
Roffen Rd ROCH ME1 ......20 C4
Rolvenden Av RHAM ME8 ......22 E3
Rolvenden Dr RHAM ME8 ......36 B3
Rolvenden Rd STRD ME2 ......15 H2
Roman Cl DIT/AY ME20 ......48 D1
Roman Rd RHAM ME8 ......33 G4
Roman Sq SNOD ME6 ......38 D2
Roman Wy STRD ME2 ......19 K2
Romany Rd RHAM ME8 ......22 D4
Rome Ter CHAT ME4 ......4 A4
Romney Cl MAID/SHEP ME15 ......55 H5
Romney Ct SIT ME10 ......36 D5
Romney Pl MAID/SHEP ME15 ......7 H4
Romney Rd WALD ME5 ......31 H3
Romsey Cl STRD ME2 ......14 C4
Ronalds Ct SIT ME10 * 37 C4
Rookery Rd STRD ME2 ......42 A4
Rookery Rw
  MAID/SHEP ME15 * 60 D2
Rook La RSIT ME9 ......35 K2
Roonagh Ct SIT ME10 ......36 E6
Roosevelt Av WALD ME5 ......31 F1
Ropemakers Ct CHAT ME4 ......4 C3
Roper Cl RHAM ME8 ......32 E5
Roper's Green La HOO/HM ME3 ......11 H2
Roper's La HOO/HM ME3 ......11 G2
The Ropery CHAT ME4 * 16 A5
Rope Wk CHAT ME4 ......4 C3
Roseacre Gdns
  MAID/BEAR ME14 ......55 H3
Roseacre La MAID/BEAR ME14 ......55 H3
Rosebery Cl SIT ME10 ......37 K4
Rosebery Rd CHAT ME4 ......20 E4
  GILL ME7 ......16 E6
Roseholme MAIDW ME16 ......6 C7
Roseleigh Av MAIDW ME16 ......53 G2
Roseleigh Rd SIT ME10 ......42 D3
Rosemary Rd E/WMAL ME19 ......45 J3
  MAID/SHEP ME15
Rosemount Cl
  MAID/SHEP ME15 ......62 A4
Rosemount Ct STRD ME2 ......15 F3
Rose St ROCH ME1 ......20 D3
Rose Yd MAID/BEAR ME14 ......7 H3
Rosslyn Gn MAIDW ME16 ......53 G1
Ross St ROCH ME1 ......3 J1
Rotary Gdns GILL ME7 ......22 B4
Rother V WALD ME5 ......31 J4
Roughetts Rd E/WMAL ME19 * 44 C1
Roughetts Rw E/WMAL ME19 * 44 C1
The Roundel SIT ME10 ......36 E6
Roundhay E/WMAL ME19 ......45 G3
Roundwell MAID/BEAR ME14 ......56 A2
Round Wood Cl WALD ME5 ......41 C1
Rover Rd WALD ME5 ......41 G1
Rowan Cl DIT/AY ME20 ......46 B4
Rowan Lea WALD ME5 ......21 H6
Rowan Wk CHAT ME4 ......16 A6
Rowbrocke Cl RHAM ME8 ......33 F5
Rowland Av GILL ME7 ......22 A5
Rowland Cl MAIDW ME16 ......22 A5
  WALD ME5
Royal Eagle Cl STRD ME2 ......3 K1
Royal Engineers' Rd
  MAID/BEAR ME14 ......48 A6
Royal Sovereign Av CHAT ME4 ......7 C4
Royal Star Ar MAID/BEAR ME14 * 7 C4
Roydon Hall Rd WBY/YAL ME18 ......58 B3
Royston Rd MAID/SHEP ME15 ......55 H3
Roystons Ct RHAM ME8 ......23 H4
Rubie Ct DIT/AY ME20 ......67 J3
Ruckinge Wy RHAM ME8 ......22 E4
Rugby Cl MAIDW ME16 ......31 J6
Rugby Cl WALD ME5 ......31 H4
Ruins Barn Rd RSIT ME9 ......42 D6
Runham La RMAID ME17 ......66 E4
Rushdean Rd STRD ME2 ......31 C5
Rushdean Dr STRD ME2 ......19 H1
Rushmead Dr
  MAID/SHEP ME15 ......62 B1
Ruskin Cl E/WMAL ME19 ......45 J4
Russell Cl SIT ME10
Russell Ct CHAT ME4 ......5 F7
Russell Rd DIT/AY ME20 ......46 D4
Russells Av RHAM ME8 ......23 J6
Russet Ct STRD ME2 ......14 D4
The Russets MAIDW ME16 * 53 G1
Russet Cl DIT/AY ME20 ......46 D4
Rutland Pl RHAM ME8 ......32 E5
Rutland Wy MAID/SHEP ME15 ......55 F6
Ryan Dr MAID/SHEP ME15 ......55 H6
Ryarsh La E/WMAL ME19 ......44 C3
Ryarsh Pk E/WMAL ME19 * 44 C3
Rycault Cl MAIDW ME16 ......6 D5
Rydal Wy RSIT ME9 ......36 D3
Ryde Cl WALD ME5 ......31 H6
Ryecroft GVE DA12 ......12 B1
Ryegrass Cl WALD ME5 ......31 J2

S

Saddlers Cl MAID/BEAR ME14 ......55 F1

Sadlers Cl *WALD* ME5 ....30 D6
Saffron Wy *SIT* ME10 ....37 F1
Sage Rd *ROCH* ME1 ....20 A5
Sailmakers Ct *CHAT* ME4 ....21 H4
St Albans Cl *GILL* ME7 ....17 F5
St Albans Rd *STRD* ME2 ....14 B6
St Andrew Rd *GILL* ME7 ....16 E5
St Andrew's Cl *MAIDW* ME16 ....53 H3
St Andrews Pk *MAIDW* ME16 ....53 F4
St Andrew's Rd *MAIDW* ME16 * 3 F3
St Annes Ct *MAIDW* ME16 ....53 G4
St Barnabas La *GILL* ME7 ....21 K3
MAIDW ME16 ....47 H4
St Bartholomew's La *ROCH* ME1 .....3 J7
St Bartholomew's Ter
ROCH ME1 ....3 K7
St Benedict Rd *SNOD* ME6 ....38 C2
St Faith's La *MAID/BEAR* ME14 .....55 J2
St Faith's St *MAID/BEAR* ME14 ......7 G3
St Francis Cl *MAID/BEAR* ME14 ....48 C6
STRD ME2 ....14 D6
St George's Rd *GILL* ME7 ....16 C5
St George's Sq *MAIDW* ME16 * 6 C3
St Helens Cnr
MAID/SHEP ME15 * 52 D6
St Helens La *MAID/SHEP* ME15 ....52 D6
St Helier's Cl *MAIDW* ME16 ....53 G4
St John's Av *SIT* ME10 ....37 F1
St John's Cl *HOO/HM* ME3 ....14 B1
St John's Rd *GILL* ME7 ....5 H7
St Johns *ROCH* ME1 ....8 B6
HOO/HM ME3 ....10 A6
St Johns Wy *ROCH* ME1 ....20 A4
St Katherine's La *SNOD* ME6 ....38 D5
St Laurence Av *DIT/AY* ME20 ....47 K4
St Laurence Cl *RSIT* ME9 ....37 K6
St Leonards Av *CHAT* ME4 ....21 F4
St Leonards Rd *MAIDW* ME16 ....47 H4
St Leonard's St *E/WMAL* ME19 .....44 E5
St Lukes Av *MAID/BEAR* ME14 ....7 K2
St Lukes Rd *MAID/BEAR* ME14 ....7 K1
St Margarets Banks *ROCH* ME1 ....3 F7
St Margarets Dr *MAIDW* ME16 ....53 G4
St Margarets *MAID/BEAR* ME8 ....32 E3
St Margaret's St *ROCH* ME1 ....3 F6
St Margaret's Ms *ROCH* ME1 ....3 F6
St Marks Cl *ROCH* ME1 * 3 G7
St Marks Ct *DIT/AY* ME20 ....39 K4
St Marks Houses *GILL* ME7 ....5 H2
St Martin's Cl *MAID/BEAR* ME14 ..49 H3
St Marys Ct *E/WMAL* ME19 * 44 E4
St Mary's Gdns *CHAT* ME4 ....16 E5
St Mary's Rd *GILL* ME7 ....16 D6
STRD ME2 ....35 G2
St Mary's Vw *STRD* ME2 ....35 G2
St Matthews Dr *CHAT* ME4 ....20 A4
St Michael's Cl *CHAT* ME4 ....4 B7
DIT/AY ME20 ....47 H1
St Michaels Ct *STRD* ME2 * 15 C4
St Michael's Rd *MAIDW* ME16 ....6 C5
SIT ME10 ....36 E4
St Nicholas Gdns *STRD* ME2 ....14 B4
St Paul's Cl *STRD* ME2 ....19 H1
St Paul's St *SIT* ME10 ....36 E3
St Peter's Br *MAIDW* ME16 ....7 F4
St Peters Cl *DIT/AY* ME20 ....46 A3
St Peters Pth *GILL* ME7 * 5 H3
St Peters Rd *DIT/AY* ME20 ....39 K4
St Peters Rd *MAIDW* ME16 ....46 A3
St Peter St *MAIDW* ME16 ....7 F2
ROCH ME1 ....3 J7
St Philip's Av *MAID/SHEP* ME15 ....21 K5
St Ronan's Cl
MAID/SHEP ME15 * 62 D1
St Saviours Rd
MAID/SHEP ME15 ....62 E2
St Stephen's Sq
MAID/SHEP ME15 ....62 E2
St Thomas Well *GVE* DA12 * 12 D4
St Welcume's Wy *MAID/BEAR* ME17 .66 D2
St Werburgh Crs *HOO/HM* ME3 ....10 C5
St William's Wy *ROCH* ME1 ....20 C3
Sakcote Rd *GVE* DA12 ....12 D1
Salem St *MAID/SHEP* ME15 ....7 J6
Salisbury Av *RHAM* ME8 ....33 J2
Salisbury Rd *CHAT* ME4 ....16 B4
DIT/AY ME20 ....40 C2
MAID/BEAR ME8 ....48 B6
Sallow Cl *CHAT* ME4 ....16 D3
Sally Port *GILL* ME7 ....23 F1
Sally Port Gdns *GILL* ME7 ....4 E1
Saltings Rd *SNOD* ME6 ....38 E3
Salt's Av *MAID/SHEP* ME15 ....62 A5
Salts La *MAID/SHEP* ME15 ....62 B4
Saltwood Rd *MAID/SHEP* ME15 ...54 A5
Samara Cl *WALD* ME5 ....31 J4
Samphire Cl *MAID/BEAR* ME14 .....55 F2
Samphire Wy *CHAT* ME4 ....16 C3
Sanctuary Rd *RHAM* ME8 ....22 C3
Sandbourne Dr
MAID/BEAR ME14 ....48 A3
Sanderling Wy *RSIT* ME9 ....26 D2
Sandford Rd *SIT* ME10 ....37 G6
Sandgate Ct *RHAM* ME8 ....33 H4
Sandhill La *HOO/HM* ME3 ....11 J1
Sandhurst Cl *RHAM* ME8 ....22 E3
Sandling La *MAID/BEAR* ME14 ....47 K3
Sandling Rd *MAID/BEAR* ME14 * 48 A4
Sandling Rd *MAID/BEAR* ME14 ....7 G1
Sandling Wy *CHAT* ME4 ....16 C5
Sandown Dr *RHAM* ME8 ....33 H4
Sandown Rd *E/WMAL* ME19 ....44 E4
Sandpiper Rd *GILL* ME7 ....31 J6
Sandringham Ct
E/WMAL ME19 * 50 D5
Sandringham Rd *RHAM* ME8 ....33 F4
Sandstone Dr *SIT* ME10 ....36 B6
Sandstone Ri *MAID/BEAR* ME14 ...41 J2
Sandway Rd *RMAID* ME17 ....64 E4
Sandycroft Rd *STRD* ME2 ....14 B5
Sandy Dell *GILL* ME7 ....32 C5
Sandy La *E/WMAL* ME19 ....44 E4
MAID/BEAR ME14 ....48 D3
MAID/BEAR ME14 ....55 J1

SNOD ME6 ....38 C4
Sandy Mt *MAID/BEAR* ME14 ....55 J1
Saracen Cl *GILL* ME7 ....36 C1
Saracen Ct *CHAT* ME4 ....21 H2
Saracen Flds *WALD* ME5 ....41 H2
Sarsen Hts *WALD* ME5 ....41 F1
Sarsens Ct *GVE* DA12 ....12 C6
Sassoon Cl *DIT/AY* ME20 ....38 E6
Satis Av *SIT* ME10 ....31 F5
Saunders St *GILL* ME7 ....16 D6
Savage Rd *WALD* ME5 ....31 H5
Sawyers Ct *CHAT* ME4 ....21 H4
Saxon Cl *E/WMAL* ME19 ....50 C4
STRD ME2 ....14 E3
Saxon Pl *STRD* ME2 ....2 A6
Saxons Dr *MAID/BEAR* ME14 ....48 C5
Saxon Shore Wy *GILL* ME7 ....17 K6
ROCH ME1 ....3 G4
ROCH ME1 ....27 H1
RSIT ME9 ....15 K4
RSIT ME9 ....26 D2
Saxton St *GILL* ME7 ....5 H3
Scarborough La *ROCH* ME1 ....39 H1
Scholars Ri *STRD* ME2 ....14 B5
Scholey Cl *STRD* ME2 ....29 F4
School Av *GILL* ME7 ....22 A2
School La *HOO/HM* ME3 ....8 B4
MAID/SHEP ME15 ....55 F5
RMAID ME17 ....66 E6
RMAID ME17 ....69 G3
ROCH ME1 ....29 H5
RSIT ME9 ....25 F4
RSIT ME9 ....35 F1
RSIT ME9 ....35 K5
RSIT ME9 ....37 K6
School Rd *SIT* ME10 ....37 H5
Schreiber Ms *GILL* ME7 * 21 K1
Scimitar Cl *GILL* ME7 ....32 B6
Scotby Av *WALD* ME5 ....31 H4
Scotland La *GVE* DA12 ....12 D5
Scott Av *RHAM* ME8 ....23 J6
Scott Cl *DIT/AY* ME20 ....46 B4
Scott Rd *GVE* DA12 ....12 A1
Scott's Ter *CHAT* ME4 ....4 B7
Scott St *MAID/BEAR* ME14 ....48 A6
Scragged Oak Rd
MAID/BEAR ME14 ....49 J2
Seaford St *ROCH* ME1 ....2 E7
Seagull Rd *STRD* ME2 ....14 C6
Sealand Ct *ROCH* ME1 * 3 G4
Seaton Rd *GILL* ME7 ....22 A3
Seaview Rd *GILL* ME7 ....5 J4
Seaview Ter *RSIT* ME9 * 25 F3
Second Av *GILL* ME7 ....22 A3
WALD ME5 ....20 B5
Secretan Rd *ROCH* ME1 ....19 K3
Sedge Crs *WALD* ME5 ....30 E4
Sedley Cl *DIT/AY* ME20 ....46 D2
HOO/HM ME3 ....9 H3
RHAM ME8 ....32 E5
Selbourne Rd *GILL* ME7 ....16 E5
Selbourne Wk
MAID/SHEP ME15 ....63 G2
Selby Rd *MAID/SHEP* ME15 ....63 G4
Selstead Cl *RHAM* ME8 ....22 D5
Senacre La *MAID/SHEP* ME15 ....63 F2
Senacre Sq *MAID/SHEP* ME15 ....63 G1
Sessions House Sq
MAID/BEAR ME14 * 7 G1
Setford Rd *WALD* ME5 ....31 J2
Settington Av *WALD* ME5 ....21 J5
Seven Mile La *RTON* TN11 ....58 B4
Severn Rd *WALD* ME5 ....31 J3
Sevington Pk *MAID/SHEP* ME15 ...62 A2
Sextant Pk *STRD* ME2 * 3 K2
Seymour Rd *RHAM* ME8 ....24 A6
WALD ME5 ....5 F6
Shackleton Cl *WALD* ME5 ....31 J5
The Shades *STRD* ME2 ....14 A5
Shaftesbury Cl *E/WMAL* ME19 ....45 J5
Shaftesbury Dr *WALD* ME5 ....30 D3
Shakespeare Rd *GILL* ME7 ....5 H6
SIT ME10 ....37 G4
Shanklin Cl *WALD* ME5 ....21 J6
Sharfleet Dr *STRD* ME2 ....14 A5
Sharnal La *SNOD* ME6 ....38 E5
Sharnal St *HOO/HM* ME3 ....11 K3
Sharon Crs *WALD* ME5 ....31 F4
Sharps Gn *GILL* ME7 ....23 F1
Sharsted Wy *GILL* ME7 ....32 C5
MAID/BEAR ME14 * 55 J1
Shaw Cl *WALD* ME5 ....30 D4
Shawstead Rd *WALD* ME5 ....31 J1
WALD ME5 ....20 B3
Sheal's Crs *MAID/SHEP* ME15 ....54 B4
Shearers Cl *MAID/BEAR* ME14 ......55 F2
Shearwater *MAIDW* ME16 ....53 G1
Shearwater Cl *STRD* ME2 ....14 B5
Sheerstone *RSIT* ME9 ....26 C5
Shelden Dr *RHAM* ME8 ....23 H6
Sheldon Wy *DIT/AY* ME20 ....45 K1
Shelley Ri *ROCH* ME1 ....20 A3
Shelley Rd *MAIDW* ME16 ....53 H4
Shenley Gv *MAID/BEAR* ME14 ......48 A2
Shepherds Ga *GILL* ME7 ....32 B3
Shepherds Gate Dr
MAID/SHEP ME15 * 55 F1
Shepherds Wy *RMAID* ME17 ....64 B6
Shepperton Cl *WALD* ME5 ....31 J4
Sheppey Rd *MAID/SHEP* ME15 ....62 A1
Sheppey Wy *RSIT* ME9 ....25 J5
Shepway Cl *MAID/SHEP* ME15 * ...54 D6
Sheraton Cl *WALD* ME5 ....30 C4
Sherbourne Dr *MAIDW* ME16 ....53 G4
Sheridan Cl *MAID/BEAR* ME14 ....47 K4
WALD ME5 ....31 J1
Sheriff Dr *WALD* ME5 ....31 G6
Sheringham Cl *MAIDW* ME16 ....47 J5
Sherman Cl *GILL* ME7 ....22 D5
Shernolds *MAID/SHEP* ME15 ....62 C1
Sherwood Av *WALD* ME5 ....31 G6

Sherwoods *WALD* ME5 * 40 D1
Shillingheld Cl
MAID/BEAR ME14 ....55 G1
Shimmin Rd *CHAT* ME4 ....42 D4
Shingle Barn La *WBY/YAL* ME18 ...60 A4
Ship La *WALD* ME5 ....3 K7
Shipwrights Av *CHAT* ME4 ....21 G4
Shirley Wy *MAID/SHEP* ME15 ....55 H3
Sholden Rd *STRD* ME2 ....15 H5
Shorefields *RHAM* ME8 ....23 J4
Shorland Ct *ROCH* ME1 * 2 E6
Shorlands Rd *GILL* ME7 ....37 G4
Shorne Ifield Rd *GVE* DA12 ....12 E2
Shorts Cl *CHAT* ME4 ....21 G4
Shorts Reach *ROCH* ME1 ....5 F7
Shorts Wy *ROCH* ME1 ....20 A4
Shottenden Rd *GILL* ME7 ....16 E5
Shropshire Ter
MAID/SHEP ME15 ....63 F1
Shrubsole Dr *MAID/BEAR* ME14 ...47 K1
Shurland Av *SIT* ME10 ....43 F1
Sidney Rd *GILL* ME7 ....16 D5
ROCH ME1 ....20 A4
Sidney St *MAID/BEAR* ME14 ....53 H4
Sienna Ct *RHAM* ME8 ....33 H4
Silchester Ct *MAID/BEAR* ME14 ....48 D5
Silver Bank *WALD* ME5 ....55 H3
Silver Birches *WALD* ME5 ....31 G5
Silverdale *MAIDW* ME16 ....52 E4
Silverdale Dr *RHAM* ME8 ....33 H2
Silverdale Gv *GILL* ME7 ....36 C5
Silver Hl *CHAT* ME4 ....4 C6
Silver Hill Gdns *CHAT* ME4 ....4 C6
Silverspot Cl *RHAM* ME8 ....33 H1
Silver Tree *WALD* ME5 ....41 G1
Silverweed Rd *WALD* ME5 ....31 G6
Simmonds La *MAID/SHEP* ME15 ...63 J2
Simpson Rd *SIT* ME10 ....36 E5
SNOD ME6 ....38 E4
Sinclair Cl *RHAM* ME8 ....33 G3
Singapore Dr *GILL* ME7 ....4 E2
Sirdar Strd *GVE* DA12 ....12 C1
Sir Evelyn Rd *ROCH* ME1 ....20 B6
Sir John Hawkins Wy *CHAT* ME4 .....4 B4
Sir Thomas Longley Rd
STRD ME2 ....3 K3
Sissinghurst Dr *MAIDW* ME16 ....53 G2
Sittingbourne Rd
MAID/BEAR ME14 ....7 K3
Skene Cl *RHAM* ME8 ....23 J5
Skinners Cl *DIT/AY* ME20 ....40 A4
Skinner St *CHAT* ME4 ....4 C6
GILL ME7 ....5 H2
Skinner's Wy *RMAID* ME17 ....64 B6
Skye Cl *MAID/SHEP* ME15 ....62 B1
Slade Rd *WALD* ME5 ....31 J5
Slatin Rd *STRD* ME2 ....15 F4
Slicketts Hl *CHAT* ME4 * 4 C4
Slip Rd *CHAT* ME4 ....16 B4
Slough Rd *RSIT* ME9 ....43 G6
Small Hythe Cl
MAID/SHEP ME15 ....55 J4
Small Profits *WBY/YAL* ME18 ....59 K4
Smeed Cl *SIT* ME10 ....37 H4
Smetham Gdns *WALD* ME5 ....31 H5
Smith Rd *WALD* ME5 ....31 H5
Smith's Hl *MAID/SHEP* ME15 ....60 B4
Smith St *WALD* ME5 ....3 B5
Snodhurst Av *WALD* ME5 ....30 E3
Snodland Rd *E/WMAL* ME19 ....38 A4
Snowdon Av *MAID/BEAR* ME14 ....54 C1
Snowdon Cl *WALD* ME5 ....31 J3
Snowdon Pde
MAID/BEAR ME14 * 54 D1
Solomon Rd *RHAM* ME8 ....23 H5
Solomons Rd *CHAT* ME4 ....4 C4
Somerfield Cl *MAIDW* ME16 ....6 C2
Somerfield La *MAIDW* ME16 ....6 C2
Somerfield Rd *MAIDW* ME16 ....6 C2
Somerset Ct *SIT* ME10 ....38 C4
WALD ME5 ....31 J6
Somerset Rd *MAID/SHEP* ME15 .....54 D6
Somner Wk *MAID/SHEP* ME15 ....63 G4
Sonora Wy *SIT* ME10 ....36 C2
Sorrel Rd *WALD* ME5 ....31 F4
Sortmill Rd *SNOD* ME6 ....39 F3
South Av *RHAM* ME8 ....23 J4
SIT ME10 ....37 G5
South Bank *WALD* ME5 ....69 G3
Southbourne Gv *WALD* ME5 ....33 J1
South Bush La *RHAM* ME8 ....33 K2
South Cers *RMAID* ME17 ....20 B5
South Eastern Rd *STRD* ME2 ....2 E1
Southey Wy *DIT/AY* ME20 ....38 D6
Southfields *ROCH* ME1 ....20 B3
Southill Rd *CHAT* ME4 ....4 B7
Southlands Rd *MAIDW* ME17 ....69 G4
South Park Rd
MAID/SHEP ME15 ....54 C5
South Pondside Rd *CHAT* ME4 ....16 B4
South St *GILL* ME7 ....16 B5
South St *MAID/SHEP* ME15 ....52 D6
Southwark Rd *STRD* ME2 ....14 C1
Southways *MAID/SHEP* ME15 ....69 F3
Southwell Rd *SNOD* ME6 ....14 B6
Southwood *MAIDW* ME16 ....52 E4
Sovereign Bvd *GILL* ME7 ....22 A4
Spade La *RSIT* ME9 ....24 B6
Spearhead Rd
MAID/BEAR ME14 ....48 A5
Speedwell Av *WALD* ME5 ....30 E4
Speedwell Cl *GILL* ME7 ....22 A1
MAID/SHEP ME15 ....62 D1
Spekes Rd *GILL* ME7 ....22 E5
Speldhurst Ct *MAIDW* ME16 ....6 B5
Spencer Cl *WALD* ME5 ....31 G3
Spencer Wy *MAID/SHEP* ME15 ....63 H1
Spenlow Dr *WALD* ME5 ....41 G1
Spicers Homes *SIT* ME10 * 37 F5
The Spillway *MAID/SHEP* ME15 .....55 J4
Spindle Cl *MAID/BEAR* ME14 ....55 D1
Spindlewood Cl *WALD* ME5 ....31 F4
Spinnaker Ct *ROCH* ME1 * 20 C5
The Spinney *MAID/SHEP* ME15 ......54 C4

The Spires *MAIDW* ME16 ....6 B3
STRD ME2 ....19 H1
Spitfire Cl *WALD* ME5 ....31 H2
Spitfire Rd *E/WMAL* ME19 ....50 C3
Sportsfield *MAID/BEAR* ME14 ....54 C1
Sportsman's Cottages
MAID/SHEP ME15 ....50 E1
Spot La *MAID/SHEP* ME15 ....55 H4
The Sprig *MAID/BEAR* ME14 ....55 H2
Springett Cl *DIT/AY* ME20 ....39 K4
Springett Wy *RMAID* ME17 ....61 J4
Springfield *MAID/BEAR* ME14 * 48 A6
Springfield Av
MAID/BEAR ME14 ....47 K6
Springfield Rd *DIT/AY* ME20 ....38 D6
GILL ME7 ....17 F6
Springfield Ter *CHAT* ME4 * 4 C5
Springle V *MAIDW* ME16 ....6 E4
Springvale *RHAM* ME8 ....32 D2
Springwood Rd *MAIDW* ME16 ....36 E2
Sprotshill Cl *MAIDW* ME16 ....6 E4
Spruce Cl *DIT/AY* ME20 ....45 K2
Spurway *MAID/BEAR* ME14 ....55 H2
Square Hl *MAID/SHEP* ME15 ....54 D6
Square Hill Rd *MAID/SHEP* ME15 ...7 K5
The Square *MAID/BEAR* ME17 * 64 C5
MAIDW ME16 ....67 J3
Squires Cl *STRD* ME2 ....14 A5
Stable Cl *WALD* ME5 ....31 J3
Stacey Cl *GVE* DA12 ....13 H1
Staceys St *MAID/BEAR* ME14 ....7 G1
Stadium Wy *SIT* ME10 ....37 J2
Stadler Cl *MAIDW* ME16 ....47 J5
Staffa Rd *MAID/SHEP* ME15 ....62 B1
Stafford St *GILL* ME7 ....5 J2
Stag Rd *WALD* ME5 ....31 H5
Stagshaw Cl *MAID/SHEP* ME15 ......54 B4
Staines Ct *MAID/BEAR* ME14 ....7 H2
Stake La *STRD* ME2 ....28 E2
Stalcham Ct *SIT* ME7 ....32 D4
Stalin Av *WALD* ME5 ....21 H6
The Stampers *MAID/SHEP* ME15 ....63 J3
Standen Cl *RHAM* ME8 ....33 G4
Stanford Dr *MAIDW* ME16 ....37 H3
Stanford Wy *STRD* ME2 ....19 G4
Stangate Rd *STRD* ME2 ....14 B4
Stanhope Av *SIT* ME10 ....37 C5
Stanhope Cl *MAID/BEAR* ME14 * 47 K5
Stanhope Rd *STRD* ME2 ....2 C5
Stanley Cl *GILL* ME7 ....22 B1
Stanley Crs *GVE* DA12 ....12 A1
Stanley Rd *GILL* ME7 ....16 D6
WALD ME5 ....31 J2
Stansted Cl *MAIDW* ME16 ....36 E1
Staple Cl *SIT* ME10 ....37 J5
Staplehurst Rd *RHAM* ME8 ....36 C3
SIT ME10 ....36 D3
Staplers Ct *MAID/BEAR* ME14 ....3 F4
Star Hl *ROCH* ME1 ....3 F7
Star La *GILL* ME7 ....22 B2
Star Mill Ct *WALD* ME5 ....21 K5
Star Mill La *WALD* ME5 ....21 K4
Starveacre La *RSIT* ME9 ....6 C2
Station Ap *E/WMAL* ME19 * 44 D2
MAIDW ME16 ....7 F5
Station Rd *DIT/AY* ME20 ....46 B5
DIT/AY ME20 ....46 E2
MAID/BEAR ME14 ....55 G1
MAID/BEAR ME14 ....61 F1
RHAM ME8 ....23 J4
RMAID ME17 ....66 C2
RSIT ME9 ....35 F2
STRD ME2 ....14 D6
WBY/YAL ME18 ....59 F6
Station St *SIT* ME10 ....37 H4
Steadman Cl *HOO/HM* ME3 ....15 F4
Steele St *STRD* ME2 ....15 H5
Steerforth Ct *ROCH* ME1 ....20 C4
Step Style *SIT* ME10 ....37 H6
Sterling Av *MAIDW* ME16 ....53 H1
Sterling Rd *SIT* ME10 ....42 D1
Stevens Cl *SNOD* ME6 ....38 D2
Stevenson Cl *MAID/SHEP* ME15 .....54 D6
Stevenson Wy *DIT/AY* ME20 ....38 D6
Stevens Rd *DIT/AY* ME20 ....39 J4
Stickens La *E/WMAL* ME19 ....45 H6
Stickfast La *RSIT* ME9 ....26 A5
Stilwater Ms *CHAT* ME4 ....38 C4
Stirling Av *RHAM* ME8 ....33 G4
Stirling Rd *E/WMAL* ME19 ....50 C3
Stockbury Dr *MAIDW* ME16 ....47 J5
Stockers Brow *RSIT* ME9 ....43 G5
Stockers Hl *RSIT* ME9 ....43 G5
Stockett La *RMAID* ME17 ....61 H5
Stockton Cl *MAID/BEAR* ME14 ......48 A4
Stoke Rd *HOO/HM* ME3 ....33 F3
Stoneacre Cl *RHAM* ME8
Stoneacre Ct
MAID/SHEP ME15 * 54 B5
Stonecrop Cl *CHAT* ME4 ....16 C3
Stonecross Lea *WALD* ME5 ....21 H5
Stonehorse La *HOO/HM* ME3 ....15 F4
Stoney Bank *MAID/SHEP* ME15 ......55 H1
Stony La *ROCH* ME1 ....30 C2
Stopford Rd *GILL* ME7 ....5 J5
Storway Ct *STRD* ME2 ....14 B4
Stour Valley Wk *RMAID* ME17 ....67 K5
Strand Approach Rd *GILL* ME7 ....17 F5
Stratford Av *MAID/SHEP* ME15 ......62 F2
Stratford Cl *GILL* ME7 ....22 E5
Stratford La *RHAM* ME8 ....32 E3
Stratford Rd *E/WMAL* ME19 ....44 D4
Straw Mill Hl *MAID/SHEP* ME15 .....54 B5
Streamside *DIT/AY* ME20 ....46 A3
The Stream *DIT/AY* ME20 ....46 A3
Street End Rd *WALD* ME5 ....21 H6
Streetfield Rd *RHAM* ME8 ....23 H5

The Street *GVE* DA12 ....12 C6
GVE DA12 ....13 H1
MAID/BEAR ME14 ....49 H5
MAID/BEAR ME14 ....55 K2
RSIT ME9 ....24 C2
RSIT ME9 ....25 F5
RSIT ME9 ....34 B4
RSIT ME9 ....34 E6
STRD ME2 ....28 C3
WBY/YAL ME18 ....50 A6
WBY/YAL ME18 ....59 K1
Strover St *GILL* ME7 ....16 D5
Strumer Ct *E/WMAL* ME19 ....50 D4
Stuart Cl *MAID/BEAR* ME14 ....48 C6
Stuart Rd *GILL* ME7 ....21 K3
Sturdee Av *GILL* ME7 ....22 A2
Sturla Rd *CHAT* ME4 ....21 G4
Sturry Wy *RHAM* ME8 ....2 D4
Style Cl *RHAM* ME8 ....33 G4
Styles La *MAID/BEAR* ME14 ....48 D5
Suffolk Av *RHAM* ME8 ....23 H5
Suffolk Rd *MAID/SHEP* ME15 ....54 E6
Sultan Rd *WALD* ME5 ....31 J6
Sunderland Cl *ROCH* ME1 ....20 A3
Sunderland Dr *RHAM* ME8 ....23 J6
Sundridge Dr *WALD* ME5 ....31 G4
Sundridge Hl *STRD* ME2 ....14 A1
Sunningdale Cl *RHAM* ME8 ....33 F2
Sunningdale Dr *RHAM* ME8 ....33 F2
Sunny Bank *SIT* ME10 ....37 H6
Sunnyfields Cl *RHAM* ME8 ....23 G6
Sunnymead Av *GILL* ME7 ....22 A1
Sun Pier *CHAT* ME4 ....4 B4
Sun Ter *WALD* ME5 * 31 H4
Super Abbey Est *DIT/AY* ME20 * 47 G2
Sussex Av *MAID/BEAR* ME14 ....48 C6
Sussex Dr *WALD* ME5 ....31 G4
Sussex Rd *MAID/SHEP* ME15 ....54 E5
Sutton Cl *MAID/BEAR* ME8 ....23 J6
Sutton Rd *MAID/SHEP* ME15 ....54 C6
RMAID ME17 ....63 K4
Sutton St *MAID/BEAR* ME14 ....56 A4
Sutton Valence Hl
RMAID ME17 ....69 F4
Swadelands Cl *RMAID* ME17 ....67 H5
Swain Cl *STRD* ME2 ....14 B4
Swain Rd *RHAM* ME8 ....32 D2
Swale Heritage Trail *SIT* ME10 ....37 J2
Swale Rd *STRD* ME2 ....15 J4
Swallow Rd *WALD* ME5 ....31 G5
Swallow Rd *DIT/AY* ME20 ....45 J2
Swan Cl *SIT* ME10 ....37 H4
Swanstree Av *SIT* ME10 ....37 H4
Swan St *E/WMAL* ME19 ....45 F4
Sweets La *E/WMAL* ME19 ....50 E1
Swift Cl *DIT/AY* ME20 ....45 K2
Swift Crs *WALD* ME5 ....31 H4
Swift Pl *STRD* ME2 * 14 C6
Swiller's La *GVE* DA12 ....13 H4
Swingate Cl *WALD* ME5 ....31 H4
Swinton Av *HOO/HM* ME3 ....15 F4
Sycamore Crs *MAIDW* ME16 ....53 H4
Sycamore Dr *DIT/AY* ME20 ....45 J2
Sycamore Rd *STRD* ME2 ....19 J3
Sydney Av *SIT* ME10 ....37 F1
Sydney Rd *CHAT* ME4 ....4 D7
Sylewood Cl *ROCH* ME1 ....10 B4
Sylvan Cl *WALD* ME5 ....41 G2
Sylvan Rd *RHAM* ME8 ....22 E6
Sylvestre Cl *STRD* ME2 ....28 E4
Symmonds Dr *SIT* ME10 ....37 C5
Symons Av *CHAT* ME4 ....21 F4

T

Tadburn Gn *WALD* ME5 ....31 H4
Taddington Wood La
WALD ME5 ....30 E4
Taillour Cl *SIT* ME10 ....37 F1
The Tail Race *MAID/SHEP* ME15 ....6 C2
Talbot Rd *MAIDW* ME16 ....47 H4
Tail Trees Cl *RMAID* ME17 ....55 E2
Tamar Dr *STRD* ME2 ....14 E6
Tamarind Ct *GILL* ME7 ....32 C4
Tamesis Strd *GVE* DA12 ....12 B4
Tanglewood Cl *RHAM* ME8 ....32 E2
Tangmere Cl *GILL* ME7 ....22 B7
Tanyard Hl *CVE* DA12 ....13 H2
Tappan Dr *CHAT* ME4 ....16 A4
Tarragon Rd *MAIDW* ME16 ....55 F1
Tasker Cl *MAID/BEAR* ME14 ....48 A6
Tassell Cl *E/WMAL* ME19 ....45 K1
Taswell Rd *RHAM* ME8 ....23 J6
Tatier Cl *WALD* ME5 ....31 G6
Taunton Cl *MAID/SHEP* ME15 ....63 G1
Taveners Rd *RHAM* ME8 ....33 H4
Tavistock Cl *RHAM* ME8 ....33 J3
SIT ME10 ....36 D2
Tavy Cl *WALD* ME5 ....41 F1
Taylor Cl *RMAID* ME17 ....66 C2
Taylor Rd *SNOD* ME6 ....38 D2
Taylors La *HOO/HM* ME3 ....8 A4
STRD ME2 ....2 E1
Teal Wy *RSIT* ME9 ....26 E1
Teapot La *DIT/AY* ME20 ....46 C1
Teasaurer Hl *MAID/SHEP* ME15 ......54 A4
Teasel Cl *MAID/BEAR* ME14 ....55 E1
Teasel Rd *WALD* ME5 ....31 G6
Tedder Av *WALD* ME5 ....31 G6
Telegraph Hl *HOO/HM* ME3 ....11 H2
Tempest Rd *E/WMAL* ME19 ....50 C3
Temple Boat Yd *STRD* ME2 * 2 A3
Temple Cl *STRD* ME2 ....19 H2
Temple Gdns *SIT* ME10 ....36 C1
STRD ME2 ....19 H2
Temple Wy *E/WMAL* ME19 ....45 J4
Ten Acre Wy *RHAM* ME8 ....33 F2
Tennyson Av *HOO/HM* ME3 ....9 G3

Tennyson Rd GILL ME7 ....5 H6
Tenterden Rd WALD ME5 * 31 H3
Terence CI CHAT ME4 ....21 G4
Terminus Rd MAIDW ME16 ....53 F4
Tern Crs STRD ME2 ....11 K4
Terrace Rd MAIDW ME16 ....6 E4
 SIT ME10 ....37 H5
The Terrace GVE DA12 ....12 C6
 ROCH ME1 ....3 G6
Terry Wk DIT/AY ME20 ....45 H2
Teston La MAID/SHEP ME15 ....60 B1
Teston Rd E/WMAL ME19 ....19 H4
Teynham Gn RHAM ME8 ....22 C2
Thackeray Rd DIT/AY ME20 ....45 K1
Thames Av RHAM ME8 ....23 G6
Thames Vw HOO/HM ME3 ....9 H3
The Thatchers MAID/SHEP ME15 ....53 G1
Thelma CI CHAT ME4 ....12 B4
Theodore PI GILL ME7 ....5 H2
Third Av CHAT ME4 ....21 J5
 GILL ME7 ....22 A3
Thirlemere CI MAIDW ME16 ....47 J4
Thirlmere CI SIT ME10 ....31 F1
 STRD ME2 ....15 H5
Thistlebank MAID/BEAR ME14 ....31 G5
Thistledown MAID/BEAR ME14 ....55 G2
Thistledown CI GILL ME7 ....32 C4
Thomas Rd SIT ME10 ....37 H4
Thomas St ROCH ME1 ....7 H5
Thompson CI RHAM ME8 ....28 J6
Thomson CI SNOD ME6 ....38 E1
Thorn CI MAID ME15 ....40 D1
Thorndale CI WALD ME5 ....30 D5
Thorndike CI CHAT ME4 * 21 F6
Thornham Rd RHAM ME8 ....48 B6
Thornhill PI MAID/BEAR ME14 ....48 B6
Thorold Rd CHAT ME4 ....5 F6
Thorpe Wk RHAM ME8 ....32 E5
Thurle Wy RHAM ME8 ....33 G4
Threshers Dr MAID/BEAR ME14 ....54 E1
Thrush CI WALD ME5 ....31 H1
Thurlestone Ct
 MAID/BEAR ME14 * 48 A6
Thurston Dr STRD ME2 ....14 C5
The Tideway ROCH ME1 ....16 D5
Tilbury Rd RHAM ME8 ....24 A4
Tile Flds RMAID ME17 ....57 G4
Tilghman Wy SNOD ME6 ....39 F1
Timber Tops WALD ME5 ....31 G2
Timber Tops WALD ME5 ....41 K2
Tintern Rd MAIDW ME16 ....47 J4
Titchfield Rd MAID/SHEP ME15 ....63 G2
Tobruk Wy WALD ME5 ....31 F2
Todd Crs SIT ME10 ....27 G6
Toddington Crs WALD ME5 ....40 D1
Toledo Paddock GILL ME7 ....21 J6
Tolgate La STRD ME2 ....2 C1
Tolgate Wy MAID/BEAR ME14 ....47 K1
Tom Joyce CI SNOD ME6 ....38 D3
Tomlin CI SNOD ME6 ....38 E2
Tonbridge Rd MAIDW ME16 ....53 G3
 WBY/YAL ME18 ....50 B6
Tonge Rd SIT ME10 ....37 J4
Toronto Rd GILL ME7 ....22 A2
Torrens Wk GVE DA12 ....12 C6
Torrington CI WBY/YAL ME18 ....50 A6
Tourmaline Dr SIT ME10 ....36 C2
Tourne Sq GILL ME7 ....17 G6
Tovil CI MAID/SHEP ME15 ....54 A4
Tovil HI MAID/SHEP ME15 ....53 K5
Tovil Rd MAID/SHEP ME15 ....54 A4
Tower CI GVE DA12 ....12 C6
Tower Gdns MAID/BEAR ME14 ....55 J3
Tower HI E/WMAL ME19 ....45 J4
Tower La MAID/BEAR ME14 ....55 H2
Tower Vw E/WMAL ME19 ....50 E3
Town CI WALD ME5 ....45 F5
Town Hill CI E/WMAL ME19 ....45 F5
Town Rd HOO/HM ME3 ....9 F4
Townsend Rd SNOD ME6 ....38 C1
The Tracies SIT ME10 ....35 G2
Trafalgar Rd ROCH ME1 ....29 G4
Trafalgar St SIT ME10 ....5 H1
Tramways CHAT ME4 ....21 J4
Trapfield CI MAID/BEAR ME14 ....55 K2
Trapfield La MAID/BEAR ME14 ....55 K3
Trapham Rd MAIDW ME16 ....53 F4
Travertine Rd WALD ME5 ....41 H1
Trelawn Crs WALD ME5 ....31 H6
Trellyn CI MAID/SHEP ME15 ....52 E4
Trenton CI CHAT ME4 ....21 G6
Trent Rd WALD ME5 ....31 H1
Tresco Rd ROCH ME1 ....20 B5
Trevarno Ter MAID/SHEP ME15 * 53 K4
Trevino Dr WALD ME5 ....31 F1
Trevor Rd MAIDW ME16 ....53 C1
Trewin CI DIT/AY ME20 ....46 C2
Tribune Dr SIT ME10 ....37 H1
Trident CI STRD ME2 ....12 A1
Trinity Rd GILL ME7 ....16 D6
 SIT ME10 ....37 H1
Troodos HI MAID/BEAR ME14 ....48 A4
Trotwood CI WALD ME5 ....31 H1
Troys Md RMAID ME17 ....57 J1
Trubridge Rd HOO/HM ME3 ....10 E5
Truro CI RHAM ME8 ....24 B4
Tudor Av MAID/BEAR ME14 ....48 C6
Tudor Gv HOO/HM ME3 ....10 A4
 RHAM ME8 ....23 G6
Tufa CI WALD ME5 ....31 H1
Tufton Rd RHAM ME8 ....23 H5
Tumblers HI RMAID ME17 ....69 H3
Tunbury Av CHAT ME4 ....31 F5
Tunbury Av South WALD ME5 ....31 F1
Tunstall Rd SIT ME10 ....42 C2
Tupman CI ROCH ME1 ....21 H1
Turgis CI RMAID ME17 ....64 B4
Turks Hall PI STRD ME2 * 28 C3
Turner CI SIT ME10 ....37 H1
Turnstone CI RSIT ME9 ....26 E2
Turnstone Rd WALD ME5 ....31 J6

Tuscan Dr WALD ME5 ....41 J1
Twisden Rd E/WMAL ME19 ....45 J4
Two Gates HI HOO/HM ME3 ....8 E5
Twydall Gn RHAM ME8 ....22 D5
Twydall La RHAM ME8 ....22 D4
Twyford CI RHAM ME8 ....23 J4
Twyford Ct MAID/BEAR ME14 ....48 E6
Tydeman Rd MAID/SHEP ME15 ....55 G4
Tyland La MAID/BEAR ME14 ......44 D1
Tyler CI WALD ME5 ....31 H5
Tyler Dr RHAM ME8 ....33 C4
Tyne CI WALD ME5 ....31 H3
Typhoon Rd E/WMAL ME19 ....50 C3

Ufton CI MAID/SHEP ME15 ....55 F5
Ufton La SIT ME10 ....36 E5
Ulcombe Rd MAID/BEAR ME14 ....64 B5
Underdown Av CHAT ME4 ....21 F4
Underwood CI MAID/SHEP ME15 ....7 G7
Union Pk CHAT ME4 ....4 D5
Union St CHAT ME4 ....4 D5
 MAID/BEAR ME14 ....7 H5
 ROCH ME1 ....3 G6
Unity St SIT ME10 ....36 E5
Unwin CI DIT/AY ME20 ....47 H1
Upbury Wy CHAT ME4 ....4 E5
Upchat Rd HOO/HM ME3 ....9 K6
Uplands CI STRD ME2 ....2 A3
Upnor Rd STRD ME2 ....15 J4
Upper Barn HI
 MAID/SHEP ME15 ....60 D5
Upper Britton PI GILL ME7 ....5 G4
Upper Bush Rd STRD ME2 ....14 B6
Upper Field Rd SIT ME10 ....37 H3
Upper Hunton HI
 MAID/SHEP ME15 ....61 F5
Upper Luton Rd WALD ME5 ....5 H7
Upper MI WBY/YAL ME18 ....51 G6
Upper Rd MAID/SHEP ME15 ....7 K7
Upper Stone St MAID/SHEP ME15 ....7 J5
Upper St MAID ME17 ....57 H5
Urquhart CI WALD ME5 ....31 G3

Vale Dr WALD ME5 ....30 D3
Valenciennes Rd SIT ME10 ....36 E5
Valentine CI GILL ME7 ....22 C5
Valentine Rd MAID/SHEP ME15 ..55 F4
Valerian CI WALD ME5 ....30 E4
Vale Rd MAID/SHEP ME15 ....61 K4
Valiant Rd WALD ME5 ....31 J6
Valley Dr GVE DA12 ....12 B2
Valley Ri WALD ME5 ....31 F6
Valley Rd GILL ME7 ....22 A2
The Valley RMAID ME17 ....61 J5
Valley View Rd ROCH ME1 ....20 B5
Vancouver Dr RHAM ME8 ....22 C5
Vanessa Wk GVE DA12 ....12 C1
Vange Cottage Ms ROCH ME1 * ..2 E7
Vange Ms ROCH ME1 * 2 E7
Vanguard Wy STRD ME2 ....15 K4
Varnes St DIT/AY ME20 ....39 K4
Vaughan Dr SIT ME10 ....37 H1
Vauxhall Crs SNOD ME6 ....38 D4
Vectis Dr SIT ME10 ....27 F6
Veles Rd SNOD ME6 ....38 D2
Ventnor CI WALD ME5 ....21 J6
Vicarage La DIT/AY ME20 ....28 E1
Vicarage La HOO/HM ME3 ....11 F6
 MAID/SHEP ME15 ....61 G1
 RSIT ME9 ....25 G3
Vicarage Rd GILL ME7 ....5 G3
 SIT ME10 ....28 E2
 STRD ME2 ....28 C3
Vicary Wy MAIDW ME16 ....6 B6
Victoria CI WALD ME5 ....30 D6
Victoria Ct MAIDW ME16 * 6 E5
Victoria Dr E/WMAL ME19 ....50 C4
 SIT ME10 ....21 H4
Victoria Rd CHAT ME4 ....2 E5
 SIT ME10 ....5 K1
 MAIDW ME16 ....6 D5
 ROCH ME1 ....2 E7
 STRD ME2 ....2 E1
Victoria St DIT/AY ME20 ....39 K4
 GILL ME7 ....5 K1
 MAIDW ME16 ....6 D5
 ROCH ME1 ....2 E7
 STRD ME2 ....2 E1
Victoria Ter ROCH ME1 ....20 A4
Victory Pk STRD ME2 * 3 K2
Vidgeon Av HOO/HM ME3 ....10 E4
View Rd HOO/HM ME3 ....9 H3
Vigilant Wy GVE DA12 ....12 C1
Viking CI STRD ME2 ....2 A1
Villa Rd HOO/HM ME3 ....14 A4
Vincent Rd DIT/AY ME20 ....40 C3
 SIT ME10 ....37 J5
The Vineries GILL ME7 ....5 G3
Viners CI SIT ME10 ....42 E1
Vines La ROCH ME1 ....3 F5
Vineyard Crs RHAM ME8 ....22 C5
Vinters Rd MAID/BEAR ME14 * ..54 E1
Vinters Rd MAID/BEAR ME14 ......54 C2
Vintners Wy MAID/BEAR ME14 ....55 F2
Violet CI WALD ME5 ....41 G2
Virginia Rd GILL ME7 ....16 D5
Vixen CI WALD ME5 ....31 J2
Volante Dr SIT ME10 ....31 K4
Vulcan CI WALD ME5 ....31 H1

Wadham PI SIT ME10 ....37 H6
Waghorn Rd SNOD ME6 ....38 E2
Waghorn St CHAT ME4 ....21 H4
Wagoners CI MAID/BEAR ME14 ..55 F2
Wainscott Rd STRD ME2 ....12 A1
Wainscott Wk STRD ME2 ....12 J1
Wakehurst CI RMAID ME17 ....61 G5
Wakeley Rd RHAM ME8 ....20 C6
Wake Rd ROCH ME1 ....20 C6
The Waldens MAID/BEAR ME17 ....66 H6
Walderslade Rd CHAT ME4 ....31 F1
Walderslade Woods WALD ME5 ..30 D5
Waldron Dr MAID/SHEP ME15 ....62 A2
Wallace Rd ROCH ME1 ....20 E6
Wallbridge La RHAM ME8 ....24 B3
Wall CI HOO/HM ME3 ....10 E3
Wallis Av MAID/SHEP ME15 ....63 F3
The Wall SIT ME10 ....36 E3
Walmer Gdns SIT ME10 ....36 D3
Walnut CI WALD ME5 ....21 H6
Walnut Tree Av
 MAID/SHEP ME15 ....63 G1
Walnut Tree CI DIT/AY ME20 ......46 A3
Walnut Tree Dr SIT ME10 ....36 B3
Walnut Tree La
 MAID/SHEP ME15 ....62 B3
Walpole CI E/WMAL ME19 ....49 J3
Walsby Dr SIT ME10 ....27 G6
Walsham Rd WALD ME5 ....41 F1
Walsingham CI RHAM ME8 ....33 F5
Walter Burke Av ROCH ME1 * 29 F2
Walters Rd HOO/HM ME3 ....11 F4
Waltham Rd RHAM ME8 ....23 G4
Warblers CI RSIT ME9 ....2 C1
Warden CI MAIDW ME16 ....6 A3
Warden Mill CI WBY/YAL ME18 ..59 H1
Warden Rd ROCH ME1 ....19 K4
Warden Ter WBY/YAL ME18 * 59 G2
Wardes RMAID ME17 ....58 E5
Wardwell La MAID/SHEP ME15 ....59 G4
Ware St MAID/BEAR ME14 ....55 H1
Warlingham Cl RHAM ME8 ....33 G4
Warmlake Rd RMAID ME17 ....68 D1
Warner St CHAT ME4 ....4 C7
Warnett CI SNOD ME6 ....38 C1
Warnford Gdns
 MAID/SHEP ME15 ....54 B6
Warren CI SIT ME10 ....37 H6
Warren La RSIT ME9 ....34 A3
Warren Rd MEO DA13 ....18 A3
 WALD ME5 ....40 D2
Warren Vw GVE DA12 ....13 H2
Warren Wood Rd ROCH ME1 ......19 H2
Warwick Crs RHAM ME8 ....18 K4
 SIT ME10 ....36 C3
Warwick PI MAIDW ME16 ....6 A3
Washington Av CHAT ME4 ....21 H4
Watchmans Ter WALD ME5 ....21 J4
Wateringbury Rd
 E/WMAL ME19 ....51 J3
Water La E/WMAL ME19 ....45 F4
 MAID/BEAR ME14 ....56 B1
 MAID/SHEP ME15 * 7 J7
 RMAID ME17 ....65 J5
Waterloo Rd CHAT ME4 ....4 D7
Waterloo St MAID/SHEP ME15 ..7 J6
Waterlow Rd MAID/BEAR ME14 ..48 B6
Watermeadow CI GILL ME7 ....32 B2
Watermill CI STRD ME2 ....12 A1
Waters Edge MAID/SHEP ME15 ..7 F7
 STRD ME2 ....2 B4
Waterside Ga MAID/SHEP ME16 * ..47 J4
Waterside CI DIT/AY ME20 * 45 K6
 STRD ME2 ....15 K6
Waterside Ms WBY/YAL ME18 ....59 J4
Watermen CI CHAT ME4 ....16 C3
Watersmeet CI
 MAID/SHEP ME15 ....54 B5
Waters PI GILL ME7 ....32 C2
Watling Av WALD ME5 ....21 K4
Watling PI SIT ME10 ....37 G5
Watling St GVE DA12 ....13 F4
 STRD ME2 ....21 K4
Watson Av CHAT ME4 ....30 D3
Watsons HI SIT ME10 ....36 C6
Watts' Av ROCH ME1 ....3 H7
Watts CI SNOD ME6 ....39 F2
Watts St CHAT ME4 ....4 E6
Wat Tyler Wy MAID/SHEP ME15 ..7 J4
Waverley CI RMAID ME17 ....61 H6
 WALD ME5 ....31 J1
Wayfield Rd WALD ME5 ....31 F1
Weald CI MAID/SHEP ME15 ....63 F3
Wealden Ct WALD ME5 ....5 G7
Wealden Wy DIT/AY ME20 ....46 B3
Wealdway STPH/PW TN12 ....58 A6
Weatherly CI ROCH ME1 ....3 H7
Weavering St MAID/BEAR ME14 ..55 G2
The Weavers MAIDW ME16 ....6 A3
Webb CI HOO/HM ME3 ....10 E4
Webster Rd RHAM ME8 ....28 J1
Wedgewood CI MAIDW ME16 ......53 C1
Wedgwood Rd WALD ME5 ....31 H1
Weeds Wood Rd WALD ME5 ......31 H1
Week St MAID/BEAR ME14 ....7 H5
Weller Av ROCH ME1 ....19 G4
Wellington PI MAID/BEAR ME14 ..48 B6
Wellington Rd GILL ME7 ....5 K2
Wellington Gn
 MAID/SHEP ME15 ....63 F3
Wellington Wy MAID/SHEP ME19 ..50 D5
Wellington St MAID/SHEP ME15 ..55 G2
Wells Rd STRD ME2 ....19 H1
Well St E/WMAL ME19 ....45 H6
 MAID/SHEP ME15 ....61 K4
Well Winch Rd SIT ME10 ....36 D3

Wemmick CI ROCH ME1 ....30 D1
Wendover CI STRD ME2 ....29 F3
Wents Rd MAID/BEAR ME14 ......55 G1
Wentworth Dr HOO/HM ME3 ....9 G2
 RHAM ME8 ....23 G4
 SIT ME10 ....36 C3
Wesley Rd MAIDW ME16 ....52 E5
Westbourne St SIT ME10 ....36 A4
Westbrook MAID/SHEP ME15 * ..62 A3
Westbrooke CI CHAT ME4 ....21 G4
Westbury Rd MAID/SHEP ME15 * ..52 E5
Westcourt St GILL ME7 ....16 A6
West Dr RMAID ME17 ....69 K3
West St RHAM ME8 ....30 D3
Westergate Rd STRD ME2 ....14 E3
Westerham CI RHAM ME8 ....22 D2
Westerham Rd MEO DA13 ....18 E1
Western Av CHAT ME4 ....16 B4
Western Rd MAIDW ME16 ....53 H5
Westfield Sole Rd
 MAID/BEAR ME14 ....41 K2
West Gn SIT ME10 ....27 F5
Westlands Av SIT ME10 ....36 B4
West La SIT ME10 ....37 G4
Westmarsh CI
 MAID/SHEP ME15 ....63 G1
Westmead MAID/SHEP ME15 ......39 G6
West Mill Rd DIT/AY ME20 ....39 G6
Westmoreland Dr RSIT ME9 ......25 F3
Westmorland CI
 MAID/SHEP ME15 ....55 F6
Westmorland Gn
 MAID/SHEP ME15 ....63 F1
West Motney Wy RHAM ME8 ......23 J5
Westmount Av CHAT ME4 ....4 D5
Weston Rd STRD ME2 ....2 B1
West Park Rd MAID/SHEP ME15 ..54 A4
Westree Rd MAIDW ME16 ....6 C5
West Rdg SIT ME10 ....36 D6
West St E/WMAL ME19 ....44 E4
 GILL ME7 ....5 K1
 MAID ME17 ....66 B2
 SIT ME10 ....36 E4
 STRD ME2 ....2 C1
Westview CHAT ME4 ....16 C2
West Wk MAIDW ME16 ....53 C3
Westway MAID/SHEP ME15 ....61 H5
Westwood Rd
 MAID/SHEP ME15 ....62 B1
Wetheral Dr WALD ME5 ....31 H4
Weybridge CI WALD ME5 ....31 J3
Wey CI WALD ME5 ....31 J3
Weyhill CI MAID/BEAR ME14 ......48 D6
Wharf Rd GILL ME7 ....16 B6
 MAID/SHEP ME15 ....7 H7
Whatman CI MAID/BEAR ME14 ..48 D6
Wheatcroft CI SIT ME10 ....37 H4
Wheatcroft Gv RHAM ME8 ....33 F1
Wheatear Wy WALD ME5 ....31 H1
Wheatfield E/WMAL ME19 ....45 H3
Wheatfields MAID/BEAR ME14 ..54 E2
 WALD ME5 ....31 K6
Wheatsheaf CI
 MAID/SHEP ME15 ....54 C6
The Wheelers RHAM ME8 ....32 D2
Wheeler St MAID/BEAR ME14 ....7 J2
The Wheelwrights
 RMAID ME17 * 66 C2
Whiffen's Av CHAT ME4 ....4 C3
Whiffen's Avenue W
 CHAT ME4 ....4 C3
Whiffen Wk E/WMAL ME19 ....46 A3
Whimbrel CI SIT ME10 ....45 J2
Whimbrel CI DIT/AY ME20 * 45 J2
The Whimbrels CHAT ME4 ....16 C3
Whitcombe CI WALD ME5 ....31 J6
Whitebeam Dr RMAID ME17 ......61 G5
Whitehall Dr WALD ME5 ....37 F6
Whitehall Rd RMAID ME17 ....65 D6
Whiteheads La
 MAID/BEAR ME14 ....55 J2
Whitehorse HI CHAT ME4 ....5 G7
White Horse La
 MAID/SHEP ME15 ....63 H2
Whitehouse CI HOO/HM ME3 ....11 F6
Whitehouse Crs ROCH ME1 ......40 A2
Whiteleaves Ri RHAM ME8 ....19 F4
White Rd CHAT ME4 ....21 G5
White Rock MAIDW ME16 ....6 E5
Whitewall Rd STRD ME2 ....3 J1
Whitewall Wy STRD ME2 ....3 J1
Whitmore St MAIDW ME16 ....6 C5
Whyman Av CHAT ME4 ....21 G5
Wickham St RSIT ME9 ....35 J2
Wickham St ROCH ME1 ....20 D3
Widgeon Rd SIT ME10 ....14 C6
Wierton La RMAID ME17 ....63 F6
Wierton Rd RMAID ME17 ....68 A1
Wigmore Rd RHAM ME8 ....32 D4
Wildred Rd RSIT ME9 ....37 H3
Wilberforce Rd RMAID ME17 ......37 H3
Wilberforce Wy GVE DA12 ....12 A1
Wildfell CI MAID/BEAR ME14 ......41 J2
Wildman CI RHAM ME8 ....33 F5
Wildwood CI RMAID ME17 ....65 H6
Wildwood Gld GILL ME7 ....32 C4
Wilks CI RHAM ME8 ....23 K4
Will Adams Wy RHAM ME8 ....22 B3
William St RHAM ME8 ....19 G4
William St RHAM ME8 ....5 K1
Willington Gn
 MAID/SHEP ME15 ....63 F1
Willington St MAID/SHEP ME15 ..55 G2
Willow Av HOO/HM ME3 ....17 F1
Willowby Gdns RHAM ME8 ....23 G4
Willow Gra HOO/HM ME3 * 10 E5

Willowherb CI CHAT ME4 ....16 D3
Willow Industries
 MAID/BEAR ME14 * 48 A1
Willow Ri MAID/SHEP ME15 ......55 G5
Willow Rd DIT/AY ME20 ....45 G5
 STRD ME2 ....14 D6
Willowside SNOD ME6 ....38 E1
The Willows CHAT ME4 ....23 G4
 RSIT ME9 ....27 F5
 SIT ME10 ....41 F1
 WALD ME5 ....31 J4
Willow Wy MAID/SHEP ME15 ......54 C3
Wilmington Wy RHAM ME8 ....22 D4
Wilson Av ROCH ME1 ....20 D5
Wilson CI GILL ME7 ....63 F4
Wilsons La MAID/SHEP ME15 ......61 F4
Wilton Dr DIT/AY ME20 ....31 H3
Wilton Ter SIT ME10 * 36 B3
Wiltshire CI MAID/SHEP ME15 ..21 J6
Wiltshire Wy MAID/SHEP ME15 ..55 F6
Wimbourne Dr RHAM ME8 ....33 F2
Winchelsea Rd WALD ME5 ....31 H3
Winchester Av WALD ME5 ....31 H3
Winchester PI
 MAID/BEAR ME14 * 7 J1
Winchester Wy RHAM ME8 ....23 J6
Winch Rd RSIT ME9 * 33 F1
Windermere Dr RHAM ME8 ....33 F1
Windermere CI STRD ME2 ....15 G3
Windmill CI STRD ME2 ....62 C5
Windmill Hts MAID/BEAR ME14 ..55 J2
Windmill La East E/WMAL ME19 ..45 J4
Windmill La West
 MAID/BEAR ME14 ....44 D6
Windmill Rd GILL ME7 ....5 J6
 SIT ME10 ....36 D2
Windmill St STRD ME2 ....15 G3
Windsor Av MAID/SHEP ME15 ..31 F4
Windsor Dr SIT ME10 ....36 C6
Windsor Rd GILL ME7 ....21 K1
Windward Rd ROCH ME1 ....22 A5
Windyridge CHAT ME4 ....23 A5
Winford Ms ROCH ME1 ....20 A4
Wingham CI MAID/SHEP ME15 ..22 E5
 RHAM ME8 ....32 C4
Wingrove Dr MAID/BEAR ME14 ..55 F1
 STRD ME2 ....3 G1
Winifred Rd MAID/BEAR ME14 ..55 F1
Winston Av E/WMAL ME19 ....50 E3
Winston Dr STRD ME2 ....32 E2
Winston Rd STRD ME2 ....19 H1
Winterfield La E/WMAL ME19 ......45 H4
Wintergreen CI CHAT ME4 ....31 G4
The Wirrals WALD ME5 ....31 G3
Wises La RSIT ME9 ....36 A5
Witham Wy STRD ME2 ....31 J3
Wittersham CI WALD ME5 ....31 H3
Wivenhoe CI RHAM ME8 ....23 J4
Wodehouse CI DIT/AY ME20 ......38 D6
Wolfe Rd MAIDW ME16 ....53 C1
Wollaston CI SIT ME10 ....53 F5
Woodbridge Dr
 MAID/SHEP ME15 ....53 K5
Woodbury Rd MAID/BEAR ME14 ..40 E1
Woodchurch CI WALD ME5 ....22 E4
Woodchurch Crs RHAM ME8 ......22 E4
Woodcourt CI SIT ME10 ....54 E6
Woodcut Rd MAID/BEAR ME14 ..48 B4
Woodfield Wy HOO/HM ME3 ....9 J6
Woodgate La RSIT ME9 ....35 C6
Woodhurst MAID ME15 ....53 G4
Woodhurst CI STRD ME2 ....19 F4
Woodland CI E/WMAL ME19 ......34 D4
Woodlands RMAID ME17 ....61 G5
Woodlands Av SNOD ME6 ....39 F1
Woodlands CI
 MAID/BEAR ME14 ....48 C5
 WBY/YAL ME18 ....59 J4
Woodlands La GVE DA12 ....13 G3
Woodlands Pde DIT/AY ME20 * ..46 B3
Woodlands Rd DIT/AY ME20 ......22 B4
 SIT ME10 ....37 H5
Woodlands Ter GILL ME7 * 2 C4
Woodland Wy
 MAID/BEAR ME14 ....48 C5
Woodlark Rd CHAT ME4 ....16 C3
Woodlea DIT/AY ME20 ....52 E4
Woodleas MAIDW ME16 ....52 E4
Woodpecker Dr RSIT ME9 ....27 F5
Woodpecker Gld RHAM ME8 ......32 E2
Woodpecker Rd DIT/AY ME20 ....45 J5
Woodruff CI RHAM ME8 ....24 B2
Woodrush PI CHAT ME4 ....16 D3
Woodside RHAM ME8 ....32 E2
Woodside Gdns SIT ME10 ....42 E1
Woodside Rd
 MAID/BEAR ME14 ....62 D1
Woodstock Rd SIT ME10 ....42 E1
 STRD ME2 ....2 E2
Wood St GILL ME7 ....63 H2
 STRD ME2 ....2 E2
Woodview Ri STRD ME2 ....14 E3
Woodville Rd MAID/SHEP ME15 ..7 J7
Woolaston CI MAID/SHEP ME15 ..55 C4
Woolbrook CI RHAM ME8 ....23 G6
Woolleys Rd RMAID ME17 ....36 E5
Woollett Rd SIT ME10 ....36 E5
Woollett St MAID/BEAR ME14 ....7 J4
Woolley Rd MAID/SHEP ME15 ....55 G6
Woolwich CI WALD ME5 ....31 F4
Wopsle CI ROCH ME1 ....30 D1
Worcester Av E/WMAL ME19 ......50 E3
Worcester CI STRD ME2 ....14 D4
Worcester Dr SIT ME10 ....27 G6
Worcester Rd
 MAID/SHEP ME15 ....62 E1
Wordsworth CI WALD ME5 ....31 H1

Wordsworth Rd
MAID/BEAR ME14 ....48 C5
Wordsworth Wy *DIT/AY* ME20 ....38 E6
Workhouse La
MAID/SHEP ME15 ....61 H4
Wormdale HI *RSIT* ME9 ....35 F5
Wormdale Rd *RSIT* ME9 ....34 E4
Worsfold Ct *MAID/SHEP* ME15 *....54 B5
Wotton Cl *MAID/SHEP* ME15 ......63 F3
Wouldham Rd *ROCH* ME1 ....29 G2
Wrangleden Cl
MAID/SHEP ME15 ....63 F5
Wrangleden Rd
MAID/SHEP ME15 ....62 E5
Wrens Cl *DIT/AY* ME20 ....45 J3
Wrens Ct *RSIT* ME9 ....42 A2

Wrens Cross
MAID/SHEP ME15 * 7 H5
Wren Wy *MAID* ME5 ....31 H2
Wright Cl *RHAM* ME8 ....22 E4
Wulfere Wy *STRD* ME2 ....15 K1
Wyatt Pl *STRD* ME2 ....2 B2
Wyatt St *MAID* ME17 ....7 J5
Wykeham St *GVE* DA12 ....12 B2
Wykeham Gv *RMAID* ME17 ......64 D1
Wykeham Rd *SIT* ME10 ....37 H4
Wykeham St *STRD* ME2 ....15 C4
Wyke Manor Rd
MAID/BEAR ME14 ....7 H3
Wyles Rd *CHAT* ME4 ....20 E4
Wyles St *GILL* ME7 ....16 D5
Wylie Rd *HOO/HM* ME3 ....10 E5
Wyndham Rd *CHAT* ME4 ....20 E4

Wyness Ct *STRD* ME2 * 15 G4
The Wytchlings
RMAID ME17 ....65 G6
Wytherling Cl
MAID/BEAR ME14 ....55 G1
Wyvern Cl *SIT* ME10 ....36 E1
SNOD ME6 ....38 E3
Wyvill Cl *RHAM* ME8 ....33 G3

Yarrow Ct *MAID/BEAR* ME14 ....55 G1
Yarrow Rd *WALD* ME5 ....30 E4
Yaugher La *RSIT* ME9 ....33 K5
Yeates Dr *SIT* ME10 ....27 C6
Yelsted La *MAID/BEAR* ME14 ....41 K3
Yeoman Dr *GILL* ME7 ....22 B5
Yeoman La *MAID/BEAR* ME14 ....55 J3
Yeoman Pk *MAID/SHEP* ME15 ....55 H4
Yeoman Wy *MAID/SHEP* ME15 ...55 J4
Yew Rd *HOO/HM* ME3 ....17 F1
Yew Tree Cl *DIT/AY* ME20 ....46 D3
WALD ME5 ....41 K1
Yoke Cl *STRD* ME2 ....15 C4
Yokosuka Wy *GILL* ME7 ....22 D1
York Av *GILL* ME7 ....5 G4
WALD ME5 ....30 E5
York HI *WALD* ME5 * 21 J4

York Rd *MAID/SHEP* ME15 ......54 D5
ROCH ME1 ....20 C3
Ypres Dr *SIT* ME10 ....27 F5

Z

Zetland Av *GILL* ME7 ....22 A4
Zillah Gdns *RHAM* ME8 ....32 D2

Index - featured places

Abbey Court School
STRD ME2 ....14 E4
Acorn Business Centre
MAIDW ME16 ....53 H4
Adult Education Centre
GILL ME7 ....5 J2
ROCH ME1 ....3 H5
Alexandra Hospital
WALD ME5 ....41 F2
Allington Primary School
MAID ME16 ....47 G5
All Saints CE Primary School
CHAT ME4 ....4 E7
MAID/SHEP ME15 ....7 H5
Anchor Business Park
SIT ME10 ....37 H2
Anchorians All Weather
Sports Club *RHAM* ME8 ....23 H5
Apiary Business Park
RMAID ME17 ....64 A6
Archbishop's Palace
MAIDW ME15 ....7 G5
Arden Business Park
STRD ME2 ....3 K1
Arden Junior School
GILL ME7 ....16 E6
The Astor of Hever
Community School
MAIDW ME16 ....6 A5
Avenue Theatre
SIT ME10 ....37 F5
Avicenna Medical Centre
E/WMAL ME19 ....45 H2
Aylesford Cemetery
DIT/AY ME20 ....46 E2
Aylesford Primary School
DIT/AY ME20 ....46 C3
Aylesford Priory
DIT/AY ME20 ....46 D2
Aylesford School
DIT/AY ME20 ....46 C3
Balfour Infant School
CHAT ME4 ....20 E5
Balfour Junior School
CHAT ME4 ....20 E4
Ballard Business Park
STRD ME2 ....2 A6
Balmoral Clinic
GILL ME7 ....5 J2
Bapchild & Tonge CE
Aided School *SIT* ME10 ....37 K5
Barming Primary School
MAIDW ME16 ....52 E4
Barnsole Infant School
GILL ME7 ....22 A2
Barnsole Junior School
SIT ME10 ....22 A2
Barrow Grove Junior School
SIT ME10 ....36 D4
BBC Radio Kent
CHAT ME4 ....4 A3
Bearsted Golf Course
MAID/BEAR ME14 ....55 J1
Bearsted Green Business
Centre *MAID/BEAR* ME14 .....55 K1
Bearsted Vineyard
MAID/SHEP ME15 ....56 B4
Beechings Way Industrial
Centre *RHAM* ME8 ....22 D2
Bell Shopping Centre
SIT ME10 ....37 F4
Bell Wood Community
Junior School
MAID/SHEP ME15 ....63 F3
Bell Wood Infant School
MAID/SHEP ME15 ....63 F3
Blacklands County Junior
School *E/WMAL* ME19 ....45 J5
Black Lion Leisure Centre
GILL ME7 ....16 C6
Blackthorn Medical Centre
MAIDW ME16 ....53 F5
Bobbing Primary School
RSIT ME9 ....36 B1
Borden CE Primary School
RSIT ME9 ....35 K5
Borden Grammar School
SIT ME10 ....36 E5
Borstal Manor Junior School
ROCH ME1 ....19 K4
Boughton Monchelsea
Primary School
RMAID ME17 ....62 C6
Bower Grove School
MAIDW ME16 ....53 G4
The Bower Mount Clinic
MAIDW ME16 ....6 C4

Bowling Alley
MAID/BEAR ME14 ....7 J3
Bowling Centre
CHAT ME4 ....4 C4
Boxmend Industrial Estate
RMAID ME17 ....63 G5
Boyd Business Centre
STRD ME2 ....3 J1
Bradfields School
WALD ME5 ....31 G2
Bredgar CE Primary School
RSIT ME9 ....42 A5
Brickmakers Industrial Estate
SIT ME10 ....37 H2
Bridge Industrial Centre
MAID/SHEP ME15 ....6 D7
Bridgewood Manor Hotel
WALD ME5 ....30 D5
Brittania Business Park
DIT/AY ME20 ....46 D4
Broadway Shopping Centre
MAIDW ME15 ....7 F4
Brompton Medical Centre
GILL ME7 ....16 B6
Brompton Westbrook
Primary School *GILL* ME7 ....4 E5
Brookfield Infant School
DIT/AY ME20 ....45 K2
Brookfield Junior School
DIT/AY ME20 ....45 J2
The Brook Theatre
CHAT ME4 ....4 C3
Brunswick House Clinic
MAIDW ME16 ....6 D2
Brunswick House Primary
School *MAIDW* ME16 ....6 D2
Bryony School
RHAM ME8 ....32 E1
Bryony School (Upper)
RHAM ME8 ....33 H3
Byron School
GILL ME7 ....5 J6
Canterbury Road Primary
School *SIT* ME10 ....37 H5
Capstone Farm Country Park
GILL ME7 ....31 K1
Casino
ROCH ME1 ....3 H5
Castlecres Industrial Park
SIT ME10 ....37 H2
Castle Remains
RMAID ME17 ....69 G3
Castle Road Business
Precinct *SIT* ME10 ....37 H1
Castle Road Industrial Estate
SIT ME10 ....37 H4
Castle View Business Centre
ROCH ME1 ....3 H3
The Cedars School
ROCH ME1 ....20 C2
Central Business Park
STRD ME2 ....3 K2
Central Hall Theatre & Cinema
CHAT ME4 ....4 C4
Chapter School
STRD ME2 ....14 C5
Charles Dickens Centre &
Eastgate House *ROCH* ME1 ..3 H5
Chart Sutton Business Estate
RMAID ME17 ....63 J6
Chatham Dockyard
(World Naval Base)
GILL ME7 ....16 A5
Chatham Girls Grammar
School *WALD* ME5 ....21 K4
Chatham Grammar Boys
School *CHAT* ME4 ....21 F5
Chatham South School
CHAT ME4 ....20 E6
Chequers Shopping Centre
MAID/BEAR ME14 ....7 H4
Child Health Centre
STRD ME2 ....14 D6
Churchill Clinic
WALD ME5 ....31 G1
Church Road Business Centre
SIT ME10 ....37 J2
City Wall *ROCH* ME1 ....3 F4
Clare House
E/WMAL ME19 ....45 J4
Cliffe Woods County
Primary School
HOO/HM ME3 ....9 H2
Cobham Primary School
GVE DA12 ....12 D6
Cobtree Manor Park Golf Club
MAID/BEAR ME14 ....47 J1

Cobtree Medical Centre
MAID/BEAR ME14 ....69 G2
Collingwood Industrial Estate
RMAID ME17 ....64 B6
Compass Centre
CHAT ME4 ....16 C4
Conquest Industrial Estate
STRD ME2 ....2 B5
Corn Exchange
ROCH ME1 ....3 G4
Cornwallis School
MAID/SHEP ME15 ....62 A5
Cottage Industrial Estate
DIT/AY ME20 ....47 G2
County Court
CHAT ME4 ....4 A4
County Primary Infant School
RHAM ME8 ....23 G6
Coxheath Primary School
RMAID ME17 ....61 H5
Crown Court Clinic
ROCH ME1 ....3 H6
Crylls Business Estate
STRD ME2 ....36 C4
Cuxton Industrial Estate
STRD ME2 ....19 G4
D2 Trading Estate
SIT ME10 ....37 H2
Dajen Business Park
CHAT ME4 ....21 J5
Dame Sybil Thorndike
Health Centre *ROCH* ME1 ....20 C2
Danecourt School
(Special School) *GILL* ME7 ...22 B4
David Lloyd Health Club
MAIDW ME16 ....7 G5
Deacon Industrial Estate
DIT/AY ME20 ....47 F2
Deacon Trading Centre
STRD ME2 ....2 C3
Deangate Ridge Athletics
Stadium *HOO/HM* ME3 ....10 D2
Deangate Ridge Golf Club
HOO/HM ME3 ....10 D3
Deanwood Primary Education
Technology School
RHAM ME8 ....33 F4
Delce Junior School
ROCH ME1 ....20 C4
Detling CE Primary School
MAID/BEAR ME14 ....49 H3
Diggerland
STRD ME2 ....19 K2
Discovery School
E/WMAL ME19 ....51 G3
Ditton CE Junior School
DIT/AY ME20 ....46 B3
Ditton Infant School
DIT/AY ME20 ....46 B3
Dolphin Sailing Barge Museum
SIT ME10 ....37 G3
East Borough Primary School
MAID/BEAR ME14 ....54 C1
East Farleigh Primary School
MAID/SHEP ME15 ....61 F2
Elaine Primary School
STRD ME2 ....14 D5
Elm Court Industrial Estate
GILL ME7 ....32 A5
The Elms Medical Centre
HOO/HM ME3 ....10 E5
English Martyrs RC Primary
School *STRD* ME2 ....15 G4
Enterprise Business Estate
STRD ME2 ....3 K2
Eurolink Industrial Centre
SIT ME10 ....37 G4
Eurolink Industrial Estate
SIT ME10 ....37 H3
European School of
Osteopathy
MAID/BEAR ME14 ....48 D1
Fairfax Business Centre
MAID/SHEP ME15 ....63 G4
Fairview Community Junior
School *RHAM* ME8 ....32 E3
The Family Medical Centre
WALD ME5 ....31 J6
Farleigh Trading Estate
MAID/SHEP ME15 ....53 K5
Featherby Infant School
RHAM ME8 ....22 C3
Featherby Junior School
RHAM ME8 ....22 C3
Flagship Brewery
CHAT ME4 ....16 A5

Fort Amherst Heritage
Park & Caverns *CHAT* ME4 ...4 C2
Fort Luton Museum
CHAT ME4 ....21 G5
Fort Pitt Grammar School
ROCH ME1 ....20 E2
Fremlin Walk Shopping Centre
MAID/BEAR ME14 ....7 G3
French Hospital
ROCH ME1 ....3 G5
Fulston Manor School
SIT ME10 ....37 F6
Gads Hill School
STRD ME2 ....14 B2
The Garden of England
Crematorium
RSIT ME9 ....26 C5
Garrison Cricket Ground Pavilion
GILL ME7 ....5 F2
Garrison Sports Stadium
GILL ME7 ....16 B6
The Gillingham College
GILL ME7 ....22 B2
Gillingham FC (Priestfield
Stadium) *GILL* ME7 ....22 A1
Gillingham Golf Club
GILL ME7 ....22 A4
Gillingham Ice Bowl
GILL ME7 ....22 C5
Gillingham Medical Centre
GILL ME7 ....22 B2
Glencoe Junior School
CHAT ME4 ....21 G4
Goacher's Brewery
MAID/SHEP ME15 ....53 K5
Gordon Primary School
STRD ME2 ....15 F4
Gore Court CC
SIT ME10 ....36 B3
Grange Moor Hotel
MAIDW ME16 ....6 C6
Grange Park College
E/WMAL ME19 ....45 F2
Greenacre School
WALD ME5 ....31 F3
Greenvale Infant School
CHAT ME4 ....21 G4
Grove Dairy Farm Business
Centre *RSIT* ME9 ....36 A2
Grove Park CP School
STRD ME2 ....36 B2
Guildhall Museum
ROCH ME1 ....3 G4
Halling Primary School
STRD ME2 ....29 F5
Harrietsham CE Primary
School *RMAID* ME17 ....66 D2
Hart Street Business Centre
MAIDW ME16 ....6 C5
Haslemere Industrial Estate
MAID/SHEP ME15 ....63 G3
Hazlitt Theatre
MAID/BEAR ME14 ....7 H3
Hempstead Infant School
GILL ME7 ....32 C3
Hempstead Junior School
GILL ME7 ....32 C4
Hempstead Valley Shopping
Centre *GILL* ME7 ....32 C4
Henley Business Park
STRD ME2 ....3 J2
Higham Primary School
HOO/HM ME3 ....8 B5
Highsted Grammar School
for Girls *SIT* ME10 ....37 F6
Hilltop Primary School
STRD ME2 ....15 H3
Historical Society Museum
CHAT ME4 ....4 B2
The Historic Dockyard
Chatham *GILL* ME7 ....16 A4
HM Prison Maidstone
MAID/BEAR ME14 ....7 J5
HM Prison Rochester
ROCH ME1 ....20 B6
Holiday Inn
WALD ME5 ....30 D3
Hollingbourne Primary School
RMAID ME17 ....57 H4
Holmesdale Community
School Technology College
SNOD ME6 ....38 E3
The Holy Family RC Primary
School *RMAID* ME17 ....63 F4
Holy Trinity Foyer
MAID/BEAR ME14 ....7 J3

Holywell Primary School
RSIT ME9 ....24 C3
Homefarm Estate
MAID/SHEP ME15 ....46 E3
Hoo St Werburgh Primary
School *HOO/HM* ME3 ....10 E5
Horsted Primary School
WALD ME5 ....30 D3
Horsted Retail Park
WALD ME5 ....30 D2
Hospital Barn Farm
MAID/SHEP ME15 ....60 E4
Howard School
RHAM ME8 ....23 F6
Hundred of Hoo School
HOO/HM ME3 ....10 D5
Indoor Bowls & Sports Centre
CHAT ME4 ....4 B2
Innkeeper's Lodge
MAID/BEAR ME14 ....7 G1
Invicta Grammar School for
Girls *MAID/BEAR* ME14 ......54 D2
Iwade Primary School
RSIT ME9 ....26 D2
John Goodhew Medical Centre
SIT ME10 ....26 E5
Kenden Business Park
STRD ME2 ....15 J4
Kent County Opthalmic &
Aural Hospital
MAID/BEAR ME14 ....7 H2
Kent Institute of Art & Design
ROCH ME1 ....3 J7
Kingfisher Community
Primary School *WALD* ME5 ..31 H1
Kingsdown Industrial Estate
DIT/AY ME20 ....46 A4
Kings Hill Golf Club
E/WMAL ME19 ....50 C3
Kings Hill Primary School
E/WMAL ME19 ....50 D3
Kings Preparatory School
ROCH ME1 ....3 F6
Kings Road Clinic
WALD ME5 ....21 K5
Kings School
ROCH ME1 ....3 G5
Kingswood Primary School
RMAID ME17 ....65 H6
Kitchener Barracks
CHAT ME4 ....4 C1
Kit's Coty House
MAID/BEAR ME14 ....40 C4
Knights Park Industrial Estate
STRD ME2 ....2 B6
Lansdowne Primary School
SIT ME10 ....37 J5
Larkfield Leisure Centre
DIT/AY ME20 ....45 K1
Larkfield Priory Hotel
DIT/AY ME20 ....45 K1
Larkfield Trading Estate
DIT/AY ME20 ....39 F5
Leeds & Broomfield CE
Primary School
RMAID ME17 ....64 D1
Leeds Castle
RMAID ME17 ....65 G1
Leeds Castle Golf Club
RMAID ME17 ....57 G6
Leybourne Business Centre
E/WMAL ME19 ....45 H2
Leybourne SS Primary School
E/WMAL ME19 ....45 H3
Library & Arts Centre
GILL ME7 ....5 G6
Lime Tree Restaurant & Hotel
RMAID ME17 ....67 J3
Lloyds
CHAT ME4 ....4 B3
Loaland Business Centre
STRD ME2 ....15 J4
Lock Meadow Leisure Complex
MAIDW ME16 ....7 G6
Lock Meadow Market
MAIDW ME16 ....7 G6
London Road Trading Estate
SIT ME10 ....36 D4
Loose Infant School
MAID/SHEP ME15 ....62 B2
Loose Junior School
MAID/SHEP ME15 ....62 B2
Lordswood Health Centre
WALD ME5 ....41 J1
Lordswood Industrial Estate
WALD ME5 ....41 J4

rdswood Leisure Centre WALD ME5 ...31 J5
wer Halstow School RSIT ME9 ...25 F4
nsford Primary School DIT/AY ME20 ...45 K2
con Infant School CHAT ME4 ...21 J4
con Junior School WALD ME5 ...21 J4
con Medical Centre WALD ME5 ...21 J4
dginford Park Infant School MAID/SHEP ME15 ...55 G4
dginford Park Junior School MAID/SHEP ME15 ...55 H4
idstone General Hospital MAIDW ME16 ...53 F2
idstone Grammar School MAID/SHEP ME15 ...7 K7
idstone Grammar School for Girls MAIDW ME16 ...6 E1
idstone Industrial Centre MAIDW ME16 ...7 F2
idstone Lawn Tennis Club MAIDW ME16 ...6 A1
idstone Leisure Centre MAID/SHEP ME15 ...54 D4
idstone Museum & Bentlif Art Gallery MAID/BEAR ME14 ...7 G2
Malling School E/WMAL ME19 ...45 J5
nor Hotel GVE DA12 ...12 A2
nor Park Country Park E/WMAL ME19 ...44 E6
plessden Noakes School MAIDW ME16 ...47 K6
rlowe Park Medical Centre STRD ME2 ...19 H1
rriott Tudor Park Hotel & Country Club MAID/BEAR ME14 ...56 A3
undeney Primary School RHAM ME8 ...31 G3
dway City Estate STRD ME2 ...3 K5
dway Civic Centre CHAT ME4 ...2 E2
dway Community College CHAT ME4 ...21 G5
dway Crematorium WALD ME5 ...40 E1
dway Heritage Centre CHAT ME4 ...4 B2
dway Little Theatre RHAM ME8 ...3 H6
dway Maritime Hospital GILL ME7 ...5 C5
dway RFC ROCH ME1 ...20 B4
dway Secure Training Centre ROCH ME1 ...30 B1
dway Towns Rowing Club RHAM ME8 ...20 A3
dway Trading Estate RHAM ME8 ...7 F6
dway Valley Leisure Park STRD ME2 ...19 J3
dway Yacht Club HOO/HM ME3 ...16 C1
Kent Business Park SNOD ME6 ...39 F2
Kent College of Further Education CHAT ME4 ...30 D2
Kent College of Higher & Further Education CHAT ME4 ...20 D3
Kent Shopping Centre MAIDW ME16 ...47 H5
rscourt Primary School RHAM ME8 ...33 H1
Hall Business Estate DIT/AY ME20 ...46 C2
on Court Primary School CHAT ME4 ...36 E2
terne Junior School RHAM ME8 ...36 D6
re Park RC Primary School E/WMAL ME19 ...45 G4
e CC MAID/SHEP ME15 ...54 C3
e Park Sailing Club MAID/SHEP ME15 ...55 F3
rway Industrial Estate DIT/AY ME20 ...47 H2
ston Infant School RSIT ME10 ...37 H4
ston Junior School RSIT ME10 ...37 H4
eum of Kent Life MAIDW ME16 ...47 J3

Music School MAID/SHEP ME15 ...7 G5
Napier Primary School GILL ME7 ...5 K4
Napier Road Secondary School GILL ME7 ...21 K2
Neptune Industrial Estate STRD ME2 ...15 K5
New Century Cinema SIT ME10 ...37 G4
New Hythe Business Park SNOD ME6 ...39 G5
Newington CE Primary School RSIT ME9 ...35 F1
Newington Industrial Estate RSIT ME9 ...34 D2
New Road Business Estate DIT/AY ME20 ...46 A4
New Road Primary School CHAT ME4 ...4 D6
North Borough Junior School MAID/BEAR ME14 ...48 A5
North Kent Magistrates Court CHAT ME4 ...4 C3
Oaklands Primary School WALD ME5 ...31 F4
The Oaks Infant School SIT ME10 ...36 D6
Oak Trees Community School MAID/SHEP ME15 ...62 E1
Oakwood Hospital MAIDW ME16 ...53 G2
Oakwood Park Grammar School MAIDW ME16 ...6 A6
Oasthouse Theatre RHAM ME8 ...23 H6
Oastpark Golf Club SNOD ME6 ...38 C4
Odeon Cinema MAIDW ME16 ...7 G5
Offham CC E/WMAL ME19 ...44 A5
Offham Primary School E/WMAL ME19 ...44 A4
Oldborough Manor Community School MAID/SHEP ME15 ...62 C1
The Old Oast Business Centre DIT/AY ME20 ...47 F2
Orchard Business Centre MAIDW ME16 ...47 H4
Orchard Industrial Estate MAID/SHEP ME15 ...63 G5
Orchard Medical Centre MAID ME17 ...61 H6
Owletts (NT) GVE DA12 ...12 C6
Palace Industrial Estate MAID/SHEP ME15 ...63 G4
Palace Wood Junior School MAIDW ME16 ...47 H6
Park Way Primary School MAID/SHEP ME15 ...54 C5
Parkwood Industrial Estate RHAM ME8 ...63 H4
Parkwood Primary School RHAM ME8 ...33 G3
Pentagon Shopping Centre CHAT ME4 ...4 C4
Phoenix Industrial Estate STRD ME2 ...3 H1
Pier Road Industrial Estate GILL ME7 ...16 E5
Pine Lodge Touring Park MAID/SHEP ME15 ...56 C4
Postley Industrial Centre MAID/SHEP ME15 ...54 B5
Premier Business Park CHAT ME4 ...21 H5
Premier Lodge WBY/YAL ME18 ...51 H6
Preston Hall Hospital DIT/AY ME20 ...46 E3
Princes Park Medical Centre WALD ME5 ...31 H2
Pumping Station Museum CHAT ME4 ...4 C4
Quarry Wood Industrial Estate DIT/AY ME20 ...46 C2
DIT/AY ME20 ...46 D5
Rainham Mark Grammar School RHAM ME8 ...23 F4
Rainham School for Girls RHAM ME8 ...22 E6
Rainham Shopping Centre RHAM ME8 ...23 H5
Regis Manor Community Primary School SIT ME10 ...36 E1
Restoration House ROCH ME1 ...3 G6
Richmond Infant School GILL ME7 ...16 D6

The Ridge Golf Club RMAID ME17 ...69 K1
Riding School E/WMAL ME19 ...52 A2
Riverside Country Park GILL ME7 ...23 F1
Riverside Primary School RHAM ME8 ...23 J5
Riverview Clinic GVE DA12 ...12 C1
The Robert Napier School GILL ME7 ...22 A3
Rochester Airport ROCH ME1 ...30 C1
Rochester Airport Industrial Estate ROCH ME1 ...30 C2
Rochester Castle ROCH ME1 ...3 F4
Rochester Cathedral ROCH ME1 ...3 F5
Rochester & Cobham Park Golf Club DA12 ...13 G6
Rochester Grammar School for Girls ROCH ME1 ...20 C4
Rochester Health Centre ROCH ME1 ...20 D3
Rodmersham Primary School RSIT ME9 ...43 H3
Rodmersham Squash Club RSIT ME9 ...43 G4
Roseacre Junior School MAID/BEAR ME14 ...55 H2
Royal Engineers Museum GILL ME7 ...16 B6
Royal Star Arcade MAID/BEAR ME14 ...7 G3
Russell Hotel MAID/BEAR ME14 ...48 C5
St Andrews School ROCH ME1 ...3 F6
St Augustine of Canterbury RC Primary School RHAM ME8 ...33 F5
St Bartholomews Hospital ROCH ME1 ...3 K7
St Bartholomews School SIT ME10 ...37 F1
St Benedicts School WALD ME5 ...31 J6
St Faiths Adult Education Centre MAID/BEAR ME14 ...7 G3
St Francis Catholic Primary School MAID/BEAR ME14 ...7 H2
St Georges Business Park SIT ME10 ...37 H4
St James Infant School E/WMAL ME19 ...45 J4
St John Fisher Catholic School CHAT ME4 ...21 F4
St John Fisher RC Comprehensive School ROCH ME1 ...20 E3
St Johns CE Infant School CHAT ME4 ...4 A6
St Johns CE Primary School MAID/BEAR ME14 ...54 E2
St Katherines School MAID/BEAR ME14 ...38 D3
St Leonard's Tower (remains) E/WMAL ME19 ...44 D6
St Margarets at Troy Town Primary School ROCH ME1 ...3 F7
St Margaret's Infant School RHAM ME8 ...23 G6
St Marks CE Primary School DIT/AY ME20 ...39 K4
St Marys Abbey E/WMAL ME19 ...45 F4
St Marys Catholic Primary School GILL ME7 ...16 E6
St Marys Island CE (Aided) Primary School CHAT ME4 ...16 C2
St Marys Medical Centre STRD ME2 ...15 G4
St Marys Primary School STRD ME2 ...15 G4
St Matthews CE Infant School ROCH ME1 ...20 A4
St Michaels CE Junior School MAIDW ME16 ...6 D6
St Michaels RC Primary School CHAT ME4 ...4 B6
St Nicholas CE Infant School STRD ME2 ...2 B1
St Nicholas' Cemetery ROCH ME1 ...20 C3
St Pauls Infant School MAID/BEAR ME14 ...48 B5
St Peters CE Primary School DIT/AY ME20 ...46 E1
St Peters Infant School ROCH ME1 ...20 C3

St Peters RC Primary School MAID ME17 ...36 D5
St Simon Stock RC School MAIDW ME16 ...53 H2
St Stephens CE Infant School MAID/SHEP ME15 ...53 K4
St Thomas More RC Primary School WALD ME5 ...31 G4
St Thomas of Canterbury RC Primary School RHAM ME8 ...22 D4
St Thomas School SIT ME10 ...37 J6
St Werburgh CP Junior School HOO/HM ME3 ...11 D5
St Werburgh Medical Centre HOO/HM ME3 ...10 C5
St William of Perth RC Primary School ROCH ME1 ...20 B4
Sandling Primary School MAID/BEAR ME14 ...48 C4
Saxon Way Primary School GILL ME7 ...16 E6
Senacre Technology College MAID/SHEP ME15 ...62 E2
Senacre Wood Primary School MAID/SHEP ME15 ...63 F1
SENCO STRD ME2 ...19 F4
Shamel Business Centre STRD ME2 ...3 G1
Sheldon Business Centre STRD ME2 ...15 J4
Shepway Infant School MAID/SHEP ME15 ...55 F6
Shepway Junior School MAID/SHEP ME15 ...55 F6
Sheridale Business Centre STRD ME2 ...2 B4
Sherwin Knight Primary School STRD ME2 ...14 D6
Shorne CE Primary School GVE DA12 ...13 H1
Shorne Wood Country Park GVE DA12 ...13 F4
Singlewell Primary School GVE DA12 ...12 A2
Sir Joseph Williams Maths School ROCH ME1 ...20 B5
Sittingbourne Adult Education Centre SIT ME10 ...36 C5
Sittingbourne Industrial Park SIT ME10 ...36 C3, ...37 F3
Sittingbourne & Kemsley Light Railway SIT ME10 ...27 H6
Sittingbourne Memorial Hospital SIT ME10 ...36 C5
Sittingbourne & Milton Regis Golf Club RSIT ME9 ...35 F5
Sittingbourne Retail Park SIT ME10 ...26 E6
Sittingbourne Sports Centre SIT ME10 ...37 G5
Skinner Street Primary School GILL ME7 ...5 H1
Snodland CE Primary School SNOD ME6 ...38 D2
Snodland Clinic SNOD ME6 ...38 E2
The Somerfield Hospital MAIDW ME16 ...6 C2
South Avenue Infant School SIT ME10 ...37 G5
South Aylesford Retail Park DIT/AY ME20 ...46 D4
South Borough Primary School MAID/SHEP ME15 ...54 B4
Spectrum Business Centre STRD ME2 ...15 K4
Spectrum Business Estate MAID/SHEP ME15 ...63 G4
Spinnens Acre County Junior School WALD ME5 ...41 K1
Spotlites Theatre Company CHAT ME4 ...4 C4
Strood Cemetery STRD ME2 ...2 A4
Strood Retail Park STRD ME2 ...2 D2
Strood Swimming Pool STRD ME2 ...2 A1
Strood Yacht Club STRD ME2 ...2 C4
Sutton Valence Preparatory School MAID ME17 ...68 E2
Sutton Valence Primary School RMAID ME17 ...69 G3
Sutton Valence School RMAID ME17 ...69 F3

Swadelands Specialist School MAID ME17 ...67 H3
Swingate Infant School WALD ME5 ...41 J1
Target Business Centre MAID/SHEP ME15 ...63 G4
Temple Mill Primary School STRD ME2 ...15 G2
Temple School STRD ME2 ...15 G3
Tennis Club MAID ME17 ...22 A3
Thames View Primary School RHAM ME8 ...23 F4
The Thomas Aveling School ROCH ME1 ...20 C6
Thornhills Medical Centre DIT/AY ME20 ...45 K3
Tovil Green Business Park MAID/SHEP ME15 ...53 K5
Travel Inn E/WMAL ME19 ...45 H1
GILL ME7 ...22 B4
MAID/BEAR ME14 ...56 D5
MAIDW ME16 ...47 G5
RHAM ME8 ...47 J3
STRD ME2 ...36 B2
Trinity Trading Estate STRD ME2 ...37 F2
Tunbury Primary School CHAT ME4 ...41 F1
Tunstall CE Primary School RSIT ME9 ...42 C2
Twenty Twenty Industrial Estate MAIDW ME16 ...47 H4
Twydall Health & Welfare Clinic RHAM ME8 ...22 D3
Twydall Infant School RHAM ME8 ...22 D4
Twydall Junior School RHAM ME8 ...22 D4
Tyrwhitt Drake Museum of Carriages MAID/SHEP ME15 ...7 F3
UGC Cinema STRD ME2 ...19 J3
University of Greenwich E/WMAL ME19 ...50 D2
University of Greenwich at Medway CHAT ME4 ...16 C4
Upbury Arts College GILL ME7 ...5 F4
Upchurch River Valley Golf Club RHAM ME8 ...24 B4
Upnor Castle STRD ME2 ...16 A2
Valley Park Community School MAID/BEAR ME14 ...54 D2
The Vine Medical Centre MAIDW ME16 ...6 B6
Vintners Park Crematorium MAID/BEAR ME14 ...48 E6
Wainscott Primary School STRD ME2 ...15 J2
Wakeley Junior School RHAM ME8 ...23 J5
Walderslade Medical Centre WALD ME5 ...31 G2
Walderslade Primary School WALD ME5 ...31 G5
Warmlake Business Estate RMAID ME17 ...69 G1
Warren Wood County Primary School ROCH ME1 ...20 C6
Watts Charity Almshouses ROCH ME1 ...20 C2
Wayfield County Primary School WALD ME5 ...31 G1
West Borough CP School MAIDW ME16 ...53 G3
West Borough Sports Centre MAIDW ME16 ...6 A5
Westfield Business Centre STRD ME2 ...3 F1
Westlands School SIT ME10 ...37 G3
West Lane Trading Estate SIT ME10 ...37 G3
West Malling CE Primary School E/WMAL ME19 ...44 E4
West Malling Industrial Park E/WMAL ME19 ...44 B2
Woodlands Primary School GILL ME7 ...22 B2
Woodlands Road Cemetery GILL ME7 ...22 B1
Woolmans Wood Caravan Park WALD ME5 ...30 C4
Wren Industrial Estate MAID/SHEP ME15 ...63 G4
Yew Tree Industrial Estate DIT/AY ME20 ...46 C2

Acknowledgements

Post Office is a registered trademark of Post Office Ltd. in the UK and other countries.

ools address data provided by Education Direct.

rol station information supplied by Johnsons

e-way street data provided by © Tele Atlas N.V. Tele Atlas

Garden centre information provided by

Garden Centre Association Britains best garden centres

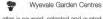

Wyevale Garden Centres

The statement on the front cover of this atlas is sourced, selected and quoted from a reader comment and feedback form received in 2004.

 **Street by Street** QUESTIONNAIRE

Dear Atlas User
Your comments, opinions and recommendations are very important to us.
So please help us to improve our street atlases by taking a few minutes
to complete this simple questionnaire.

You do not need a stamp (unless posted outside the UK). If you do not want to remove this page from your street atlas, then photocopy it or write your answers on a plain sheet of paper.

Send to: The Editor, AA Street by Street, FREEPOST SCE 4598,
Basingstoke RG21 4GY

ABOUT THE ATLAS...

Which city/town/county did you buy?

_____

Are there any features of the atlas or mapping that you find particularly useful?

_____
_____
_____

Is there anything we could have done better?

_____
_____
_____

Why did you choose an AA Street by Street atlas?

_____
_____
_____

Did it meet your expectations?

Exceeded ☐   **Met all** ☐   **Met most** ☐   **Fell below** ☐

Please give your reasons

_____
_____
_____
_____

ML178z

continued overleaf

Where did you buy it?

For what purpose? (please tick all applicable)

To use in your own local area ☐   **To use on business or at work** ☐

Visiting a strange place ☐   **In the car** ☐   **On foot** ☐

Other (please state)

LOCAL KNOWLEDGE...

Local knowledge is invaluable. Whilst every attempt has been made to make the information contained in this atlas as accurate as possible, should you notice any inaccuracies, please detail them below (if necessary, use a blank piece of paper) or e-mail us at _streetbystreet@theAA.com_

ABOUT YOU...

Name (Mr/Mrs/Ms)

Address

                                                    Postcode

Daytime tel no

E-mail address

Which age group are you in?

Under 25 ☐   **25-34** ☐   **35-44** ☐   **45-54** ☐   **55-64** ☐   **65+** ☐

Are you an AA member?   **YES** ☐   **NO** ☐

Do you have Internet access?   **YES** ☐   **NO** ☐

Thank you for taking the time to complete this questionnaire. Please send it to us as soon as possible, and remember, you do not need a stamp (unless posted outside the UK).

We may want to contact you about other products and services provided by us, or our partners (by mail, telephone) but please tick the box if you DO NOT wish to hear about such products and services from us by mail or telephone. ☐

ML178z